Family-Run Universities in Japan

Globally, private universities enrol one in three of all higher education students. In Japan, which has the second largest higher education system in the world in terms of overall expenditure, almost 80 per cent of all university students attend private institutions. According to some estimates up to 40 per cent of these institutions are family businesses in the sense that members of a single family have substantive ownership or control over their operation. This book offers a detailed historical, sociological, and ethnographic analysis of this important, but largely understudied, category of private universities as family business.

This updated edition of *Family-Run Universities in Japan* examines how such universities in Japan have negotiated a period of major demographic decline since the 1990s: their experiments in restructuring and reform, the diverse experiences of those who worked and studied within them and, above all, their unexpected resilience. It argues that this resilience derives from a number of 'inbuilt' strengths of family business which are often overlooked in conventional descriptions of higher education systems and in predictions regarding the capacity of universities to cope with dramatic changes in their operating environment. This book offers a new perspective on recent changes in the Japanese higher education sector and contributes to an emerging literature on private higher education and family business across the world.

JEREMY BREADEN is Associate Professor of Japanese Studies at Monash University, Australia. His previous works include *The Organisational Dynamics of University Reform in Japan* (2013), *Internationalising Japan as Discourse and Practice* (2014), and *Articulating Asia in Japanese Higher Education* (2018).

ROGER GOODMAN is Nissan Professor of Japanese Studies and Warden of St Antony's College at the University of Oxford. His previous publications include *Japan's 'International Youth'* (1990), *Children of the Japanese State* (2000), *Family and Social Policy in Japan* (2002), and *A Sociology of Japanese Youth* (2011).

'a comprehensive and illuminating analysis of private higher education in Japan and worldwide, a focus on the understudied phenomenon of family-owned universities in Japan, a case study of Japanese family-owned university, and a discussion of the likely future of Japanese private higher education. All of this is cogently argued, engagingly written, and packaged into a 224-page volume... without question a landmark contribution'

Philip G. Altbach, *Japanese Studies*

'It provides perhaps the most succinct depiction of contemporary Japanese higher education available in English, and it illuminates the little-known phenomenon of family-run educational enterprises. The unique dynamics described by the authors illuminate facets of higher education in Japan and in private sectors worldwide.'

Roger L. Geiger, *Higher Education Quarterly*

'*Family-Run Universities in Japan* is well-written, exceptionally researched, and provides much food for thought. It offers a wealth of data, insights, and micro-level theorizations that will provide numerous jumping off points for further study in a range of different fields.'

Christopher D. Hammond, *Higher Education*

'The authors give a thorough historical overview of Japanese private university management and use statistical data to get to the heart of the problem... it is notable that this book is practically the first to study the theme with reference to private universities. As a researcher who has been engaged in the anthropology of business administration, I hope that this co-authored work will open up a new arena for investigating the resilience and perpetuation of family businesses in general.'

Hirochika Nakamaki, *Journal of Royal Anthropological Institute*

'Even though the book is about family-run universities in Japan, their findings and conclusion give courage, confidence, and hope to those who are involved in governance, management, and administration of those in the Asia-Pacific region.'

Kazuhito Obara, *Asia Pacific Journal of Education*

'An enormously profound picture of the Japanese higher education system... An enormous wealth of information on higher education and society in a single country—discussed as well as being not just typical for a single country—is well collected and convincingly presented with a lesson: a specific social phenomenon can be understood well, if one is ready for the adventure of getting to know in detail the enormous complexity of conditions.'

Ulrich Teichler, *Contemporary Japan*

Family-Run Universities in Japan

Sources of Inbuilt Resilience in the Face of Demographic Pressure, 1992–2030

JEREMY BREADEN AND ROGER GOODMAN

OXFORD
UNIVERSITY PRESS

OXFORD
UNIVERSITY PRESS

Great Clarendon Street, Oxford, OX2 6DP,
United Kingdom

Oxford University Press is a department of the University of Oxford.
It furthers the University's objective of excellence in research, scholarship,
and education by publishing worldwide. Oxford is a registered trade mark of
Oxford University Press in the UK and in certain other countries

Published in the United States of America by Oxford University Press
198 Madison Avenue, New York, NY 10016, United States of America

British Library Cataloguing in Publication Data

Data available

Library of Congress Cataloging in Publication Data

Data available

ISBN 978-0-19-886349-6 (Hbk.)
ISBN 978-0-19-887975-6 (Pbk.)

Acknowledgements

Although we only started writing this book in 2017, it is based on material which we have separately been collecting on the Japanese private higher education system since the early 2000s. At that time, Breaden was working in a Japanese private higher educational institution which he went on to describe in detail in his 2013 ethnography *The Organisational Dynamics of University Reform in Japan*. Goodman spent the Japanese academic year 2003–4 undertaking anthropological fieldwork at an institution which in this book is called Meikei Gakuin University (MGU, for short) which he has drawn on in a number of publications over the past decade (for example, Goodman 2009). He is particularly grateful to the President, who had both the confidence and the interest in academic scholarship to allow him to spend a year researching freely in his university, as well as to the many members of staff (academic and non-academic) and students who spent hours expressing their views of the institution.

MGU does exist as an institution and we have outlined faithfully what we understand to be its key features, philosophy, and policies, as an exemplar of a family-run university. Since we do only want to use it as an exemplar, however, we have also disguised certain features as well as the name of the institution while demonstrating its 'typicality' by reference to other family-run universities in Japan. In the case of the latter, we have drawn mainly on publicly available sources and hence we use the actual names of the institutions. While elements of our account of family-run universities in Japan may appear critical, we believe overall that our account is a positive one—certainly much more positive than the general external view (in as much as there is one) of such universities in Japan—and we express our sincere thanks to all those in such institutions across Japan who helped us with this project while respecting the fact that some of them would prefer not to be publicly acknowledged.

This is the second project on which we have worked together and we would like to thank the co-organizers of the 2011 Japan Studies Association of Australia conference, Carolyn Stevens and Stacey Steele, who brought us together to work on the first. At that conference we discovered a mutual interest in the media reporting of the experiences of foreign students in Japan following the so-called 'Triple Disaster' of earthquake, tsunami, and nuclear meltdown of 11 March 2011. The paper that we subsequently published, under the title 'The Dog That Didn't Bark: 3/11 and International Students in Japan' (Breaden and Goodman 2014), signals some of the embryonic thinking which drove the current project.

Since this project has some twenty years of gestation, it follows that we have both incurred many debts along the way which it is good to be able to acknowledge here while reinforcing the traditional disclaimer that we alone are responsible for all the mistakes (both of fact and analysis) which we are sure must remain in this text. Among the many colleagues who have helped us with either collecting or analysing data, we would like to thank the following (in alphabetical order and Japanese names with surnames first except where the individual concerned has expressed a different preference). Sadly not all of them are still with us, but we hope that each of those that are will know the part that they played in this project even if, in some cases, it was many years ago: Amano Ikuo, Daryl Arakaki, Arimoto Akira, Robert Aspinall, Harumi Befu, William K. Cummings, Leonardo Davoudi, Deguchi Akira, Ronald Dore, Jeremy Eades, Ehara Takekazu, Fujita Hidenori, Fukui Yu, Hamana Atsushi, Harano Yukiyasu, Hatakenaka Sachi, Hirakawa Makiko, Futao Huang, Iiyoshi Atsuo, Imoto Yuki, Inaba Yushi, Ishida Hiroshi, Itō Daiichi, Kaneko Keiko, Kaneko Motohisa, Kariya Takehiko, Kawano Mako, Kawashima Tatsuo, Curtis Kelly, Terri Kim, Earl Kinmonth, Kitamura Kazuyuki, Kitamura Wataru, Kiyonari Tadao, Kobayashi Tetsuya, Kuratani Nao'omi, Maeda Sanae, Marina Lee-Cunin, Maruyama Fumihiro, Chris McKenna, Brian McVeigh, Morozumi Akiko, Diane Musselwhite, Nagashima Nobuhiro, Nakamura Tamio, Oba Jun, Ogata Fusako, Ohmori Fujio, Ota Hiroshi, Gregory Poole, Stephen Ryan, Saito Kiyoshi, Sato Yuriko, Paul Scott, Michael Shackleton, Paul Snowden, Sukigara Matsuaki, Tanioka Ichiro, Tsuzaki Tetsuo, Ushiogi Morikazu, David Willis, Tom Wright, Yamada Reiko, Yamamoto Shinichi, Yamamura Satoshi, Yamanoi Atsunori, Yamashita Noboru, Yasuhara Yoshihito, Yoneyama Toshinao, Yonezawa Akiyoshi, Yoshida Aya, Yoshikawa Eiichiro. We would particularly like to thank Philip Altbach and colleagues who have allowed us to draw on their project on family-owned/managed universities which went to press at the same time as this book.

Several people have played key roles in turning this manuscript into a publishable form. Carolyn Dodd, as well as making suggestions based on her own knowledge of Japan, smoothed out any differences between British and Australian English to such an extent that neither of us can remember any more who originally wrote which sections. Hiroko Levy brought a keen eye for detail to referencing and formatting. Colleagues at OUP—Jenny King, Christina Fleischer, Ganesan Kanmani, Deva Thomas, and copy editor Phil Dines—have, as ever, all been a pleasure to work with. Finally, we are very grateful to Adam Swallow for encouraging us to publish this book in the Oxford University Press *Business and Management Series*. All our previous work has been published in monograph series, edited volumes, or specialist journals aimed at colleagues in our primary areas of academic specialism, Japanese studies, educational studies, and social anthropology. While we, of course, hope that this book will also prove of interest to those audiences—as well as more general audiences in Japan and elsewhere—we have been keen to engage with the newly emerging interest in family businesses in the management studies world. We hope that those colleagues will find this an interesting contribution.

Jeremy Breaden
Roger Goodman

January 2020

Contents

List of Figures

List of Tables

A Note on Sources and Conventions

Much of the account in this book of the higher education system in Japan in the mid-2000s comes from newspaper and popular magazine archives from that period. We use the abbreviations below for those newspapers and popular magazines. When articles are bylined, the name of the author is also included, e.g. Hino, *AS*, 26 May 2004.

AE   AERA (in Japanese)
AJ   Asahi Journal (in Japanese)
AS   Asahi Shimbun (in Japanese)
EJ   Economist (in Japanese)
G   The Guardian (UK)
GB   Gendai Business (in Japanese)
I   The Independent (UK)
JT   Japan Times (Japan)
KN   Kyodo News (Japan)
KS   Kobe Shimbun (in Japanese)
MS   Mainichi Shimbun (in Japanese)
NKS   Nihon Keizai Shimbun (in Japanese)
NYT   New York Times (US)
SA   Shūkan Asahi (in Japanese)
SD   Shūkan Diamond (in Japanese)
SG   Shūkan Gendai (in Japanese)
SM   Sunday Mainichi (in Japanese)
SS   Sankei Shimbun (in Japanese)
STK   Shūkan Tōyō Keizai (in Japanese)
TA   Time Asia (Hong Kong)
YS   Yomiuri Shimbun (in Japanese)

We have followed the standard rules of Romanization for ordinary words in the Japanese language, including italicization and the use of macrons for long vowels. We have made an exception for words which have been taken from Western languages, e.g. *manejimento* (for management) or *gabanansu* (for governance). This is to avoid unnecessarily confusing people who do not know Japanese and who might be interested in the number and type of such Western loanwords which figure in discussions about higher education in Japan. As a result, such Western loanwords are romanized in their original form, but italicized, e.g. *management, governance*.

Japanese proper nouns have been rendered in English in accordance with the preferences of the people and organisations concerned or, in the case of place names, in accordance with common convention in English (e.g. Tokyo, Osaka, Kyoto). The Japanese Ministry of Education has undergone a number of reorganizations in recent decades. In this text, we refer to it either by its current preferred title, MEXT, or as the Ministry of Education or simply as the Ministry.

All monetary values are expressed in yen when discussing financial issues in Japan since translations into pounds or dollars are complicated by the fluctuating exchange rates between countries. For the purposes of comparison, however, £1 was around ¥230 in 1990, ¥165 in 2000, and ¥140 in early 2020; US$1 was about ¥150 in 1990, ¥105 in 2000, and ¥108 in early 2020.

Introduction

This book started out with a social science puzzle.

There was much discussion in the mid-2010s in Japan about an issue involving Japanese universities which became known as the '2018 *mondai*' (2018 problem). The Japanese word for university (*daigaku*) covers, as we shall see, an extremely broad range of institutions, from world-class establishments with several thousand students to local colleges with fewer than fifty. Since the mid-2000s, the number of 18-year-olds in Japan had remained constant at about 1.2 million, but from 2018 the number would begin to fall year by year until 2030 to just over one million. The figures were easy to calculate since Japan has almost no immigration and the cohort which would turn 18 by 2030 had already been born. The reduction in the number of 18-year-olds would particularly affect universities, since over 95 per cent of all those entering universities for the first time were either 18- or 19-year-olds and around 80 per cent of this age cohort attend some form of higher education in Japan—one of the highest figures in the world. The impact would, it was predicted, particularly be felt by private universities which educated around 80 per cent of all students but were generally both less competitive to enter and much more expensive than the national or local public universities which educated the remainder. In the mid-2010s, Japan had roughly 600 private universities and predictions varied widely about how many would still be operating in 2030.

The respected scholar of higher education in comparative perspective, Ogawa Yō (2016), published a widely reviewed book entitled *Kieyuku 'Genkai Daigaku': Shiritsu Daigaku Teiinware no Kōzō (Vanishing 'Universities on the Brink': The Framework of Insufficient Enrolment at Private Universities)* in 2016, in which he showed that about 130 (20 per cent) of the total number of private universities in Japan were already below 80 per cent of their enrolment targets. This, he suggested in a radio interview on the TBS radio programme Session 22 (TBS Radio 2017), meant that if they did not get their numbers up they could go bankrupt. In the prologue to his 2017 book entitled *Shiritsu Daigaku wa Naze Ayaui noka (Why Private*

Family-Run Universities in Japan: Sources of Inbuilt Resilience in the Face of Demographic Pressure, 1992–2030. Jeremy Breaden and Roger Goodman, Oxford University Press (2020). © Jeremy Breaden and Roger Goodman.
DOI: 10.1093/oso/9780198863496.001.0001

Universities are at Risk), Watanabe Takashi, economist and former chairman of a private university board of trustees, offered a premonitory narrative of 'University X', a (fictional) large private university which does indeed go bankrupt in the year 2030 as a result of under-enrolment, compounded by a series of failed investments and poor management decisions. Watanabe (2017: 14) concludes his narrative by saying that the sad case of University X 'marks the start of an era of mass culling of private universities, which had on numerous previous occasions been a topic of discussion in the sector, but had never before amounted to much in practice'.

The '2018 problem' also became a popular topic of discussion, with mainstream news outlets declaring 'the era of university bankruptcy will soon be a reality' and 'universities are in breakdown' (Sankei Digital 2018; Toyo Keizai 2018). Journalist Kimura Makoto (2017), the author of a long-running series of books and numerous articles on the financial crisis in private universities, suggested that over one hundred universities would disappear within the next fifteen years. Titles in Kimura's book series became more agitated as the decade progressed, from *Private Universities at Risk and those which will Survive* (2012) to *Universities which will Sink and those which will Flourish* (2014), *The Era of Mass University Bankruptcy* (2017), and finally *The Great University Collapse* (2018).

This book does not set out primarily to explore what is likely to happen to the private higher education system in Japan over the next twelve or so years of declining numbers of 18-year-olds in the population, although we believe it will provide some tools for those who want to investigate this question. It may be that Ogawa's prediction of 20 per cent, or Kimura's prediction of 17 per cent, of these institutions going out of business will be borne out.[1] If so, and in either case, it will certainly be the largest and most spectacular implosion of a higher education system ever seen in absolute terms and probably the most spectacular in relative terms in peacetime.

Instead, this book looks backwards at what has happened to higher education, particularly private higher education, in Japan over the past fifteen years. It was the accounts of the '2018 problem' that independently reminded each of us of the dire predictions of the collapse of Japanese universities which had aired in the early 2000s (when we were both studying the higher education scene) and which brought us together to work on this project.

---

[1] Galan (2018: 34), in a recent overview in English of the experience of young people in Japan, also concludes that due to the so-called '2018 problem' in Japan 'Universities will inevitably be forced to close'.

We both remembered that the literature from the early 2000s has contained what looked like a statistical conundrum. Between 1992 and 2002, the number of 18- and 19-year-olds in the Japanese population *decreased* by around 30 per cent. At both the start and end of this period, 18- and 19-year-olds made up over 95 per cent of those attending university. The number of four-year (i.e. full) universities in Japan, however, over this same period had *increased* by around 30 per cent.

The most immediate answer to this conundrum could be found in the 30 per cent increase in the proportion of 18- and 19-year-olds who were going to four-year universities in 2002 (48.6 per cent) compared to 1992 (36.9 per cent). Many of these new students were women who had previously gone to two-year junior colleges (where the number of students declined by almost exactly half between 1992 and 2002).

But 2002 was not the end of the decline in the number of school leavers. Numbers were set to continue to decline by almost another 20 per cent over the next eight years. All things being equal, supply and demand for university places would be absolutely balanced in 2007. After 2007, there would be a surfeit of places and, since private universities relied on fees for 80 per cent of their income, the only possible outcome was an implosion in the system. The only questions were: how many universities would disappear, in what order, and exactly when.

The implosion in Japan's universities, however, never materialized. Indeed, the number of private universities in 2018 was almost 15 per cent more than in 2003 (Table I.1). Student enrolments in them increased by 6.4 per cent over the same period, and the proportion of university students enrolled in private (as opposed to national or local public) universities also grew, from 73.5 per cent to 77.4 per cent. These increases were matched by growth in revenue from

Table I.1 Vital statistics of private universities, 2003 and 2018

	2003	2018
Number of universities	526	603
Number of students	2,016,113	2,144,670
Share of university students overall	73.5	77.4
Number of full-time academic staff	84,296	107,425
Revenue*	3,037.8 billion yen	3,431.4 billion yen
(from student fees)	(2,360.4 billion yen)	(2,656.3 billion yen)
Government subsidies	283.115 billion yen	296.031 billion yen

* Revenue figures are from 2017 (latest available).

Sources: MEXT 2018a (University and student numbers); PMAC 2018c (revenue); PMAC 2019a (subsidies).

student fees, and subsidies from government—although the latter decreased slightly on a per-capita basis, for reasons we shall examine later.

At the same time, many of the predicted knock-on effects did not materialize. University credentials were not devalued in the marketplace as expected; competitive admissions systems and a selectivity-based hierarchy of institutions were still very much in place; there was little evidence of the development of new markets or even of radically different modes of operation. Most conspicuous of all was how few universities had actually disappeared altogether. In Chapter 5, we show that just eleven (less than 1.5 per cent) of all the private universities which existed in Japan in 2000 had disappeared completely by 2018. Overall, the situation in Japanese universities was remarkably similar in 2018 to that of 2003 or indeed 1992 when the number of 18-year-olds in the population peaked.

The puzzle behind this book therefore is: What did happen in Japan over the past fifteen years which prevented this implosion and why did so many commentators and experts get their predictions about the future of Japanese private higher education so wrong in the early 2000s?[2]

We tackle this puzzle on several different levels.

At the micro level, we examine many of the mechanics of the Japanese higher education system: the relationship between the national, public, and private sectors; the market for higher education; the expectations of the sector by government, professors, students, and families; the system's relationship with the world of work and the world beyond Japan. We explain how the system as a whole has come under pressure to be more 'productive' in the light of economic, political, and demographic forces and how it responded to this with new initiatives throughout the late 1990s and early 2000s. This overview of the local operation of the higher education system is essential for

---

[2] We need of course to include ourselves in this account, since we have also been guilty of propagating the image of an imploding higher education system to audiences outside Japan. For example, in a *Guardian* interview in 2008, Goodman predicted that up to 40 per cent of Japanese universities could go bankrupt (Shepherd, G, 16 January 2008). He is also featured in a similar report in the *Japan Times* (Hollingworth, *JT*, 28 February 2008). Both of these reports were the subject of a careful and, in hindsight, justified critique by Charles Jannuzi in his blog site *Japan Higher Education Outlook* (Jannuzi 2008) where he accuses Goodman of drawing on and propagating tired stereotypes in his analysis of the future of Japanese higher education—that Japan's universities are playgrounds or that most Japanese have lifelong employment in one company—and ignoring several key features which would help private universities weather the demographic crisis they appeared to be facing in 2008. Most important, he suggests, is that '(I)f there is one sector of education in Japan that can avoid the devastation of the demographics, it is higher education. This is because it enjoys much greater administrative freedom to develop diversified business plans.' Significantly, most of Jannuzi's predictions from 2008 about the next decade for higher education in Japan have proved to be accurate, as explained in Chapter 5.

understanding the options available to those facing the most severe challenges in this period.

Two variables in particular stand out as important for understanding the resilience of Japan's universities in the face of these challenges. The first is the role of the private sector. Japan has had the second largest higher education system in the world in terms of financial investment over the past thirty years, but the majority of accounts (in both Japanese and English) have focused on the national (*kokuritsu*) universities, which account for less than 20 per cent of students (even if they account for most of the research outputs). Our account is very much taken from the perspective of the private sector. This is mainly because, for reasons which we outline, the private universities were the ones under the greatest pressure in the past two decades, but it is also because we believe that the downplaying of the importance of the private sector in Japan may have misled some commentators about some of the key dynamics within the overall system. Indeed—and here our study moves to a more macro level— we believe that the private higher education sector has been understudied on a global level. This is despite the fact that, globally, private universities currently enrol one in three of all higher education students, a proportion which is growing rapidly.

The second key variable which this study brings to light is the role of family businesses in running higher education institutions, another topic which, for reasons we will explore, appears to be understudied on a global stage. As Altbach and colleagues (2019) point out, there is an almost complete absence of studies on the role of family business in relation to universities. This is perhaps particularly conspicuous in the case of Japan since the role of family kinship systems has been identified by many authors, as we will see, as particularly important in the case of Japanese business. Few businesses historically are as robust as family business and nowhere in the world has family business been as successful over such long periods of time as in Japan.

The role of family business in Japan, however, is seen as old-fashioned and feudalistic and, according to some commentators, borders on the taboo when it comes to the discussions of higher education institutions which some feel should not be seen as businesses at all, let alone family businesses. According to the only academic article (Obara 2019) on the topic, 40 per cent of Japanese private universities (i.e. more than 30 per cent of all universities) are family owned or managed. As we shall see later, the figure of 40 per cent is probably an exaggeration—since it includes institutions which are still in the first generation and succession plans are not clear—but it suggests that this is a real and significant phenomenon. The fact that no official figures are published on the number of family-run universities in Japan today is interesting in its own right. Japan is a society which loves to understand itself through statistics and if such statistics have not been collected it is often, as in the case of minority groups in Japan, because it is felt better not to do so.

We will argue that the fact that so many private universities, particularly those which were among the most vulnerable institutions, were family businesses gave them an element of what we call 'inbuilt resilience'. They may have changed size, changed their offerings, changed their location, run at a loss, and been cross-subsidized by other institutions within the family corporation. They may have even changed their name. They have not allowed themselves, however, to be closed, since to do so would place at jeopardy the whole family business enterprise (of which they are often the flagship) as well as the family occupation and reputation. In an unusually explicit comment in 2008, the head of the a study group into the predicament of some private educational corporations, Kiyonari Tadao expressed his frustration about this state of affairs:

> Even when we urge private university corporations to stop recruiting new students because they are in a business situation where recovery is difficult, the head of the governing board (*rijichō*) who is the founder will sometimes say that he wants to continue and will not listen. The feeling that they do not want to end the family business in their generation is stronger than in the case of companies, and this is leading to deepening the wounds (*kizu o hirogeru*).
>
> (*AS*, 21 January 2008)

Rather than seeing family-run universities as an anachronistic leftover from a pre-modern time which is unworthy of serious study, we suggest that they need to be understood as a dynamic and entrepreneurial class of institutions which have, of course, their weaknesses and vulnerabilities, but also important strengths in an increasingly complicated higher education marketplace. This explains not only the growth of such institutions globally but also why they may be welcomed by countries which are under pressure to increase their provision of higher education centrally.

An Outline of the Book

Chapter 1 tells the story of Japanese higher education from 1992 to 2010, from a period of great stability to one of anticipated implosion. What is conspicuous is the uniformity of agreement among commentators about both the key features of the system and its role in the socialization of young people to become fully fledged members of society. In 1992, there was a peak both in the number of 18-year-olds in the Japanese population and in the global power of the Japanese economy. As the economy went into slowdown and then stagnation and the number of 18-year-olds shrank precipitously, so the voices of those predicting a dire future for many of Japan's universities became louder. There were a number of curious aspects to these accounts. The first was that while the bursting of the economic bubble might not have been adequately foreseen, the potential impact of the decline in the number of school leavers after 1992 had been pointed out from the late 1980s. The second was the uniformity of views as to what the outcome of the above would be. Everyone agreed that there would be an implosion in the private higher education sector in Japan. Indeed, there seemed to be general agreement that the government, with its neoliberal agenda, was happy for this to happen. Some academics, including university heads, also seemed to think it would be good for there to be a major shake-up in the sector, and it was pointed out that other countries which had been though such crises had come out stronger as a result.

Chapter 2 provides further context for the ethnographic case study which follows. Accounts of the predicted implosion of Japanese private higher education have tended to see it as a uniquely Japanese story. Chapter 2, however, suggests that it should be looked at in a broader, comparative perspective. Part of that framework is the development and role of private higher education globally. Private higher education is an increasingly significant, ramified, and yet still conspicuously understudied topic. The chapter sets out various established and emerging models of private higher education, explaining key concerns such as the relationship with state authority, diversity of institutional structures and modes of governance, and the interplay of social and commercial missions (profit versus non-profit institutions), all of which can shift in line with economic and demographic change.

Chapter 2 then asks where the Japanese system fits within these models and suggests that the Japanese private higher education sector shares a number of important features with other countries, particularly in Asia. One of these features is the reliance of the state on the private sector to complement public investment in higher education, especially in periods of rapid growth in participation rates. The result has been the entrenchment of a demand-absorbing role for private institutions—not one which is peripheral to the public system but rather the dominant mode of higher education provision. The chapter proceeds to develop a more Japan-specific profile of the private sector. It begins by establishing the definitional scope of private higher education in Japan and presenting data which places the numerical dominance of the private sector in direct contrast with its absolute disadvantage in terms of public investment. It also explains that, despite this financial handicap, private institutions do enjoy certain privileges in terms of governance structures, taxation, and scope of operations, and also boast distinctive educational strengths which allow them to mount strong arguments for more favourable treatment by the state.

To provide a context for understanding these features, the final section of the chapter constitutes an in-depth history of the Japanese private university. This is offered as a conscious alternative to more orthodox historical accounts which tend to place national universities in the limelight and treat their private counterparts as a cast of supporting characters. The headings of the individual sections give an indication of the trajectory of this history: post-war reforms and growth; mass higher education and the rise of the private sector; expansion and diversification; from golden age to recruitment hell.

What this history shows is the complex relationship that the private universities in Japan have had with the state, which has managed to combine elements of laissez-faire with high levels of interference; why they have been seen as attractive investment opportunities by entrepreneurs; and how they have developed a strong sense of independence. All three factors are important for understanding the resilience of private universities in the face of the dramatic changes of the 1990s and 2000s. They also have the potential to enrich existing comparative models of private higher education by proposing a more nuanced and sympathetic engagement with the category of entrepreneurial institutions, of which the case study in the following chapter is one.

Chapter 3 is the first of two ethnographic chapters describing the situation at the institution we call Meikei Gakuin University (MGU) as it was about to hit the bottom of a rapid decline in the number of applications and students. As anthropologists, we draw on kinship studies, anthropological theory, and ethnographic methods in constructing this account. The ethnography of MGU sets out to recapture the atmosphere there in the academic year 2003/4 (Japanese academic years run from April to March) when the original fieldwork was carried out. It sets out the background history of the institution and the way it had positioned itself in the private higher education sector. It outlines the key features of its academic faculty, support staff, and students. It shows how well it was doing at the height of the 18-year-old population in 1992 and how badly by the mid-2000s. It then looks at how students were recruited in 2004 and the efforts which were invested in retaining them in the face of rapidly falling applications and enrolments. When a 'crisis report' was circulated in 2003, MGU was receiving just 10 per cent of the applications of ten years earlier. Its junior college was receiving just 2.5 per cent.

In particular, the account highlights two features. The first is that MGU was a family-run institution which was part of a conglomeration of family-run institutions.[3] The second is the general level of dissatisfaction among staff towards management as the institution faced an increasingly insecure future combined with an equal level of frustration of management towards staff who would not change their practices to confront the problems the institution faced. These two features were perceived to be linked. Staff claimed that they had no information about the real state of affairs because of the tendency of management towards secrecy and hence felt powerless to do anything to change the institution. Management claimed to feel—reflecting the priorities of the classic kinship system in Japan—that it was their personal responsibility to sort out the problems of the institution; they felt a sense of duty towards those who had set MGU up, those currently running it and its linked institutions, and those who would take over in the future. Overall, these mutual perceptions led to a divided community, and it was hard to see how MGU would be able to rescue itself.

Chapter 4 is an account of MGU's recovery. It starts by telling the tale of the establishment of the MGU Law School, which was by far its most major reform project undertaken in the mid-2000s. It sets the story in the context of the history of law education in Japan and the debate in Japan over many decades over how many lawyers the society needed. It gives an outline of the new graduate law schools and then tells the story of the establishment and disestablishment of the MGU Law School. It is concluded that the law school experiment in Japan was an interesting example of, for once, allowing free market forces to play out by not limiting the number of applications to establish a law school. It concludes that in the case of MGU, it was almost certainly better institutionally that the university had opened a law school rather than it had not, even though it closed after just ten years.

The rest of Chapter 4 looks at the other reforms which MGU introduced from the mid-2000s. It reduced its official admissions quota (which protected

---

[3] One of the curious features of studies of family business is how little it draws on anthropological theory and method. In his summaries of the field, Stewart (2003: 383), for example, argues that 'The greatest underutilized resource for advancing the field of family business studies is the large anthropological literature on kinship and marriage' and that (Stewart 2014: 66) 'cultural and social anthropology can advance family business studies thanks to well developed literature in three areas: kinship theory, relevant research, and ethnography (up-close field research using participant observation).'

its government subsidy); it reduced the number of its full-time staff by not replacing those who retired; it reduced its fees. The attached junior college was redesignated as a programme within the undergraduate curriculum; staff bonuses were cut; changes were made in the facilities, from the closing of high-profile retail outlets on campus and the heavy subsidy of one overseas connection to minor decisions such as the reduction of free newspapers on campus. Teaching and the student experience were taken much more seriously by the academic staff. Changes were made in courses and course names; a new programme for foreign students and one taught in English for Japanese students was introduced, and the opportunities to study overseas were greatly expanded. These and other reforms aside, there was a significant generational shift within MGU's owning family, as a new generation emerged and as the family itself sought to lead by example in the reform process.

Chapter 5 returns to the dire predictions made in 2004 for the future of private higher education in Japan and finds that while individual examples can be found on a micro level which support them, on a macro scale the evidence almost all points in the opposite direction. The number of private universities, students in private universities, the proportion of students going to private universities, full-time academic staff, revenue from student fees, and government subsidies are all greater and larger in 2018 than they were in 2004. The value of a university credential can be argued to have improved rather than to have been devalued. Many universities are still operating competitive admissions systems, and the hierarchy of institutions, while it has seen some changes, remains in place and widely used. The development of alternative markets and modes of operation have been much more muted than predicted. Finally, predictions of the number of universities which would go bankrupt have proven spectacularly inaccurate. Chapter 5 not only outlines these trends but also explains some of the reasons for them at the macro level.

The final section of Chapter 5 examines some of the key actions which have allowed private universities to survive the last fifteen years. It suggests that the power of various actors (especially the government, local and central, and the universities themselves) to contend with the macro forces challenging universities in the early 2000s was greatly underestimated. This is in line with many of the accounts of Japan in that period which were still dominated by theories of society which emphasized the power of society rather than that of the actors; or, in theoretical terms, a functionalist (or occasionally a Marxist) rather than a social action theory model. It may well have been the dominant theoretical assumptions which commentators and academics brought to their analysis in the early 2000s which explains why their predictions for private higher education have proven to be so wrong.

The importance of family ownership in this account only emerged as clearly as it did during the writing-up phase of the project. Indeed, we were at first unsure if we were overemphasizing its significance even though it was clearly indicated in our field notes and was consistent with accounts of other areas of Japanese society such as medical and welfare institutions. We were greatly reassured therefore by a project undertaken by Altbach et al. (2019) which, for the first time, collected a number of global case studies of family owned/managed higher education institutions (FOMHEIs, as they call them) and developed a series of generalizations about such institutions. Our cases studies from Japan fitted almost perfectly within these broader frameworks.

In Chapter 6, therefore, we explain how Japanese family businesses in general, and family-run universities in particular, operate in practice and some of the negative and positive tropes with which they are frequently associated. These features include a high level of centralization, little voice for employees, top-down decision-making, and a particular concern over succession. How these can all be both strengths and weaknesses is clear from the case of MGU. The literature on family-run universities also highlights some of the potential conflicts between, on the one hand, family-oriented management approaches and, on the other, assumptions regarding the collegial and public-spirited nature of academic institutions.

Chapter 6 ends with a short discussion of possible outcomes of the '2018 problem' with which this project started. The rate of decline in 18-year-olds between 2018 and 2031 is 80 per cent less per year than it was in the period 1992 to 2009, but decline there will be. The scope for increasing the proportion of school leavers going to university is much reduced since it is already so high in Japan. Even the most optimistic scenarios predict a drop in university entrants from the figure in 2017 of 10 per cent by 2033 and 20 per cent by 2040. The most evident government intervention appears to be pushing for greater top-down management in line with the need for universities to rethink their role in society in the face of changing technologies and market demands. Despite the reappearance of the doom-mongers, however, it may well be that the private university sector in Japan, with its inbuilt resilience and long experience of reacting to crises, will survive better than the public sector.

1

The Predicted Implosion of Japan's Private Higher Education System

This book explores how Japanese private universities have responded, and are responding, to a crisis of dramatic demographic change, major structural reform, and shifting understandings of the social and economic role of higher education. Had such a book been planned as this crisis unfolded in the 2000s, it would almost certainly have been imagined as a story of how the private university sector collapsed in the face of insurmountable challenges. But the story which now demands telling is not one of demise so much as survival. While specific circumstances varied greatly and many different fates befell individual institutions, as a whole Japanese private universities have, contrary to all predictions, proven extraordinarily resilient. In this book we set out to account for this resilience.

In order to understand the gravity of the situation which faced Japan's private universities in the 2000s, it is necessary to begin in 1992, when the population of 18-year-olds (the standard age of entrance to university in Japan) reached its highest level since the 1950s. This population had grown immensely throughout the 1980s, at the same time as the Japanese economy matured and demand for university-educated workers burgeoned. Universities were blessed with an abundance of students competing for admission in a 'hell' of undergraduate entrance examinations for which Japan gained international notoriety. But the country was about to enter a severe demographic decline. It is not difficult to paint a statistical picture of the remarkable speed at which this change progressed and, in turn, at which the surfeit of applicants that universities once enjoyed turned into a deficit. The population of 18-year-olds in Japan increased by 30 per cent between 1980 and its peak in 1992, then decreased by 40 per cent by the mid-2000s (see Figure 1.1). This decline was expected to continue—albeit with some fluctuations—through to 2040 at least, and was to leave the higher education sector, which had increased capacity in line with the population growth of the 1980s, desperately short of students.

Family-Run Universities in Japan: Sources of Inbuilt Resilience in the Face of Demographic Pressure, 1992–2030.
Jeremy Breaden and Roger Goodman, Oxford University Press (2020). © Jeremy Breaden and Roger Goodman.
DOI: 10.1093/oso/9780198863496.001.0001

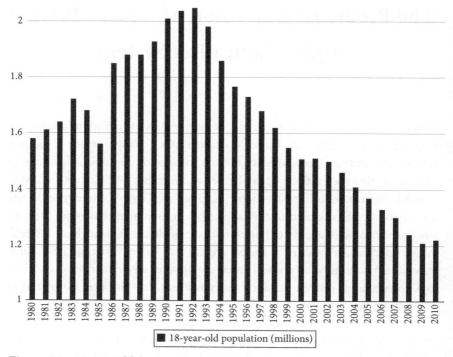

Figure 1.1. 18-year-old (university entrance age) population in Japan, 1980–2010. *Source*: Created by the authors from MEXT 2017a.

What made this change even more momentous was the fact that when it began, Japanese higher education was enjoying unprecedented success not only in scale but also in stability even if some foreign scholars such as the American academic John Zeugner (1984) concluded that the Japanese higher education system was best described as a 'puzzle' because its underlying principles were so different from comparable institutions in most western societies at the time.

At the beginning of the 1990s, Japan had the second-largest higher education system in the world in terms of financial investment, and almost 60 per cent of high school leavers went on to some form of higher education— including 25 per cent who entered 4-year undergraduate degree programmes at universities (*daigaku*; see Chapter 2 for a full typology of higher education institutions in Japan). Within the university sector, private institutions were numerically dominant: they outnumbered both national and local public universities combined by around three to one and enrolled 75 per cent of all university students.[1] Moreover, this huge private university sector was funded mostly by private contributions, with nearly 80 per cent of revenue deriving from student fees and little more than 12 per cent from government subsidies.[2]

There was also widespread agreement over the distinguishing features of university education in Japan. These features are worth outlining as they offer a point of departure for the changes which followed. Japan had a *clearly defined hierarchy* of universities. As a leading scholar of comparative private higher education (Geiger, 1986: 35) put it: 'Most national systems of higher education possess some degree of institutional hierarchy, but Japan's is the most explicit in the world. Furthermore, because employers abide by this hierarchy and because first jobs tend to be lifelong jobs, its effects may be more consequential for life chances than in any other system.' This hierarchy was a composite of the reputational attributes, such as founding origins, size, and geographical location, coupled with the more direct question of how difficult it was for students to gain admission. Public, especially national, universities were generally higher in the hierarchy than private institutions. The hierarchy allowed even people with little knowledge or experience of university education in Japan to confidently pronounce, for example, that the University of Tokyo—a large, comprehensive national university with a long history located in a major metropolitan zone—was indubitably an excellent institution. On the other hand, a small, single-discipline, recently established private university in rural Kyushu was likely to be considered low-quality, no matter how excellent its education and research may actually have been.

The prime determinant of a university's position in the hierarchy was selectivity, as determined through the *hensachi* index. *Hensachi* is essentially a standard deviation score which indicates a prospective university applicant's position relative to her/his peers, as determined through mock entrance exams conducted by major supplementary education providers.[3] These providers

---

[1] Unless specified otherwise, basic data on universities and student numbers in this section are drawn from the Ministry of Education, Culture, Sports, Science and Technology's Basic Schools Survey (*gakkō kihon chōsa*) (MEXT 2018a).

[2] The heavy reliance on private investment in private higher education meant that overall the proportion of the gross domestic product (GDP) assigned to the public subsidy of higher education in Japan was the lowest among members of the OECD and less than half the OECD average (Fukudome 2019: 43). Put the other way around, Japanese households contribute roughly twice the OECD average towards the costs of higher education. On the other hand, Japanese investment in public elementary and junior high schools is relatively high. At these levels, almost everyone attends public institutions (OECD 2017).

[3] *Hensachi* is calculated by subtracting the population mean from an individual raw score, dividing the difference by the population standard deviation and adding the mean score. The *hensachi* range is

published the *hensachi* of students admitted to different universities and departments each year, a system originally intended to help applicants make decisions about where to apply based on their likelihood of success (by comparing their own *hensachi* with the previous year's results), but also inevitably generating a simple and ostensibly transparent ranking of departments based on their selectivity (Dore and Sako 1998: 21–37; Goodman and Oka 2018).[4]

Intuitively, hierarchy should have been reflected in tuition fee levels, with the top-ranked universities able to charge the highest fees. This was not the case in Japan, however. According to Yonezawa and Baba (1998: 151), 'the more selective a university is, the less it charges for tuition fees.' National universities, highly subsidized and entrenched at the top of the reputational pyramid, charged modest fees—around 375,000 yen annually in 1992—while private institutions charged at least double that amount.[5] *Demand for university education was relatively inelastic*—higher prices did not drive demand down—which means that in many cases it was the middle- and lower-tier institutions which charged the highest fees.[6] It is perhaps not surprising that a higher proportion of children from wealthier families went to university; a University of Tokyo survey in 2007 showed that while 61 per cent of children from families with incomes of ¥10 million or more went to university, only

from 20 to 80, and 95.4 per cent of the population fall within the 30–70 range. Since *hensachi* is not an officially condoned system but a mechanism developed by cram schools to help students and parents calculate to which institution they should apply, there is some variation in the figures and calculations used. Two well-known and trusted sites are Daigaku Hensachi.biz and Daigaku Hensachi Jōhō. In the former, all 751 universities in 2018 are divided into eight categories. A small group of fifteen supercompetitive institutions, called S, have an institutional *hensachi* (i.e., the average of all the departmental *hensachi*) of between 65–70. These are followed by thirty universities in the A group (*hensachi* 59–65); fifty in the B group (54–59); 135 in the C group (49–54); ninety-five in the D group (44–49); 120 in the E group (39–44); 265 in the F group (34–39) and forty in the G group (31–34). In 2018, none of the 171 national or public universities were in a group lower than C (i.e., they were all in the top 30 per cent of most competitive universities to enter). Put the other way around, all the universities in the four lowest ranked categories were private.

⁴ *Hensachi* is also a reflection of the overall competitiveness to get into university. The average *hensachi* which was needed to get into university in 1992 (at the peak of competition) was 47; by 2000 it was down to 39 (Daigaku Mirai Mondai Kenkyūkai, 2001: 104).

⁵ In the case of private universities, as Yonezawa and Huang (2018: 432) point out, what they call 'demand absorbing universities' generally charged higher fees than 'selective universities'. The top private universities set relatively low tuition rates, in order to compete with the top national universities for the best students.

⁶ Teichler (2019: 6) describes the higher fees that students who pay at lower level, generally private, universities as a 'fine' for being less successful in the education system. Kariya (2011) shows that while this investment in paying higher fees has generally not paid off as well as it has for those who go to higher level universities, significantly, it has paid off as an investment compared to those who do not go to university at all, particularly during the economic problems of the 1990s and 2000s. This has allowed private universities to continue to charge higher fees.

34 per cent of those with incomes of ¥4 million did so (*NKS*, 2 September 2007). What is perhaps more surprising is the compelling evidence that students paying the highest fees often came from the poorest families (Ishida, 2007).[7]

Many of the other most widely discussed features of the Japanese university system of the late twentieth century related to admission and enrolment. One particularly well-known axiom was that *universities were difficult to enter, easy to exit (hairi-nikui, de-yasui)*. The first half of this statement can be explained by reference to the rapid development of a mass demand for university education in the context of regulated supply and a low level of public investment—facts which are examined in more detail in Chapter 2 of this book. University admission became the pinch point of the education system and entrance exams assumed an importance outweighing educational goals themselves. Ronald Dore (1976: 48) famously described the result as 'an enormously elaborated, very expensive intelligence testing system with some educational spin-off, rather than the other way around.'

The second part of the formulation references the view that university programmes were easy to complete (*de-yasui*). Undergraduate degrees were earned through completion of a prescribed number of course credits, which may have included mandatory subjects, but there was no such thing as a 'graduation exam' in the sense understood in some other university systems. The drop-out rate was extremely low and *university education was viewed as a period of incubation or 'breathing space'* between entrance exam pressures and the demands of the working world, rather than a rigorous academic experience in its own right (Refsing 1992: 118; Tsuda 1993).[8] This tendency, combined with university academics' inclination (discussed later in this section) to view themselves as researchers rather than educators, meant that teaching quality was not given high priority. It was difficult to speak of a distinctive style of university teaching because classrooms tended to be viewed as the exclusive domain of individual instructors and subject to little scrutiny or standardization. The one distinguishing feature of undergraduate teaching and learning

---

[7] The cheapest fees are at the national universities, attended by students who are, on average, wealthier and where individual students receive over forty times the amount of government subsidy of those who go to private universities. This constitutes a massive cross-subsidy of wealthier families by poorer families through the taxation system.

[8] According to the World Competitiveness Yearbook of 2001, Japan ranked lowest among forty-nine economies surveyed with regard to university education meeting the needs of the economy (Arita, *JT*, 26 December 2001). In his comparison of global higher education systems, McLean (1995: 169) cited the most distinctive feature of the Japanese system as being the extent to which it allowed the student a moratorium period for self-development but largely required the consumer to pay for the privilege.

was the *zemi*, a small-group seminar class offered in the final (and sometimes penultimate) year of study, in which students pursued self-directed research projects under the close supervision of a professor (Lee-Cunin 2004: 134; Poole 2010: 65–6, 152).

The simple formulation of graduation as 'easy' could be modified by saying that graduation was the student's prerogative, not the university's. *Graduate employment was the critical entry point to the labour market*, and smooth entry was crucial to one's long-term career prospects (Ohta, Genda, and Kondo 2008). For this reason, some students elected to stay on at university (*ryūnen*) rather than graduate in years when the job market was depressed, but at other times expected to be graduated on time for precisely the same reason. Obstruction of either choice by a university itself could be a newsworthy occurrence.[9]

Ease of graduation in this sense was indicative of the fundamental positioning of universities in the structure of transition from school to work. Conventionally, universities were not required to equip students with vocation-specific skills: employers were more interested in malleable generalists who nonetheless had proved their intelligence and capacity for hard work through their success in entrance examinations. Thus in labour market terms *the function of a university education was to provide a credential rather than a set of concrete capabilities* (see, for example, Amano 2011). As Geiger (1986: 50) pointed out, the fact that the Japanese higher education system was in large measure a device for screening manpower was a 'considerable impediment to the goal of raising academic quality'. Honda (2004) suggested the academic culture inside a university was not going to be put under pressure to improve when employers believed that the performance of students in university entrance exams was still the best indicator of their 'trainability' in the employment place.

A closer look at the university student population in 1992 reveals several other key features. The most notable were that around 95 per cent of students started university at the age of 18 or 19, meaning that universities were *highly geared to catering for school-leavers*,[10] and that the great *majority of these students were enrolled in undergraduate social science and humanities*

---

[9] In one famous case in 1991, more than one hundred students of the Meiji University law faculty were held back from graduating in the requisite four years owing to failure to pass the final examination in a single subject, an event which led not only to protests from the students themselves, but also to widespread public consternation and even bewilderment from the professor in charge of the subject, who stated, 'I am more surprised than anyone' (Sankei Shimbun Shakaibu 1992: 19–20).

[10] Japan has always had one of the lowest percentages of students aged over 25 attending higher education institutions. This is currently around 2 per cent compared with an OECD average of 20 per cent.

programmes. Disciplinary distinctions were especially significant for Japanese undergraduates, as vertical divisions between faculties tended to be strong. Enrolment quotas were determined at departmental and faculty level and admissions processes were therefore faculty-specific rather than university-wide. Inter-faculty transfer was difficult, meaning that the initial choice of course was decisive and it was often easier to drop out and begin again if that choice proved unsatisfactory.

Another telling figure was the *extremely low proportion of students continuing to graduate education*, especially in the social sciences and humanities. In the 1980s, for example, while as many as 200,000 students took an economics undergraduate degree, often with an eye on a career in business, fewer than 2,000 (one in one hundred) went on to graduate work at either master's or doctoral level (Clark 1995: 171–2). In areas like physics, where larger numbers went on to graduate work, in the late 1980s only around 8 per cent of master's students went on to do a doctorate. In general, companies in Japan preferred to take new staff directly from their undergraduate degree and train them in-house in the company-specific way of working. This made it more difficult for employees to take their skills elsewhere and also reduced the pressure on companies to help pay for a national graduate education system. While many universities in Japan offered graduate programmes, therefore, the number of students actually taking graduate degrees was in fact very small as a proportion of all students, leading to some commentators to brand these graduate schools as the 'empty shop window' (Clark 1995: 167).

A further distinguishing feature of the Japanese university student body in the early 1990s was its *gender imbalance*. Changes such as gender equality legislation in the 1980s were beginning to prompt a rise in women's participation, but women were greatly under-represented overall, accounting for 30 per cent of undergraduates and 19 per cent of postgraduates. Rather than going to university, many women instead enrolled in 2-year associate degrees at junior colleges (*tanki daigaku*) studying mainly humanities and domestic science. The gender imbalance was even more pronounced among university academic staff. Women accounted for less than 10 per cent of full-time university academics in 1992 and were overwhelmingly located in humanities and social science departments. Only 5 per cent of full professors and 4 per cent of university presidents were women.

One other notable feature of the Japanese professoriate was the *high rate of academic 'inbreeding'*, whereby universities preferred to recruit their own graduates to new faculty appointments. While 'inbreeding' originated in systems of departmental hierarchy and patronage at the pre-war former imperial universities, as the university sector expanded, senior imperial university professors tended to cultivate intellectual 'colonies' through placement of their former students at other universities, pursuing an accentuated concern with maintaining disciplinary lineage through personnel appointments throughout the sector (Horta et al. 2011). The preference for home-grown academic staff was also sustained by the managerial reasoning that the loyalty of inbred staff contributes to organizational stability and coherence (Yamanoi 2007). As Yonezawa (2015) shows, the proportions of alumni faculty were particularly high in fields such as law, humanities, and engineering and much lower in fields such as economics.

'Inbreeding' was a source of university identity and prestige, related to the fact that *academic identities were connected primarily to research, not teaching*. Academics had a strong sense of autonomy and scholarly collegiality as opposed to a centralized, institutionally bound identity (Ehara 1998). Academics also enjoyed high social status. According to a survey from the early 1990s cited by Yamamoto (1999: 314–15), the social prestige of university professors was on a par with that of lawyers, doctors, and members of the Parliament and considerably higher than that of company presidents. A comparative survey by Altbach and Lewis (1995: 57) suggested that university academics in Japan felt that they were more influential opinion leaders than in almost any other country except South Korea. Despite the high social status of academics and the importance of research to academic identity, universities were routinely criticized for lack of industry-oriented research productivity, and the balance of funding between university-based and industry-based research (conducted in corporate research laboratories) was weighted very highly in favour of the latter (Coleman 1999; Hatakenaka 2010).

Universities had also made *slow progress on internationalization*, which had been identified as one of the main weaknesses of Japanese higher education since at least the 1970s. Japanese students were becoming more internationally mobile with close to 40,000 studying abroad in 1992, but the vast majority were doing so independently rather than through university-arranged programmes (MEXT 2014). Despite enjoying almost continuous growth through the 1980s, international student numbers still stood at little more than 1 per cent of the overall university student population, while non-Japanese nationals accounted for around 2 per cent of full-time academic staff. Research output in international journals was also limited, partly as a product of the highly developed Japanese-language publishing industry and the self-sufficient character of domestic academic communities (Eades 2000; 2005).

Japanese university education in the early 1990s was far from flawless, but the flaws were nonetheless emblematic of a highly developed and relatively stable system. Ten years later, however, the story was very different, as virtually all these well-established attributes were under serious threat.

The Implosion Scenario of the Early 2000s

University Collapse, Universities in Turmoil, Universities Gone Astray, Cliff-Edge Universities, Disappearing Universities, University Revolution, University Bankruptcy, Universities Going Bust: this is just a small selection of titles from a new genre of publications which appeared on the shelves of Japanese bookstores around the turn of the millennium (Asahi Shimbun Kyōiku Shuzaihan 2003; Kawanari 2000; Kuroki 1999; Nakamura 2002; Tada 2001; Shimano 1999; Sugiyama 2004; Yomiuri Shimbunsha 2002). They carried a compelling message: our universities are in serious trouble. The origins of the trouble outlined in such gleefully fatalistic terms in these publications were manifold. One issue was the impending corporatization of Japan's national universities: a 'big bang' which would upend the operating logic of institutions accustomed to nestling comfortably under the wing of the education ministry, thus opening up a new era in which all universities, public and private alike, would compete for the same pool of government funding and revenue from student fees and research contracts. Another issue was the flow-through effect of changes made to the primary and secondary education curriculum in the early 2000s, which would require university professors to contend with a less academically capable student body. Yet another was the growing pressure for universities to contribute more to Japanese industry, producing work-ready graduates and commercially relevant research which would support Japan's overdue economic recovery.

The most apocalyptic tone, however, was saved specifically for the private university sector, which, as has already been stated, at the time enrolled around 75 per cent of all university students and was funded largely through student fee income. With a high proportion, by global standards, of Japan's school leavers already going to university and seemingly little prospect that university entrance rates would rise sufficiently to counterbalance the decline, a point would soon be reached at which the number of applicants to university would be fewer than the overall number of university places available. This point, originally forecast for 2007 and later revised to 2009, would mark a complete reversal of the fundamental principle of excess demand on which higher education had previously operated in Japan.

In the new era, anybody would be able to get a place at university, and the 'hellish' pressure would no longer be on students seeking admission but on universities persuading them to do so. While the elite echelon may actually benefit from this situation as applicants rushed to secure places in the few institutions that remained truly selective, the vast majority of private universities would be forced into a desperate fight for survival and many casualties could be expected. The entirety of this clear-cut logic is encapsulated in the title of a special feature in the Japanese *Economist* magazine in March 2000: 'Decline in 18-year-old Population Drives Open Access to University: Under-Enrolment Will Make University Bankruptcy a Reality' (Kuroki, *EJ*, 21 March 2000). As the decade went on, the concern was borne out by data: 25 per cent of 4-year universities were in deficit in 2002 (*AS*, 10 June 2001); 29.1 per cent of 4-year universities failed to enrol their full quotas of new students in 2004 (*AS*, 4 August 2004). In spring 2006, 40.4 per cent of private universities missed their targets (*SK*, 25 August 2006). In the spring of 2008, around 47 per cent of all 4-year universities were under-enrolled (*SS*, 19 April 2009) and 32 per cent of all private universities were in the red (*AS*, 21 January 2008).

A common topic of speculation therefore was the proportion of under-enrolled private universities which would actually be forced to close their doors. The estimates in the publications noted earlier tended to range from 15 per cent to as high as 40 per cent. Yamada (2001: 287), for example, writes that 'It is estimated that approximately 40 per cent of the private colleges will face financial crisis in 2004.' Though they tended to be somewhat lower, university leaders weighed in with their own estimates. The President of Hosei University, Kiyonari Tadao, put the figure at 30 per cent (interview on 3 February 2004). Yamamoto Shinichi, Director of the Centre for University Studies at the University of Tsukuba, suggested 20 per cent (interview on 24 February 2004). A symposium of deans from seven well-known universities gave estimates of the number of universities which would have stopped accepting new students over the next 10 years averaging out at around sixty, or 10 per cent (*AS*, 25 June 2005). A similar figure was arrived at in a larger-scale survey of private university leaders by the Nihon Keizai Shimbun newspaper (31 October 2005).

Most scholars of higher education refused to be drawn on an actual figure, but nonetheless acknowledged the dire conditions the private sector would face in the coming years, and foresaw a combination of closures, mergers, and new alliances. 'The number [of private universities] which will survive intact is a matter of speculation', wrote the doyen of higher education studies Amano Ikuo in 2004, when there were 526 private universities in Japan. 'It could be 400, it could be 350—nobody knows for sure. What is certain at this stage is that the shift over the next ten years, or even five, will be remarkable' (Amano 2004: 229).

Mainstream news media too became somewhat intoxicated by the scenario of university collapse. The Nihon Keizai Shimbun's 2004–5 series of articles on 'universities in turmoil' (*daigaku gekidō*), for example, included instalments on 'the 2007 shock', 'imminent bursting of the bubble', and 'the impact of university failure' (3 August 2004, 23 October 2004, 8 November 2005). The Yomiuri Shimbun predicted 'the greatest transformation of universities since the postwar reforms' (14 November 2004). New terms came to prominence in the journalistic lexicon. Most notable was *zennyū jidai*, literally the era of university admission for all, referring to the imminent turning point when university places would outnumber students seeking admission. Another was *teiin-ware* or enrolment below the government-approved quota—an obvious sign of danger for fee-reliant private universities. The blanket term for university reform, *daigaku kaikaku*, also enjoyed a peak in popularity in the 2000s (see Figure 1.2).[11]

By 2007, with the very first casualties of the universal admission era starting to appear, the tone became even more agitated. '40 percent of universities are already under-enrolled, 27 private university corporations on the brink of bankruptcy', reported the *Economist* magazine (16 January 2007), while the *Asahi Shimbun* wrote of 'the vanishing alma mater: successive bankruptcies of private university corporations' (*AS*, 16 April 2007). 'The market will be halved! Death knell is sounding for universities', predicted the *Shūkan Tōyō Keizai* magazine (13 October 2007). Representatives of the private university sector were not inclined to refute these statements. 'We are entering an era of survival of the fittest', agreed Nishii Yasuhiko of the Promotion and Mutual Aid Corporation for Private Schools of Japan. 'We need to find ways to let weaker universities close without disrupting the education of their students' (Fackler, *NYT*, 22 June 2007).

The heads of some of the universities under threat (see, for example, Fukui 2004) began to talk about the need for 'survival strategies' (*survival senryaku*). What new strategies could universities adopt in an era of cutthroat

---

[11] A catalogue search of the National Diet Library in Tokyo reveals no fewer than 119 books and 845 periodical articles with the Japanese words 'university reform' (*daigaku kaikaku*) in the title published between 1995 and 2004, compared to just twenty-one and 167 respectively in the previous decade.

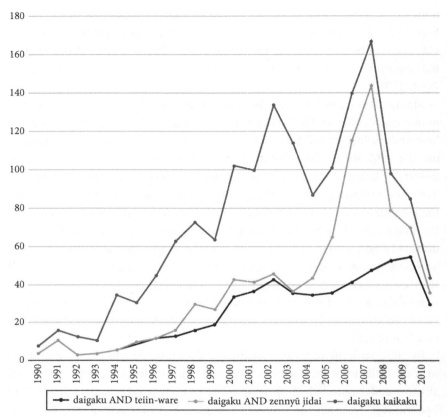

Figure 1.2. Appearance of key terms in *Mainichi Shimbun* newspaper articles, 1990–2010.

Source: Mainichi Shimbun *Maisaku* database, accessed 1 November 2018. Y axis is number of articles including the search term in headline and/or body text.

competition? How would families sending children to university be able to identify those with the best prospects of survival? Would a university degree be worth anything in the job market anymore? What impact would the changes have on secondary education, and on the huge supplementary education (*juku* and *yobikō*) industry which prepared students for university entrance exams? Would the government step in to prop up failing universities, or would it, in the neoliberal spirit permeating so many other domains of policy at the time, leave them at the mercy of the market? These are just some of the many questions which preoccupied not only researchers and educators but also university applicants, their parents, and a wide spectrum of the Japanese reading public in the early to mid-2000s.

At first glance, it is puzzling why people in Japan appeared so surprised by the imminent implosion of the higher education system. The scenario posed no great challenge for demographers. With very little immigration and an infant mortality rate close to zero, population change could be forecast with relative ease. It was difficult to understand why action had not been taken earlier to avert the impending disaster. This question becomes even more pertinent in light of some of the discussions which had taken place a decade earlier, just before the decline in the 18-year-old population began. A publication of the Japan Association of Private Colleges and Universities in 1987 refers to demographic change as 'The Impending Storm', explaining that rather than allowing themselves to become preoccupied with the short-term rise in demand they were currently enjoying, universities should be planning for the long-term decline which would follow. A 1987 article in the *Japan Quarterly*, for example, states: 'The private colleges anticipate a decline in enrolments after 1992, when the 18-year-old population reaches a peak, so school administration policy is focused instead on how to survive when the time comes. Rather than expanding enrolments to meet the current demand, the aim is to attract highly qualified students and improve the school's reputation in order to survive the lean years ahead' (Nishimura 1987: 182). A 1989 book edited by leading higher education scholar Kitamura Kazuyuki is full of expectations for dramatic change 'as the myth of permanence in universities' is shattered (Kitamura 1989).[12] A 1991 report of the University Council, the government's main advisory body on university policy, directly addressed the question of 'how best to equip higher education for a period of rapid decrease in 18-year-old population' and recommended that 'new establishments and expansions should in principle be curbed' (University Council 1991).

The Literature of Crisis and Reform in the Early 2000s

It was the combination of demographic with other political, economic, and social changes taking place in the 1990s and early 2000s which appeared to catch everyone off guard. For example, the employment situation for young people in Japan was completely different in the early 2000s than it had been

---

[12] Just a decade later, Kitamura (2002, see also Clark, 2003) was writing with some regret about a 'lost decade' which many universities had squandered, and now found themselves woefully unprepared for the coming crisis.

in the early 1990s before the 'economic bubble' burst. The percentage of final-year university students securing a job offer by the December before graduation—a critical point in Japan's highly formalized graduate employment system—dropped to an all-time low of 73.5 per cent in 2003 (*NKS*, 14 January 2004). The downturn was even more concerning because it coincided with a shift in white-collar employment practices. The high school leavers of the 1980s and 90s had fought hard for their places at university, but as graduates they profited from a culture of stable and long-term white-collar employment. By the early 2000s a combination of economic recession and labour market deregulation was prompting employers to eschew this culture in favour of limited-term appointments and casual outsourced labour. In 2005, 33 per cent of the workforce was classified as 'non-regular' (*hiseiki*; casual, part-time, temporary, short-term, etc.), compared to 19 per cent at the start of the Heisei era in 1989 (Statistics Bureau 2014). It was difficult to see how a university degree could retain its value as a credential when virtually anybody could enter university. The fundamental nexus between education and socio-economic status, the key feature of Japanese meritocracy, would surely be undermined: employers would need to find other ways of selecting candidates and graduates would need new strategies for distinguishing themselves in the job market.

Adding to the insecurity around job prospects after graduation was the notion that the initial step of selecting a 'good' university to which to apply would be more complex in the *zennyū* era. As outlined earlier, Japan's universities had come to operate within a well-established hierarchy based primarily on the degree of difficulty of their entrance examinations. In the new era, with places at university available to all who wanted them, entrance exams would surely lose their relevance for all but the elite echelon, and the selectivity-driven logic of the existing hierarchy would be shattered. Fine differentiations based on entrance examination results would be replaced by a more dramatic polarization (*nikyoku-ka*) of the university sector, firstly between those elite universities which had the luxury of remaining selective and those grateful to fill their classrooms with any willing applicants, and secondly between institutions with the managerial ingenuity to adjust to the *zennyū* era and those unable or unwilling to do so. This polarization scenario was encapsulated in the title of many popular publications around the turn of the millennium, such as *Tsubureru Daigaku, Nobiru Daigaku* (Universities that will go bust and those that will flourish; Umezu 2001) and the *Abunai Daigaku, Kieru Daigaku* (Universities at risk and those that will disappear; Shimano 1999) series, which is still being published annually at the time of writing. The terms *kachi-gumi* and *make-gumi* (winners' circle and losers' circle) were also invoked widely in this account (Nakai 2002).

Students, parents, and high school teachers would need new criteria for distinguishing between these categories. The above-mentioned publications themselves provided starting points, but more sophisticated approaches were also being developed. One of the pioneering, and still most popular, initiatives in this field was the Asahi Shimbun's annual *Daigaku Ranking* (University Rankings), launched in 1994, which ranked universities on a wide variety of criteria ranging from reputation among secondary school teachers to research income and community outreach activities (Asahi Shimbunsha 2002). Another well-known contribution was the annual feature in the business magazine *Shūkan Tōyō Keizai* on 'truly strong universities' (*hontō ni tsuyoi daigaku*), which gave especial emphasis to financial health and graduate employment prospects (*STK*, 16 September 2000). Many of these new rankings ended up closely mirroring the traditional selectivity-based hierarchy, but others celebrated the distinctive successes of small, non-elite universities in adapting to changing conditions. A substantial portion of the literature on university reform in this period, profiled below, was similarly directed to consumers seeking an answer to the question of how to appraise university quality without relying on entrance exam selectivity.

The sense that universities were in the midst of a great upheaval was further enhanced by the changes underway in the public sector. National universities were facing the watershed of corporatization (*hōjinka*) in 2004, a transformation which would see them untethered from the educational bureaucracy and compelled to compete for funding in a more open market (Goodman 2010). Observers suggested that this would lead to a more 'borderless' or 'single-dimensional' higher education landscape in Japan, which would quickly make it very difficult for all but the top few private universities to compete, especially in a period of market contraction (AFCSPU 2004; Ichikawa 2000; Kiyonari and Hayata 2005). One commentator even proclaimed that national university corporatization alone would spell the demise of 300 private universities (Nakamura, C, 2001).

Thus the tightening of the market through demographic change seemed to be highly consistent with the government's wider vision for higher education reform shaped by market forces, not government regulation. 'The decrease in potential student population could have a positive effect on Japanese universities in that it will create a competitive environment among them and make them conduct reforms to meet the needs of students', commented Goda Takafumi, director of the university division of the education ministry's higher education bureau in 2003. 'It is a fact that they may face bankruptcy, but ultimately I think it good that, in order to survive, the universities will be forced to change.' (*JT* 6 October 2002). This was the feeling among some private university leaders, too. 'When private universities go bust, it won't be because somebody makes them do so', said Kato Hiroshi of Chiba University of Commerce. 'They will go bust because they can't attract enough applicants. And when they do, closures and amalgamations will be possible' (Amano 2004: 179).[13]

There was also widespread concern over the impact on educational practice, as struggling private universities moved to admit students of a calibre previously considered unsuited for higher education and poorly prepared for university-level content. The teaching of such students was already an acknowledged problem: a 3-year nationwide survey conducted in the late 1990s highlighted serious gaps in basic scholastic abilities, including large numbers of university students unable to solve primary school-level mathematics problems (Tose and Nishimura 2001). New approaches to the task of teaching and managing university classrooms became a very common topic (Furusawa 2001; Kinukawa and Tachi 2004; Tokai Higher Education Research Institute 2001). A new academic society, the Japan Association for Developmental Education, was established in 2005 specifically to formulate remedial strategies for students unprepared for university classes (*SS*, 23 March 2005).[14] There was even a series of books devoted to pressing questions such as how professors could deal with students whispering and using electronic devices in their lectures (see, for example, Shimada 2002). This interest in changing student profiles was connected to a high-profile reform of primary and secondary education, namely the 2003 introduction of a *yutori kyōiku* or 'relaxed' educational curriculum, which had paradoxically led to a widespread panic over declining scholastic standards. 'The 2006 problem'—referring to the year in which the first wave of students educated under the new curriculum would enter universities—became a common shorthand for the challenges facing university educators (see, for example, *YS*, 8 November 2004).

---

[13] This drive to allow the market to sort out issues in the higher education sector in Japan was very much in tune with the views of external agencies which looked at the Japanese system. A major report by the OECD (Newby at al. 2009: 49) expresses this very clearly, where it writes: 'MEXT has shown commendable restraint in permitting private universities to enter bankruptcy, the first of which occurred in 2005.'

[14] Nearly a fifth of the students at private universities had the reading ability expected of 13- to 15-year-olds, according to a survey of 13,000 first year students carried out by the National Institute of Media Education (NIME) (Johnson, G, 25 November 2004). In 2006, around 30 per cent of all universities provided some form of remedial education (*SK*, 18 April, 2008).

Narratives of university crisis thus drew on a wide range of concerns circulating beyond the immediate sphere of university education, all of which would contribute to the imminent implosion.

There was also, however, a substantial body of work affirming the implosion as an opportunity at last to undertake serious reform of educational practice at universities. Amano described this optimistically as 'the first time in the history of the university in Japan that true reform in university teaching and learning had begun' (Amano and Poole 2005: 697). New centres of higher education studies were established, along with postgraduate programmes designed to cultivate a new generation of professional university administrators (Oba 2009). 'It's ironic, but it took this crisis to make universities realize they actually have to educate their students', observed Hamana Atsushi, President, Kansai University of International Studies (Fackler, NYT, 22 June 2007). According to Murakami Kiyoaki from the Mitsubishi Research Institute, 'Ruthless competition will ultimately be good for students' (Walsh, TA, 4 July 2005).

Many university professors themselves were eager to capitalize on the crisis, perceiving how it could force their universities finally to confront long-standing problems such as misalignment with industry needs, bureaucratic inefficiency, and academic traditionalism, or even simply to weed out some of the inferior products of expansion of the university sector in the 1980s and 90s (Kusaka et al. 2003; Nishida 2000; Sato 2001; Takeda 2001). A number of foreign scholars working in the Japanese education system tended to concur with these pronouncements, finding that the scenario of collapse fitted neatly within their critiques of the desultory and static nature of university organizations and the broader dysfunctional tendencies of Japan's academic culture (Hall 1998; McVeigh 2002; 2006).[15] One North American professor with a long career in Japanese academia offered the following memorable (unpublished) caricature of university student life, which effectively highlights the areas in most urgent need of reform:

> Bakataro arrives at the International University of Virtue Creation and Information Studies after a 90 minute commute from his parents' house where he got four hours of sleep after finishing one of his three part time jobs. He has not been to the university in six weeks but figures that since it is near the end of the term, he should find out whether there is an exam and when it is.

[15] Excoriating reviews of Hall's book by Ramseyer (1999) and McVeigh's by Kinmonth (2008) accuse the authors of being self-serving, relentlessly negative about Japan, and ethnocentric.

Details of the exam were on the course syllabus, but he has not read the syllabus let alone any of the assigned or suggested readings. He thinks he may still have a copy of the syllabus but is too tired to look for it.

When he gets to the classroom, he is 15 minutes late but he does not worry about missing anything because he knows the professor never shows up until at least 20 and often 30 minutes after the nominal start of class. He looks around the classroom to see if there is anyone he knows, but there isn't, so he sits in the back so that the lecturer's voice is less likely to disturb his nap once he has heard any announcement about the exam. The fact that he is at an 'international university' but all the students in the classroom are Japanese is not something that he has ever thought about. He has heard that there were some Chinese students who were studying humanities and social science subjects at the university, but they have decamped to a larger city with more chances for earning money through side jobs.

Much of the literature in the early 2000s was focused on the search for new models of university management. Scholars of comparative higher education pointed out that the predicament of Japan's private universities was not entirely without precedent, and university leaders and policymakers would do well to examine similar periods of transition in other countries (Ehara and Sugimoto 2005). The successes of universities in the United States in stream-lining their operations and opening up new markets for both education and research furnished an especially persuasive reference point (Aoki et al. 2001; Kitamura 1997; Tachi 1997).[16] Common themes included reforming bureau-cratic processes and top-heavy academic personnel structures, restructuring finances, and developing systems for organizational 'crisis management' (Aoki et al. 2001; Kawahara 2004; Maruyama 2002; Nakamura 1997; Obinata 2001). The activities of reform-minded private universities within Japan, such as Hosei and Ritsumeikan, were proffered as inspiration to university leaders struggling to come to terms with the reform agenda. Acknowledging that the work done to date would not be enough to navigate a course through the impending disaster, Hosei's President envisaged a 'new operating model' for

---

[16] A collection of papers by commentators on Japanese higher education (Daigaku Mondai Mirai Kenkyūkai, 2001: 40–3) pointed out that in the 1970s and 1980s more than eighty institutions of higher education in the United States went bankrupt and that the era was characterized by a large number of mergers and acquisitions when weak universities were taken under the wing of stronger ones. It also compared, albeit very briefly and with little data, the situation of Japanese universities with that of Japanese banks in the 1990s, which led to multiple tie-ups between previously inde-pendent institutions.

universities: managed efficiently, focused on educational quality and student well-being, well connected with the local community and industry, technologically savvy, and, above all, entrepreneurial enough to look beyond the shrinking pool of high school leavers in Japan and attract clientele from other parts of society (Kiyonari 2001 and 2003; see also Nakamura, K. 2001). These recommendations echoed in many ways the measures recommended by the aforementioned University Council report on planning for higher education in the post-1992 contraction period (University Council 1991).[17]

The exploitation of non-traditional markets for university education was a focal point of discussion. One way of turning population change from a curse into a blessing would be to develop new offerings for mature students, especially the over-60s—Japan's largest and most affluent demographic. These 'lifelong education' programmes would be especially efficient as they could make use of universities' existing teaching personnel and campus resources (Yamamoto 2012). Meanwhile, trends such as globalization and technological advancement were transforming business and professional domains in Japan. Universities could capitalize on these changes by developing more flexible postgraduate offerings, both degree-based professional education and short-term modules tailored for corporate clients in fields such as executive training. Another major revenue stream for universities in developed countries, international education, remained largely unexploited in Japan. The recruitment of fee-paying international students could surely go some way toward replenishing the dwindling pool of Japanese high school graduates.

Some scholarly assessments were less optimistic, however, pointing to the vast and uncoordinated assortment of discrete initiatives lacking integration and overall transformative effect (Arimoto and Yamamoto 2003; Yamagishi 2001). Private universities, other than the few which were blessed with significant financial reserves and strong leadership structures, also faced considerable constraints on their capacity to pursue reform. Amano's (2000) collection of interviews with university presidents demonstrates these problems vividly. The scenario of contraction and potential university collapse had clearly been

---

[17] Snoddy (1996) in his comparative analysis of strategies to maintain enrolments at Japanese and American private institutions of higher education outlines three basic courses of action available: expansion of traditional clientele, expansion of non-traditional clientele, and increasing the retention rate. He (1996: 58) says that that there was very little investment in the third of these—retention—because there were few dropouts in Japan based on academic performance (efforts were made to ensure all students can pass and graduate) and there were no mechanisms for re-entry with advanced standing after a student drops out. His survey (1996: 93, 98–100) also suggests that most administrators did not know how to increase the number of non-traditional students, meaning that the emphasis on retaining student numbers was focused almost entirely in the mid-1990s on recruiting traditional school-leaver students by improving the attractiveness of university offerings and their recruitment processes.

internalized by all those interviewed, but it simply marked the point of departure for highly divergent accounts of what should be done in response. Some looked forward to dramatic change, others looked back to long-standing principles; some embraced the challenge personally, others looked elsewhere for answers. Perhaps most surprisingly, the sense in all these works is of a challenge which lies ahead—despite the fact that the major change, demographic decline, had been underway since 1992.

A major survey of private university leaders conducted in 2005 (Nihon Keizai Shimbun 2005) offers some quantitative sense of the peculiar combination of anxiety and aimlessness which pervaded the sector. More than half of respondents reported that their operating conditions had worsened in the 5 years up to 2004. When asked to predict what would happen as competition became even fiercer, the only issue on which more than 50 per cent concurred was that 'more institutions will become under-enrolled, and there will be many bankruptcies and closures'; other popular responses (40 per cent and above) included 'there will be amalgamations and transfers', 'there will be more outsourcing and other forms of rationalisation', and 'academic and administrative staff expenses will be cut'. Eighty per cent agreed that there were 'too many' universities in Japan; only 15 per cent thought that the number was 'appropriate' and 4.4 per cent that there should be more. The majority (55.9 per cent) agreed that 'there are not many people in universities who really understand management.'

To summarize: the millennial literature, both popular and scholarly, evidences unanimous agreement that Japan's private university sector would experience a major implosion in the near future. Demographic change would trigger a dramatic drop in enrolments and revenue, sending many universities into the red and forcing a substantial minority to close or at least merge. There was also widespread speculation regarding the impact of this scenario. Clearly, there would be winners and losers, and the line between them would become better defined than ever. To secure a place on the positive side of the ledger, universities would need urgently to develop alternative markets and modes of operation.

The concern, however, was not only the fate of universities themselves. The implosion scenario also prompted reconsideration of some of the most well-established features of the Japanese university system outlined at the start of this chapter, as selectivity-based hierarchies were upset and the value of a university degree inevitably called into question. Possibly the most concentrated distillation of these wide-ranging concerns is found in an array of expert predictions regarding the future of Japan's universities compiled in 2001 by the magazine publisher Tōyō Keizai (Daigaku Mirai Mondai Kenkyūkai 2001). Articles in this compilation include not only predictable candidates such as the onset of hyper-competition to recruit students and a rapid increase in university bankruptcies, but also the demise of entrance examinations and *hensachi*, the end of public subsidies for universities, dropout rates of more than 30 per cent, the entry of new market players such as for-profit businesses and foreign universities, strategic alliances with supplementary education schools and professional training colleges, the rise of postgraduate education and professional schools, large-scale recruitment of international students from Asia, and the introduction of performance pay for professors. Virtually all the taken-for-granted distinguishing features of Japanese university education were under threat.

In the chapters which follow, we examine what actually did happen to Japan's universities following the predicted implosion scenario of the early 2000s—and why. To do so, we need to step back from the immediate case studies and set the Japanese higher education system in a broader comparative and historical context. The story of what happened in Japan has resonances and lessons for other sectors of Japanese society as well as higher education systems in other countries. In the next chapter, we look at Japan's private universities in comparative perspective.

2

Japanese Private Universities in Comparative Perspective

Comparative Frame: Private Higher Education

In April 2018, in an op-ed on the widely read blog site, *Inside Higher Ed*, Daniel Levy[1] (2018a) provides a good summary of the current state of understanding and research on private higher education:[2]

> Private institutions enroll one in three of the world's higher education students. By 2010 private enrollment reached 57 million, today surely pushing toward 70 million...Ten countries account for nearly 70 per cent of global private enrollment but fewer than 10 of nearly 200 countries have no private enrollment. Asia has easily the largest private enrollment,... but each of the world's seven regions has more than one in ten of its students in private institutions...Private higher education is thus too large, too ubiquitous, too permanent, and too intertwined into various parts of society to minimize, to treat as if it were peripheral...The world's higher education cannot be understood without understanding its private sector.

As Marginson (2018) points out, part of the problem in talking about typologies of private higher education has been the diverse use of the words 'private' or 'privatization' in this context and the fact that definitions are constantly challenged and change over time. In Continental Europe in the early 2000s, for example, these terms covered both the emergence of genuinely private new institutions in Central and South Eastern Europe as well as the process by

---

[1] Daniel Levy directs the Program for Research on Private Higher Education (PROPHE), one of the most active research centres globally on private higher education.

[2] The article was produced to accompany the first-ever comprehensive global private–public dataset on higher education, see: http://www.prophe.org/en/global-data/. The findings have since been published in the scholarly journal *Higher Education* (Levy 2018b).

Family-Run Universities in Japan: Sources of Inbuilt Resilience in the Face of Demographic Pressure, 1992–2030.
Jeremy Breaden and Roger Goodman, Oxford University Press (2020). © Jeremy Breaden and Roger Goodman.
DOI: 10.1093/oso/9780198863496.001.0001

which public institutions were forced to compete for funding sources in so-called quasi-market structures (Dima 2004).[3]

Despite confusion over the differing use of terms such as 'independent', 'non-profit', 'non-state' in different countries, there have been several notable attempts at standardization. The *OECD Handbook for Internationally Comparative Education Statistics* (2004: 58), for example, proposes that, 'An institution is classified as private if ultimate control rests with a non-governmental organization (e.g. a church, trade union or business enterprise), or if its Governing Board consists of members not selected by a public agency.' It further proposes (OECD 2004: 59) two subcategories of private institutions: 'government-dependent', which either receive 50 per cent or more of their core funding from governmental agencies or whose teaching personnel are paid by a government agency (directly or through government), and 'independent', where those conditions do not pertain.

In the 1980s, two typologies of public–private sectors in higher education institutions were produced which have dominated the thinking in the field ever since. Geiger (1986) proposed a tripartite model based on a comparative study of private education in eight countries based on their relationship with public or national sectors: *mass private sectors* (Japan, Philippines); *parallel private sectors* (the Netherlands, Belgium); and *peripheral private sectors* (France, Sweden, UK). The private higher education sector in the US did not fit neatly into any of these three categories, so Geiger discussed it as a fourth type, the *American private sector*, on its own. In the US, until the mid-nineteenth century, private higher education institutions had been in the overwhelming majority, and while in pure numbers this is still marginally the case, the mass expansion of huge public higher education institutions from the mid-1970s means that in total today private institutions account for less than a quarter of total higher education enrolments. Expansion in the US, therefore, has been mainly in the public sector, while in Japan it has been in the private sector.

At almost the same time as Geiger produced his tripartite model above, Levy (1986) proposed an alternative typology based on a broader set of criteria and resulting in a more complex typology of five 'patterns'. The first two of these patterns are essentially based around higher education being a single sector

---

[3] The terms 'private' and 'privatization' in relation to higher education have become particularly complex in the case of the UK where universities are still generally regarded as public even though the vast majority of their funding for teaching now comes through loans which students take out to pay for their education. The picture is complicated even further by the recent opening up of higher education to new private providers, both for-profit and non-profit, most of which are small scale and many of which are very short-lived: 50 per cent of private HE providers which operated in the UK in 2014 were no longer in operation three years later (Hunt and Boliver, 2019).

and the latter three around it being made up of dual sectors. These patterns can be characterized by the following features and exemplars:

Statist: almost no privately funded universities; funds received from the state; strong role of ministries in distributing funds (i.e.: communist nations, most of Western Europe, much of former French Africa)

Public-Autonomous: almost no privately funded universities; previously mixed private–public funding, now mainly public; 'buffer organizations' between state and universities (i.e.: Australia, UK, Israel, New Zealand, Nigeria)

Homogenized: traditionally two sectors, funded differently; evolved towards mostly public funding for private as well as public sectors; sectoral distinctiveness based now on tradition and possibly governance rather than funding (i.e.: Belgium, Canada, Chile, the Netherlands)

Distinctive, minority private: private sector more than 10 per cent but less than 50 per cent of enrolments; private sector relies mostly on private finance; public sector relies mostly on public finance (i.e.: most of Latin America)

Distinctive, majority private: private sector has more than 50 per cent but less than 100 per cent of enrolments; private sector relies mostly on private finance; public sector relies mostly on public finance (Examples: Brazil, India, Japan, Philippines).

The main critiques of Levy and Geiger's models of the 1980s were that they were static and synchronic. While they provided a framework into which any country could be placed at any one point in time, they did not explain how this had come about or give any indication as to how they might develop in the future. Levy (2008) addressed these critiques to some extent at a conference he attended in Tokyo in 2008 comparing the trajectories of private higher education systems across a number of East Asian countries. He identified the fact that, increasingly, different regions of the world were exhibiting different patterns of private higher education: Western Europe had the lowest number of private institutions; the US, which had long been thought to be the model for others, now had less than the average; Eastern Europe saw huge growth, especially in countries like Poland, immediately post-1989 as demand for tertiary education soared after the collapse of Communism; the Middle East, North Africa, and sub-Saharan African all also saw rapid growth in the 1990s and early 2000s (though unlike Eastern Europe this was at the initiative of, or with promotion from, government); and Latin America grew to around 40 per cent of higher education provision by around 1980 and has maintained the same level ever since with, in subsequent decades, public and private higher education growing at roughly the same rate.

In terms of common patterns across the regions of the world, Levy (2008: 14–16) picked out a number of key points. The first is that world rankings of leading universities contain almost none outside the US that are private, and even those, in terms of funding, are more public than private. To reinforce this point, he proposes the use of the term 'semi-elite' to categorize the leading private universities outside the US. In almost all countries, the best students leaving secondary school still put the top public universities as their first choice. Second, he points towards what he calls 'demand-absorbing private institutions' as the largest growth type by far in the world: they thrive because in so many countries across the world demand for higher education exceeds public supply, in large part because of the global trend for the state to put a hold on its public expenditure accounts. A third type that he identifies, he calls 'culturally pluralizing' private institutions, most of which are culturally conservative and many of which are religious in the wake of increased secularization of the education system. Finally, he points out that private higher education has often played a key role for women, both progressively in bringing more of them into higher education but also conservatively by offering an alternative form of higher education, as in the case of women-only institutions in Japan.

Levy (2008: 21) points to a number of challenges which threaten to inhibit further growth of the private higher education sector globally. There is a continued perception in parts of the world that private higher education is 'strange and seems illegitimate'. There is also opposition from the public sector which feels under threat. Government policy which has tried to impose regulation—such as tuition caps or through the accreditation of programmes dominated by the models of the public institutions—is a threat to the existence of the private higher education sector. At the same time, the increasing privatization of public institutions, such as the conversion of Japanese national universities into independent administrative entities in the early 2000s, allows public universities to enter into areas of entrepreneurship, such as working with industry or competing for students, which had previously been the preserve of the private sector. Another threat to the current private universities may come from the increasing development of for-profit higher education institutions, such as Laureate Education, which often bypass state accreditation processes and allow the market to determine their success or failure. The success of the for-profit sector in countries like Brazil has encouraged the state to push more private universities into becoming for-profit because it allows it to tax them on their profits. The final challenge which Levy identifies as threatening the private higher education sector across the developed world is a demographic one.[4]

The demographic threat to private universities in many parts of the world that Levy describes is particularly interesting when so much of the literature on the threats faced by Japanese private higher education, reviewed in Chapter 1, suggests that it is a situation somehow unique to Japan. As Huang (2019) shows, very little of the research undertaken by higher education scholars in Japan connect Japanese experiences with those of higher education systems elsewhere. Where comparisons are made with the Japanese situation, this is almost always within an Asian context and it is instructive to consider this literature too before turning to the Japanese case itself.

According to Altbach (2014: 15), while many Asian countries can point to higher education institutions which long pre-date the institutions of western societies—Confucian academies in China, traditional madrasahs in India, and similar institutions in Vietnam, Cambodia, and Thailand—'no Asian university is truly Asian in origin—all are based on European academic models and traditions, in many cases imposed by colonial rulers, and in others (e.g., Japan and Thailand) on voluntarily adopted Western models.' When those countries that had been colonized regained their independence, none of them abandoned the academic models which they had developed in their colonial period; indeed, they continued to look abroad, especially to the US, for new ideas to develop their institutions. This background has had a major impact on how such institutions have subsequently developed and to a large degree explains why, historically, they have been peripheral players internationally in terms of scientific and research leadership.[5]

There have been a number of commonalities across East and South East Asian societies in relation to the development of their education systems which Cummings (1997a) has delineated in his 'J-Model'. The 'J' stands for Japan as the country which was the first architect of the following key components of the model: state coordination of education and research development and utilization of human resources in manpower planning;

---

[4] The widespread nature of this phenomenon has been masked somewhat by the fact that it does not pertain in the United States where its immigrant and minority populations continue to grow. In 2013 *The Independent* reported that '77 per cent of university leaders (in the UK) interviewed believed a number of universities will fail or go bankrupt as a result of ... dwindling student applications (due to) rising fees coupled with a fall in the birthrate' (Garner, *I*, 24 June 2013).

[5] Another common feature of the development of higher education across Asia has been the role of Christian missionaries. Indeed, with the exceptions of the Philippines and possibly South Korea, it could be argued that the missionaries were far more successful in creating educational institutions than they were in making converts.

priority of universal primary education; heavy investment by individual students, their families, and the private sector. The origins of these elements can be traced back to the need for Asian societies to meet western threats— such as Japan did in the Meiji period with the development of a centralized state and investment in primary education—but their full impact was first realized in the 1960s with the beginning of what came to be called the 'Japanese economic miracle'. Cummings (1997a: 279) developed his model into a 'flying geese' framework, with Japan at the front, and its colonies of Korea and Taiwan following in one wake, and Thailand, Singapore, Malaysia, and Indonesia (which had all by the 1980s consciously determined to follow Japan) in the other.

The J-Model concept of a strong, centralized but lean state is well documented, as is the emphasis on primary education focusing on basic skills and national priorities and the instruction to learn from western models and to combine them with Asian values to drive development. The fact that the state expected 'society' to fill the gaps which were not covered by state provision is perhaps somewhat less well understood. As Cummings (1997a: 284–5) says: 'Rather than contain... popular demand, the state assumed a permissive policy, only intervening when the private response began to conflict with public objectives. Thus a vigorous private sector often emerged to complement the public sector.' This private education sector took a number of forms: pre-school private education (*yōchien* in Japan); supplementary private education for those in schools and between schools (*juku* and *yobikō* in Japan); and private schools and universities themselves, set up by educational entrepreneurs to accommodate the sometimes very sizeable 'excess demand' which existed in these countries (James and Benjamin 1988).

In a broader comparative analysis of thirteen East and South East Asian countries in the same volume as his work on the J-Model, Cummings (1997b: 144) identified five enabling factors for the development of a private educational sector—indigenous institutional heritage; indigenous entrepreneurs; mission schools; foreign colonial policy; foreign influence—and examined the extent to which these existed in different countries. Only Japan unequivocally met four of these criteria (it was not colonized).

Cummings (1997b: 150–2) also set out some common policy implications which can be gleaned from the general experience of private education across the region:

- 'Privateness' can breed more 'privateness': as private sectors get started they experience economies of scale through expansion;
- Large private sectors can thwart the achievement of certain public goals: in a democracy individuals can buy education which improves their

chances and which undercuts state concerns to maintain an educational meritocracy;
- Private schools may recruit critical staff from the public sector;
- Private schools may be corrupt: the need to survive may make them susceptible to accepting gifts in return for entrance;
- Private schools may promote controversy: the entrepreneurs who establish private schools may not always see eye to eye with government policy;
- The existence of a moderate-sized private sector tends to stimulate greater efficiency in the public sector; once the private sector exceeds 40 per cent, however, this impact declines.

In his brief summary of the private higher education system in Asia, Altbach (2004: 24–6) picks out the following key features: they are generally found at the lower end of the prestige hierarchy; they rely on tuition fees for the vast majority of their funding; they have little tradition of private philanthropy (in part because the tax regime does not reward private donations to non-profit organization such as universities); and, many are family owned, a phenomenon which we will pick up on again in Chapter 3.

Finally, Umakoshi (2004) provides an analysis of private higher education in Asia by building on the earlier work of Geiger and proposes that countries be classified in one of three categories: 'private-peripheral', 'private-complementary', and 'private-dominant'. He links these respectively to Trow's classic differentiation between elite, mass, and universal higher education. For the first category, he gives the examples of China, Vietnam, and Malaysia; for the second, Indonesia and Thailand; and, for the third, Japan, South Korea, and the Philippines. The implication is that there is an expected progression from the first, through the second to the third, and certainly the massive growth of private higher education in China and Vietnam since the early 2000s might seem to support that theory. Umakoshi (2004: 47–8) is somewhat pessimistic about the future for the private-dominant model within Asia. As private institutions become more dominant, he is worried they will become increasingly diversified and it will be harder to maintain consistent levels of quality.

Private Higher Education in Japan

As outlined above, the classifications of 'private' and 'public' are fundamental to understandings of higher education across the world. The evolution of the

Japanese higher education system, discussed later in this chapter, has occurred in such a way as to blur these classifications, at the same time as entrenching them in policy and administrative processes, and in both the popular and scholarly understandings of the system. While the Japanese 'private university' can be understood within the comparative framework outlined above, there are also specific considerations which need to be taken into account in order to position the Japanese case more precisely within the global landscape.

As this book deals primarily with private *universities*, it is necessary first to distinguish this type of institution from other institutions of higher education in Japan. In everyday usage, the term 'university' (*daigaku*) in Japan refers to institutions which confer 4-year undergraduate (Bachelor) and/or postgraduate degrees.[6] There are 782 of these as of 2018, and they enrol the vast majority

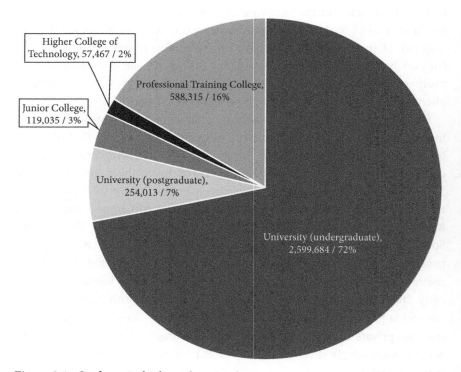

Figure 2.1. Students in higher education by institution type, 2018.
Source: Created by the authors from MEXT 2018a.

---

[6] There is a small number of 'graduate universities' (*daigakuin daigaku*) which offer graduate degrees only. Most of these are either research-intensive national institutes or small-scale operations catering for professional niches.

(around 80 per cent) of all students in higher education in Japan (see Figure 2.1). Almost 90 percent of these students are undertaking undergraduate degrees. Universities (*daigaku*) are sometimes referred to more specifically as 4-year universities (*yonen-sei daigaku*), to distinguish them from a second type of institution, *tanki daigaku* (commonly abbreviated to *tandai*), literally short-term universities, but generally known in English as 'junior colleges'. These junior colleges award 2-year associate degrees predominantly in the fields of domestic science, humanities, and teaching, and cater for an over-whelmingly female student body. A distinctive product of the post-war reorganization of higher education in Japan (discussed later in this chapter), these institutions have declined in number considerably since the 1990s and now enrol little more than 3 per cent of all students in higher education.

Universities and junior colleges are considered to be the academic arm of Japan's post-secondary education system. The other arm is made up of institutions which offer advanced curricula as part of a larger vocational training system which straddles both secondary and tertiary levels. These institutions can be divided into two types: higher technical colleges (*kōtō senmon gakkō* or *kōsen* for short) which provide qualifications leading mainly to occupations in engineering, science, and technology and enrol just under 2 per cent of students in higher education; and the much more numerically significant professional training colleges (*senmon gakkō*), technically a specific class of specialized training college (*senshū gakkō*) which offer post-secondary courses (*senmon katei*) across a very wide range of occupational fields gener-ally over a 3-year programme. These professional training colleges enrol around 16 per cent of all students in higher education but are defined by the OECD as offering 'non-university qualifications' and hence are generally omitted in comparative statistics of the proportion of students going to university. If one adds the participation rates of those going to such schools to those of university undergraduate programmes, junior colleges, and higher technical colleges, then nearly 80 per cent of the age cohort in Japan is enrolled in some form of post-secondary education. This is one of the highest partici-pation rates in the world (Yonezawa and Huang, 2018: 426).

Advanced entry systems now exist which allow universities to admit graduates of all three of the other institutional types—junior colleges, higher technical colleges, and selected courses in advanced vocational schools—creating a considerable degree of movement between the vocational and academic streams. Around 40 per cent of higher technical college graduates, for example, transfer to university, as do around 10 per cent of junior college graduates (MEXT 2018a). It is even possible at some professional training colleges to gain qualifications allowing direct progression to a university graduate programme. Movement in the opposite direction appears to be inconsequential—only around 1 per cent of university graduates proceed directly to enrol in professional training colleges—but quite a large number do attend them concurrently in order to earn specialist vocational qualifications. This will be discussed later in more detail.

In 2019, the line between academic and vocational higher education in Japan was blurred further with the creation of a new category of vocational universities (*senmonshoku daigaku*) and vocational junior colleges. These are to offer undergraduate courses and confer degrees just like existing universities and junior colleges, but with an emphasis on practical training with direct connection to specific vocational fields, placing them somewhere between the conventional university system and the professional training college system. At the time of writing, the government had approved three out of fourteen applications for establishment of vocational universities in 2019.

In Japan, the category of 'university' itself covers an immense variety of institutional sizes, curricular offerings, missions and modes of operation. This high degree of heterogeneity, many aspects of which will be addressed in the course of this chapter, has led some scholars writing in English to eschew the English term 'university' in favour of the original Japanese *daigaku* when referring to these institutions (see, for example, McVeigh 2002 and 2006; Breaden 2013). Due to this high level of diversity, when determining where a university is positioned among its peers, several very fundamental questions are often asked: how large the university is, where it is located, and when it was established. The answers to any of these questions alone may not offer a great deal of insight but, in combination, they are likely to provide at the very least a starting point for classifying the university in question.

The most basic index of difference is size. Universities in Japan range from single-department undergraduate colleges with only a few hundred students to institutions offering a full range of undergraduate and postgraduate degrees and student populations in the tens of thousands. On average, private universities are roughly half the size of national universities. In 2019, only forty private universities (7 per cent) had student populations in excess of 10,000; the bulk (close to 60 per cent) had between 1,000 and 9,999, and the remainder had fewer than 1,000. The largest was Nihon University with 67,353 students and the smallest two were Tokyo Union Theological Seminary (*Tōkyō Shingaku Daigaku*) and Nagaoka Sutoku University (*Nagaoka Sūtoku Daigaku*) with just forty-three students each.

Universities can also be categorized by reference to their age, using the major points of transformation of the modern university system as dividing lines.[7] As explained later in this chapter, the major reorganization of Japan's higher education system in the post-war period enabled a distinction to be made between those universities which were established under the pre-war system and those established under the new system instituted in the late 1940s, with the latter group further divided according to in which part of the post-war era they were established. The popular perception is that the older institutions are the more respectable.

The over-concentration of people, resources, and power in the Tokyo metropolitan area (*Tōkyō ikkyoku shūchū*) is readily apparent in many areas of Japanese society and university education is no exception. Around 41 per cent of all university students in Japan are enrolled in universities in Tokyo and its adjacent three prefectures alone (Chiba, Kanagawa, Saitama); this proportion is even higher, 49 per cent, in the private university sector specifically (MEXT 2018a). Japan's other major metropolitan corridor, the Keihanshin (Kobe-Osaka-Kyoto) region, accounts for a further 19 per cent of student enrolments overall and 21 per cent in the private sector. This concentration has become even more pronounced over the past three decades, despite some attempts by the government to discourage universities from establishing or expanding metropolitan campuses.

The simplest way to bring these factors of size, age, and location into a single generalization is to say that larger universities tend to be older and located in major centres of population; smaller ones tend to be established more recently

---

[7] There is no organization which represents all of Japan's higher education institutions. The divide between universities founded pre-war and post-war is reflected in the existence of two separate national associations of private universities each with a distinct membership. The oldest and largest is the Association of Private Universities of Japan (APUJ; *shidaikyō*), which was established in 1948 and counts around two-thirds of all private universities as its members. The other is the Japan Association of Private Universities and Colleges (JAPUC; *shidairen*). This association was established later, in 1951, by a group of pre-war institutions (Aoyama Gakuin, Chuo, Doshisha, Jochi, Kansai, Kwansei Gakuin, Keio, Meiji, Nihon, Rikkyo, Ritsumeikan, Waseda) which appear to have felt that their influence within APUJ and the capacity of that organization to represent their interests was diluted by the growing number of newly-established universities. Owing to the presence of the aforementioned and other large and well-resourced private universities in its membership, JAPUC is actually the larger organization on measures such as overall student enrolment and research revenue. It was sometimes said that the JAPUC was more focused on quality and gaining equal status with the national universities, while the APUJ was more focused on the development of quantity. But both have attracted many new members in the decades since their establishment and these days there is no obvious critical ideological divide between the two. The headquarters of APUJ and JAPUC are on different floors of the same building. There is also much resource-sharing and collaborative advocacy, mainly through the Federation of Japanese Private Colleges and Universities Associations (*Shidai Rengōkai*), which is a joint body for both APUJ and JAPUC, founded in 1986. Around seventy-five private universities are not affiliated with either of these two associations.

and located in suburban or rural areas. All of the twenty largest private universities, for example, have major campuses in greater Tokyo or the Keihanshin (Kobe/Osaka/Kyoto) metropolitan area, and all but one of these twenty was established prior to 1950. These correlations are predictable in light of the historical development of the Japanese university system reviewed later in this chapter, especially the expansion of the 1980s and 90s.

The Private Versus Public Modes

The dominant typology of Japan's highly diverse university sector today is constructed on the basis of the public/private distinction and more specifically the mode of establishment (*setchi keitai*). The category of 'private universities' (*shiritsu daigaku*) which is the primary subject of this book refers to those established by private school corporations (*shiritsu gakkō hōjin*; referred to simply as '*gakkō hōjin*' throughout this book) under the Private Schools Act (*shiritsu gakko hō*) of 1949. A *gakkō hōjin* is a type of not-for-profit corporate entity subject to certain minimum requirements for capital, facilities and equipment, limitations on for-profit activity, standard governance structures, and auditing requirements. It is established by an endowment from its founders and following the approval of its articles of endowment (a constitutional document similar to articles of association for a company) by the national education minister or prefectural governor depending on the types of educational institutions it intends to establish. One minor exception to the rule that private universities are operated by *gakkō hōjin* is the category of corporate universities (*kabushiki kaisha ritsu daigaku*), which was created in 2003. Universities in this category numbered just four at the time of writing.

Private institutions have been numerically dominant throughout the history of Japanese higher education, and they currently enrol around 74 per cent of students in universities, 95 per cent in junior colleges, and 96 per cent in professional training colleges. Of the 782 universities in Japan overall in 2018, 603 were private, eighty-six national, and ninety-three local public (MEXT 2018a). These are unusually high proportions by international standards. A recent large-scale cross-national study placed the average proportion of students enrolled in the private higher education globally at 32.9 per cent. South Korea (80.6 per cent) was the only other country among the ten largest higher education systems with a proportion similar to Japan (Levy 2018b).

Japan's public higher education sector, meanwhile, is made up of two types: national (*kokuritsu*) and local public (*kōritsu*). The former type of institution is established by the national government and used to be under its direct control (their employees were classified as civil servants), but since 2004 have operated as 'independent administrative corporations' (*dokuritsu gyōsei hōjin*). This corporatization has afforded them more scope to determine their own institutional identities and directions, as well as requiring them gradually to become more financially autonomous, with the government incrementally cutting management expense grants by a cumulative total of close to 12 per cent in the first decade after corporatization. Nonetheless, national higher education institutions are still largely government-funded and retain many ties to the national educational bureaucracy. Currently, national universities enrol 21 per cent of Japan's university students.

The other 5 per cent of students not in the private sector are at local public universities, which were established and funded by prefectural or city governments. The day-to-day operations of most of these universities are now separated from the local bureaucracy under a corporatized structure similar to that applied to national universities since 2004. Adoption of this structure is not mandatory, however, and a small minority (twelve out of a total of ninety in 2017) continue to be operated directly as an arm of the municipal government. Local public universities all proclaim distinctively local missions, but in practice they vary considerably in their orientation: some are large comprehensive institutions not unlike national universities, while others are more focused operations directly connected to local agendas for economic revitalization and talent retention.

Mode of establishment aside, the factor which distinguishes private universities most clearly from their public counterparts is their revenue structure. This structural difference is worth examining briefly at the outset both because it is a crucial part of private universities' institutional identity and because it provides a basic frame for understanding other distinctions made within Japan's highly heterogeneous university sector.

Japanese private universities are private not only in terms of their establishment and operation, but also in the sense that they are funded largely through private means. Government subsidies make up just 9 per cent of private university revenue, while student fees account for almost 77 per cent (see Figure 2.2 below). In contrast, national universities derive close to 50 per cent of their revenue from subsidies and less than 20 per cent from fees. Moreover, Japan has a comparatively low level of absolute expenditure on higher education both per student and as a proportion of GDP (Figures 2.3 and 2.4). This makes for what is sometimes described by advocates who speak on behalf of the private university sector as a 'dual-layered discrepancy' (*nijū*

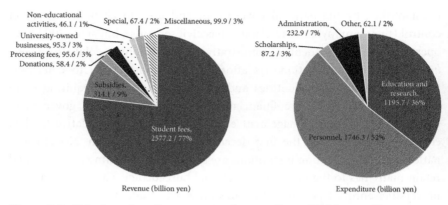

Figure 2.2. Private university revenue and expenditure (2016, overall).
Source: MEXT 2018b.

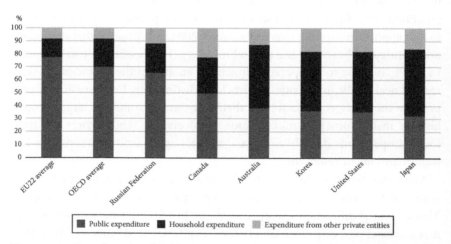

Figure 2.3. Distribution of public and private expenditure on tertiary education, 2015.
Source: Created by the authors from OECD 2018a: 273.

no mujun), whereby private universities get a disproportionately small slice of a pie which is already small in comparative terms. This is evidenced most starkly in the comparison of public expenditure per student in Figure 2.4, which shows that national university students are funded thirteen times higher than their private counterparts per student (1.99 million yen versus 160,000 yen). Part of this is due to the fact that a much higher proportion of students in national universities are studying high-cost subjects such as medicine, science, and engineering. Even so, the Federation of Japanese Private Colleges and

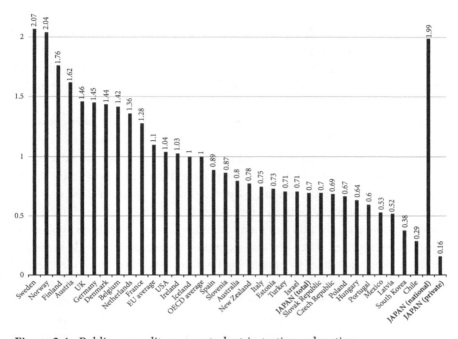

Figure 2.4. Public expenditure per student in tertiary education.

Unit: million yen.

Source: Federation of Japanese Private Colleges and Universities Associations 2017.

Universities Associations (2017) estimates that bringing per-student funding in the private sector up to the same level as national universities would require an additional budgetary commitment in the order of 710 billion yen (6.4 billion US dollars) annually.

Inevitably, private universities are forced to charge higher student fees than their public sector counterparts, but the difference is far less than the funding deficit: annual undergraduate fees at private universities average just over 1 million yen, compared to ¥535,000 in national and ¥538,000 in local public universities.[8] Private university operators thus face far greater constraints on expenditure which are reflected in student–teacher ratios. In humanities

[8] Undergraduate fees at private universities includes annual tuition averaging 900,000 yen and an annual 'facilities fee' averaging 181,000 yen (MEXT 2018c). There is considerable variation in both fees across disciplines. Annual tuition, for example, averages around 750,000 yen in faculties of humanities and social sciences, a little over 1 million yen in science and engineering, and close to 3 million yen in medicine. To this, in the initial year of enrolment, must be added an admission fee averaging around 250,000 yen, which is also charged (at slightly higher rates) by national and public universities.

faculties the average ratio is 26.9 to 1 in private universities and 14.3 to 1 in nationals; engineering is 26.4 versus 15.0; law 36.8 versus 17.4, and pharmacy 23.1 versus 8.4 (Kawaijuku 2016: 21). Similar comparisons can be made of per-student campus space: 452 square metres per student at Nihon University, the largest private, as against 3,777 square metres at Kyoto University and an extraordinary 23,332 square metres at the University of Tokyo, although much of this relates to research institutions which have nothing to do with under-graduate education (Sankei Biz 2017).

It is all too easy to conclude that private universities are the poor cousins of their national counterparts, and that is certainly true in terms of access to public funding, but such a conclusion ignores the fact that the educational corporations which found and operate private universities also enjoy signifi-cantly preferential status among corporate entities in Japan. Revenue from their educational activities is exempt from taxation, and they are excused from consumption tax collection and many other tax-related obligations applying to business enterprises. They are also permitted to engage in a wide variety of profit-making activities to which highly favourable taxation rules apply.[9] Moreover, well-established *gakkō hōjin* are likely to have significant reserves in the form of cash deposits, securities, and real estate, and can raise capital through management of these assets as well as the issuing of bonds. As we shall see in the next chapter, the operation of multiple educational institutions enables a degree of cross-subsidization, and *gakkō hōjin* can provide capital for the establishment of private companies, creating extensive networks of business interests.

While private universities in Japan are supposed to be non-profit, paradox-ically they are often spoken of as highly profitable. According to Maruyama (2010: 62), one of the leading experts on how to read university financial accounts,

the net surplus or deficits in the statements of income and expenditure of private universities should be read with caution. The accounting system allows this manipulation of the accounts to help institutions show appropri-ate reasons for raising tuition fees and supressing wage increases, thereby

---

[9] The range of acceptable business activities is determined by MEXT on advice of its Private Schools Council. The scope is very wide, ranging from agriculture and fisheries to wholesaling, insurance and real estate (MEXT 2016). The reduced 'small and medium enterprise' corporate tax rate is applied to revenue from these activities (MEXT, n.d.a), and up to 50 per cent of the profits can be repurposed as tax-deductible-deemed contributions to the *gakkō hōjin*'s endowment (Corporation Tax Act Art. 35(1) and (5); enforcement regulations Art. 73 (3)).

enabling the private universities to insist that they are not in a satisfactory financial situation even if, in reality, they are. Private universities are classed as non-profit organizations but reserve their 'profits' in the Basic Fund.

Morozumi (2010) identifies this capacity to reserve profits as one of the key distinguishing features of the Japanese private higher education system and explains that it is central to the ability of *gakkō hōjin* to respond to market changes, by building a large reserve and drawing on it alternatively to expand in boom times and to weather downturns.

Another feature deriving from the *gakkō hōjin* model is the degree of vertical continuity of schools and universities. *Gakkō hōjin* which also operate their own primary and secondary schools or have close affiliations with other private school operators are able to create 'escalator' systems whereby students graduating from an affiliated school can enter university through a special admission track (usually termed 'admission by recommendation' or *suisen nyūgaku*), thereby avoiding the regular university entrance exams. The point of greatest competition for entry to elite institutions, therefore, is often not the university entrance examination but rather the screening for admission to secondary schooling, and in extreme cases primary institutions.[10] Vertical affiliations do exist in the national and local public university sector too, but the vast majority of affiliated schools are at primary and lower secondary level (there are only seventeen senior high schools affiliated with national universities), precluding the scale of the escalator phenomenon seen in the private sector.

Another way in which public and private universities in Japan can be differentiated is in terms of what Clark (1983) has called 'modes of authority differentiation'. He (1983: 125–31) describes the differences between a 'continental mode' (which combines a guild-like faculty with state bureaucratic control but without a strong autonomous administrative element between the two); a 'British mode' (with faculty guilds and, until recently, influence from trustees and administrators more than the state); and, an 'American mode' (where the faculty are relatively weak, the trustees and administrators relatively strong, and the bureaucracy highly localized). The 'Japanese mode', he (1983: 131) describes as a 'fascinating mixture of contrary forms of organization and authority' with Continental patterns in the public universities and American patterns in the private sector.

---

[10] The entrance examination to Yochisha, a primary school in the Keio University system, is one of the most notoriously rigorous (Clavel, *JT*, 16 February 2014).

A more recent account by Whitley (2019) also distinguishes between three kinds of university management. In many ways, the corporatization plan for national and public universities in the early 2000s in Japan was designed to convert them from what Whitley (2019) calls 'hollow universities' (with hardly any independent decision-making authority separate from state universities) to 'state-chartered universities' (with conditions of employment and promotion comparable to those in private companies and with discretion over how they used their block grant from the state). Significantly, it did not succeed in converting them to the third category of university which Whitley identifies, 'corporate universities', which were much more independent from the state, with authority concentrated in the hands of the president and their senior staff and with academic staff having little say in the distribution of resources or decisions over priorities. The dominant example of such 'corporate universities', according to Whitley (2019: 71) has been the privately run university in the US. It has also been the dominant model among privately run universities in Japan.

Independence from government brings important benefits to the private universities in Japan. The national associations of private universities present some strong arguments related especially to the educational strengths of private universities in comparison with their public counterparts (Association of Private Universities of Japan 2004; Federation of Japanese Private Colleges and Universities Associations 2017; JAPCU 1987). One is their capacity to develop original and progressive educational curricula, guided by their distinctive missions, and to foster greater variety and vibrancy in university education as a whole. Their reliance on fee revenue makes them particularly responsive to changing employment trends and consumer preferences and highly focused on the academic growth of their students. Moreover, academic personnel structures and hierarchies tend to be less rigid than in the national university sector, thus facilitating the exploration of innovative teaching and, sometimes, research. They also enjoy scope for flexibility in student admissions, providing a diverse range of subjects and pathways to recognize individual aptitudes and circumstances. These self-proclaimed strengths can of course be seen in a different light as the very features which render private universities inferior to their public counterparts: curricular innovation as a cavalier attitude to academic conventions; a student-centred ethos as an overly consumer-driven mindset; and flexibility in student admissions as a lack of selective rigour. Indeed almost all that is characteristic of private universities can be claimed as both weakness and strength, depending on perspective.

Private University Governance

The governance of private universities is a vast and complex topic in its own right and the subject of numerous volumes in Japanese, both scholarly and practitioner-oriented (see, for example, Maruyama 2002; Mito 2014; Morozumi 2010; Saneto 2015; Saito & Aoki 2009; Yamazaki et al. 2018; Yonezawa 2011). One of the most distinctive features is the dualistic character of governance. A private university actually comprises two entities: an institution of education and research—the university proper, as it were—and the *gakkō hōjin* (private school corporation) responsible for founding and operating that institution. The former has features which are relatively familiar to an international audience: a president, deans of undergraduate faculties and other principal organs of education and research, and councils of academic staff affiliated with these organs. Meanwhile the *gakkō hōjin* is governed by a board of trustees (*rijikai*), headed by a chair (*rijichō*) who is the trust's legal representative and effective chief executive officer. A board of councillors (*hyōgiinkai*) and auditors (*kanji*) theoretically function as checks on the power of the board of trustees, advising the board on important matters such as budgets and financing and amendments to the *gakkō hōjin*'s act of endowment. The scope of these checks, however, is rather limited[11] and it is the board of trustees, and often the individual who chairs it, which runs the *gakkō hōjin* in a practical sense.[12]

---

[11] While councillors must be at least twice as numerous as trustees and include both employees of the *gakkō hōjin* and graduates of its schools, trustees can serve concurrently as councillors and, given that board of councillors' decisions are made by a simple majority at meetings which are in quorum with a simple majority of councillors present, it is quite foreseeable that all decision-making councillors may in fact also be trustees. In any case, the law is vague as to the practical effect of the board of councillors' decisions: the exact wording is simply that the chair of trustees 'must hear the opinions' (*iken o kikanakereba naranai*) of the board of councillors. The auditors (*kanji*), of which there must be at least two, are more independent: they cannot serve concurrently as trustees, and are empowered autonomously to make recommendations to the boards of trustees and councillors. Proactive intervention by auditors, however, appears to be rare. A survey published in 2015 showed that only 14 per cent of *gakkō hōjin* operating universities had received recommendations from their auditors to address major operational issues at any time in the 3-year survey period (PMAC 2015).

[12] In a 2012 survey of members of the Association of Private Universities of Japan, around 65 per cent of respondents stated that they operated under the 'strong individual leadership' of the board chair, and around the same proportion said that meetings of the board of trustees were held only a few times a year to discuss basic management issues such as budgets (RIIHE 2012). Even where the chair does not dominate, power may be held by a small group of trustees. A *gakkō hōjin* is legally required to have a minimum of five trustees who are charged with 'assisting' the chair and together deciding on important matters of the *gakkō hōjin*'s business. The average number of trustees in practice is eleven (PMAC 2019b), but this often includes external and quasi-honorary appointments, with the *gakkō hōjin* actually steered by a much smaller group of full-time trustees (*jōnin riji*) who also hold executive posts within the universities and other educational bodies operated by the corporation.

A key problem here, as pointed out by Oe (2003), is that most boards of trustees have limited management ability: 36 per cent of board chairs in *gakkō hōjin* operating universities are from the academic faculty, and a further 17 per cent from the administrative staff; while 19 per cent previously held appointments in companies or other private organizations (PMAC 2019b). The mobility of executive-level staff is also extremely low: only 5 per cent of board chairs previously held the same post in another *gakkō hōjin*. Moreover, very few *gakkō hōjin* nominate strengthening of managerial capacity as a priority issue, and leadership education for executive officers is not yet common (Morozumi et al. 2018).

Harmonizing the dual governance structure of *gakkō hōjin* and university is a challenge in all private universities and the way it is approached generates important differences in institutional character. The Japan Association of Private Colleges and Universities (JAPCU 1987: 127) suggests that there are three basic approaches. The first is the 'strong president approach' in which the university president[13] has primary authority over all matters, financial and administrative affairs included, and devolves his/her day-to-day powers to various academic and administrative organs within the university. The president is answerable to the *gakkō hōjin*'s board of trustees, of which s/he (along with other senior university officials) is usually a member, but the board respects the autonomy of the university proper. Secondly, there is the 'separation of academic and administrative affairs model' where the university president's responsibilities are limited largely to matters related to education and research at the university, and university financial and administrative affairs are entrusted to a separate, typically non-academic, management team. Coordination between the academic and administrative arms is the responsibility of the *gakkō hōjin* board of trustees and its chair. Finally, there is the 'chairman of the board-cum-president approach', in which the chair of the board of trustees (*rijichō*) serves concurrently as the university president,

---

[13] Procedures for selection of the president vary from unilateral appointment by the board of trustees to popular ballot. In a 2018 survey, 40.2 per cent of private universities named the *gakkō hōjin* board of trustees as the body having the most influence over the presidential selection and 33.1 per cent used a presidential selection committee; only 19.7 per cent said that ballot was the most influential factor (PMAC 2019b). According to Kobayashi (2008), there have historically been three routes for becoming a university president in Japan: internal election, external invitation, and succession within the founding family (*sōritsusha ichizoku*). Internally elected presidents, according to Kobayashi, used to be essentially decorative (*o-kazari gakuchō*) but presidents brought in from outside had generally been expected to play a very active role in revitalizing the education, research, and management of the university. Kobayashi (2008: 68) gives a detailed account of the appointment of Yamaoka Keiichiro, who was at the same time the president (*gakuchō*) and chair of the board of trustees (*rijichō*) of Heian Jogakuin University, who he says was likened to Carlos Ghosn, the former CEO of Nissan who took drastic action in the 1990s to rescue the company when it was on the verge of bankruptcy.

strengthening the board's control over the university's operations. This approach is also known as the 'one-man (or owner) management' (*one-man kei or owner-kei*) model because so much power is concentrated in the chair-cum-president.[14] According to a large survey of 608 *gakkō hōjin* (PMAC, 2019b: 5), almost 22 per cent of them currently follow this latter pattern.

Indexed to this typology based on the power of the board and president is the degree of autonomy granted to academic councils (*kyōjukai*—literally 'professors' councils' but membership can and typically does include associate professors and other full-time academics) which dictates the scope for members of academic staff to influence the running of the university. The law is vague on the role of academic councils, with Article 93 of the School Education Act simply stipulating that they should 'discuss' (*shingi suru*) education and research activities undertaken within their faculty or other arm of the university and 'give opinions' (*iken o noberu*) on student admissions, graduations, curricula, and conferral of degrees, as well as other 'important matters concerning education and research' as nominated by the university president. It is common in the 'chairman-cum-president' approach—and often in the 'strong president approach', especially in small universities—for the role of the academic council to be confined to a bare minimum of legally mandated duties, leaving rank-and-file academics rather disconnected from information on the university's administrative operations and not privy to decision-making within the president's inner circle.[15]

In older and larger universities the notions of academic freedom and collegial self-governance are likely to be more well developed; academic councils will often deliberate on a very wide variety of matters and have an effective veto over the decisions of the president and board of trustees—even though it is the latter which is ultimately responsible for the financial effects of those decisions. The governance principle of these universities is termed *kyōjukai-shihai* or 'academic council rule', in contrast to the *rijikai-shihai* or 'board of trustees rule' operating elsewhere (Ehara 1998). In the public university sector the *kyōjukai-shihai* model has always been dominant, but is increasingly seen as a constraint as they move to a 'strong president' model

---

[14] In one of the very few pieces of research which includes '*owner-kei*' (owner-run) as a form of governance in private universities, Miyajima Koji (2016) concludes that no single governance model is inherently superior to any other.

[15] Surveys by PMAC (2019a) suggest that the only issues on which the academic council's opinion holds significant weight in *gakkō hōjin* decision-making are educational planning (the council's opinion was nominated as the most important by 42 per cent of *gakkō hōjin*; 39 per cent nominated the university president) and the recruitment of academic personnel (28 per cent; university president 45 per cent).

under a corporatized structure. The fact that the academic council had decision-making authority but not fiscal responsibility was seen as increasingly problematic for the running of national universities and was one of the driving forces behind the 2004 corporatization (*hōjinka*) of national universities (Yamamoto 2005). Very similar arguments were made by administrators about the role of the academic council in those private universities where the latter also had decision-making power, and there were attempts to limit that power to the school boards of trustees (Kinukawa 2002; Ushiogi 2002).[16]

A final consideration which is often overlooked in scholarly accounts of university governance is the position of the administrative organization (*jimu-soshiki, jimu-kyoku,* or *jimu-bu*). Where the administration is organized roughly in parallel with the university's academic organs, it is more likely to serve the interests of the professoriate and facilitate academic council rule, with administrative staff members (*jimu shokuin*) patently subordinate to their academic counterparts. In many private universities, however, the administrative organization is much more closely aligned with the structure of the *gakkō hōjin*, which has the effect of separating important lines of decision-making (such as those concerning finances and new projects) from the academic council, while also subjecting many day-to-day university operations to a distinctively bureaucratic logic impenetrable to many academics (Breaden 2013; Poole 2016). A strong administration thus operates in concert with the *rijikai-shihai* or board of trustees model.[17]

---

[16] The trope of the recalcitrant academic council (*kyōjukai*) is an important one in the literature on university reform. Daigaku Mirai Mondai Kenkyūkai (2001: 200) gives a good flavour of the nature of this critique: 'University management tends to be controlled by the *kyōjukai*. The *rijikai* makes decisions but it cannot do anything if it is opposed by the *kyōjukai*. The result is endless meetings...Professors have no experience or expertise in management and refuse to depart from general principles; they simply pile argument upon argument, as if reaching a pragmatic compromise would be the most abhorrent thing to do. This approach has long been considered the cornerstone of academic freedom...The *kyōjukai* is the cancer (*gan*) of university administration'. Barretta's (1987) study of Rikkyo University in Tokyo is a classic example of a *kyōjukai-shihai* university where the fact that each of the six colleges of the university had its own academic council (what she called a 'senate') tended to hinder university wide reform. Even when a Dean's Council was formed to coordinate university-wide decision-making, it could not operate with any authority without the full consensus of its members, which it was rarely able to achieve, as its members owed their primary loyalty to the college and only secondarily to the university. Indeed, she argues, the six 'senates' also had more power than the Board of Trustees. Hall (1975) describes the same process at the University of Tokyo in the 1970s as 'organizational paralysis'.

[17] This collaboration is reflected in *gakkō hōjin* responses to PMAC survey questions about decision-making. The administration is more likely than the board chair to have final say on matters of financial planning (43 per cent of respondents nominated the administration, 31 per cent the board chair), facilities/infrastructure (36 per cent administration versus 28 per cent board chair), and non-academic personnel (46 per cent versus 16 per cent), and has only slightly less influence than the board chair (29 per cent versus 30 per cent) on medium- and long-term planning. An administrative officer or secretarial unit (*hishoshitsu/rijichōshitsu*) is by far the most common form of support for the board chair (nominated by 64 per cent of university *gakkō hōjin*, in comparison with just 20 per cent nominating a deputy chair) (PMAC 2019b).

Thus far we have seen that the private higher education institutions exist as a relatively well-defined, if under-researched comparative category, and Japanese private universities fall clearly within it. They also, however, have some distinctive features: they constitute the largest category of institution in the Japanese higher education system; they are highly heterogeneous; they receive little government support and the role of government in their operation is ambiguous; they conform to a standard governance structure which nonetheless allows for considerable variety in approaches to management and the distribution of power. In order to make sense of why private universities have taken this form in Japan, some historical knowledge is essential.

Historical Overview of Private Universities in Japan

The history of Japanese universities which follows is told from the perspective of the private sector, as a conscious alternative to the more orthodox version which tends to place national universities in the limelight and treat their private counterparts as a cast of supporting characters. What this approach highlights is: the complex relationship that the state has with private universities in Japan, combining elements of both laissez-faire and high levels of interference; why they have been seen as attractive investment opportunities by entrepreneurs; and how they have developed a strong sense of independence. All three factors are important for understanding the resilience of private universities in the face of the dramatic changes of the 1990s and 2000s.

Foundations of the Japanese Private University

The orthodox history of the modern Japanese university usually begins with the founding of 'imperial universities'—later to become national universities— in the late 1800s, following the Meiji Restoration which ushered in Japan's modern era (see for example, Nagai 1971: Chapter 2). This starting point often sets the tone for the remainder of the history, which focuses heavily on the construction and reform of a centralized, state-funded university system. A history of Japanese private higher education which was published by the Japan Association of Private Universities and Colleges[18] (JAPCU 1984; later

---

[18] The organization's name in Japanese is *Nihon Shiritsu Daigaku Renmei*, commonly abbreviated to *shidairen*. Note that the English name of the organization as it appears in the 1984 and 1987 books cited

also published in English: JAPCU 1987) emphasizes that this is no more than a small piece of the much larger historical tapestry of Japanese higher education, one which is, and always has been, populated primarily by private educational institutions.

According to the JAPCU view of the world, the origins of private higher education in Japan can be traced to the establishment of a school in Kyoto in the ninth century by the Buddhist monk Kūkai (Kōbō Daishi). This was a clear divergence from the central and regional schools for training public servants (*daigakuryō* and *kokugaku*) which had a strictly Confucian curriculum and were open only to a small circle of nobles and government officials. By the time of the Tokugawa Shogunate (1603–1868) there were many religious schools in major centres and thousands of small village and temple schools (*terakoya*) scattered across Japan, as well as a variety of other private academies offering more advanced education (for which a variety of Japanese words were used, including *shijuku*, *kajuku*, and *shigaku*) (JAPCU 1984: 14; JAPCU 1987: 4; Anderson 1975: 14–15). Some of these were centres of Confucian or European scholarship such as Tekijuku (from which Osaka University was founded), which taught Western medicine and other sciences, and Kangien in present-day Oita prefecture, which taught not only the Confucian classics but also mathematics and astronomy. Others were later creations responding to growing demand for vocational education in late feudal Japan (Rubinger 1982).

At the time, there existed no national education 'system' in a modern sense: schools were not systematized into distinct tiers or credential types, and the precise value of education was not widely recognized across society. Private schools had a wide clientele ranging from the samurai class—especially those less privileged and more distant from centres of political power, and therefore with stronger aspirations for self-improvement—to the growing urban population of merchants and artisans, for whom access to modern ideas and technologies was of material importance (Amano 1990; Dore 1965).

The feudal system ended with the Meiji Restoration of 1868 and was replaced by a modernist state committed to rapid industrialization through the adoption of western ideas and technologies. The benefits of higher education became patently clear, and new private academies sprang up to cater for burgeoning demand in professional fields such as medicine, engineering, and law. Private higher education by this time had a considerable support base

in this section (Japan Association of Private Colleges and Universities, JAPCU) differs slightly from the name now used in the organization's official English-language materials (Japan Association of Private Universities and Colleges, JAPUC).

among the landholding and new urban middle classes, as well as political opponents to the Meiji regime (Kaneko 2004: 121–4).

The government at first afforded no recognition to these private academies, and instead busied itself with establishing a new national university system. The first government-backed higher education institution to be established was the present-day University of Tokyo, which had roots in a Confucian Studies school established by the Tokugawa Shogunate in the seventeenth century and various early Meiji experiments inspired by the French Grandes Ecoles system. Ultimately, however, it took a form closely resembling the German university, with considerable academic autonomy but also a clear function as a centre for talent development and research serving state interests (Bartholomew 1989: 89–124; Kaneko 2004: 117–18). The Imperial University Ordinance of 1886 stated the aim of these imperial universities as 'to provide instruction in the arts and sciences and to inquire into the mysteries of learning in accordance with the needs of the state' (Nagai 1971: 21). Ultimately a total of nine imperial universities were established under the ordinance: seven in Japan proper and one each in the Japanese colonies of Korea and Taiwan. Their presidents were appointed by imperial order, and staff members had the status of national civil servants. The ties of the imperial universities to the centre of state power were further strengthened by the fact that the elite posts in government were overwhelmingly occupied by their graduates.

The formal regulation of private educational institutions, on the other hand, began with the issuing of the Private Schools Ordinance (*shiritsu gakkō rei*) of 1899, which placed them under the control of regional government heads (*chihō chōkan*), who not only authorized the establishment of new institutions but also had broad powers to intervene in practical operations—teaching included—and to close those judged to pose a risk to public order. This move reflected a balance between two potentially contradictory attitudes toward educational governance which had developed among the Meiji leaders: firstly, the desire to exercise governmental control over the entire education sector as part of a broader statist/nationalist political agenda and, secondly, a notion, seen widely in other areas of Meiji society, of a hierarchy determined by distance from state power, which positioned private academies as naturally inferior to the elite imperial universities and precluded the possibility of placing them within the same frame of direct state control.

In 1903, the government passed another ordinance to create a national system of professional training colleges (*senmon gakkō*) under the jurisdiction of the national Education Ministry. Many private academies applied, and were permitted, to become part of this new system, thereby gaining official state endorsement—albeit one rung lower than the universities established under the Imperial University Ordinance. The professional training college system was designed to provide practical qualifications for middle-level professionals, not academic titles. Some private colleges nonetheless sought to situate their offerings closer to the imperial university system, referring to themselves as 'universities' (*daigaku*)—a practice which was tolerated informally by government officials.

A system for the formal recognition of private academies as *daigaku* was finally legislated in the University Ordinance (*daigaku rei*) of 1918. This move to expand the university sector beyond the imperial university system reflected the growing demand for higher education outside the elite echelons of society for which the imperial universities catered, as the industrial sector sought more highly skilled human resources and Japan's system of government evolved to engage a wider expanse of civil society (Itoh 1999). As Geiger (1986: 22) has pointed out, the fact that meeting excess demand was the primary motivation for granting private universities legal status meant that from the very beginning they were viewed to have lower status than the public institutions. The perception that private institutions were secondary to national ones (*kankō shitei*) continues to colour views of the Japanese university sector to the present day.

Initially only a small handful of private academies had the resources to attain university status, as the government required candidates to provide a 'deposit' of at least ¥500,000 and more if multiple departments were being established. Candidates also needed to be operating pre-university courses (*daigaku yoka*) which demanded considerable investment in facilities and staff. Even the most well-resourced of the private academies, such as Waseda and Keio Gijuku, appear to have struggled to meet these requirements (JAPCU 1987: 17–19), despite in some cases being granted ad hoc government subsidies to offset costs in the first years of operation (Amano 1986: 83; see also Morikawa 2007). Only eleven private academies had converted to official university (*daigaku*) status by 1920. Many other academies remained within the professional training college system, while a few others instead established 'higher schools' (*kōtō gakkō*), providing education at a lower level of the multi-tiered system of pre-war Japan.

By 1938, however, the number of officially recognized private universities had grown to twenty-five, with a combined student population of over 44,000—about two-thirds of the total university student population—while another 75,000 students were enrolled in 119 private professional training colleges (Table 2.1). The vast majority of these students were men: some private universities did offer places to women, but few women were yet able

Table 2.1 Universities and students in pre-war Japan

Fiscal Year		Universities				Private Professional Training Colleges
		Private	Imperial (National)	Local Public	Total	
1918	Institutions	0	5	0	5	63
	Students	0	9,040	0	9,040	33,918
1923	Institutions	16	11	4	31	75
	Students	21,944	15,149	1,638	38,731	37,145
1928	Institutions	24	11	5	40	93
	Students	36,251	22,586	2,665	61,502	59,552
1933	Institutions	25	18	2	45	110
	Students	41,560	27,901	1,432	70,893	63,802
1938	Institutions	25	18	2	45	116
	Students	44,017	28,034	1,466	73,517	75,734

Source: Created by the authors from Japan Association of Private Colleges and Universities, 1987: 11–12.

to access the kind of education which would prepare them for university entrance. Moreover, a number of alternative higher-education pathways had been established specifically for women, including government-established women's normal schools and private women's professional training colleges (Iida 2013). With less than 1 per cent of women advancing to higher education, however, these institutions remained a marginal presence (Inagaki 2007).

As well as mandating the creation of Japan's first official private universities, the 1918 Ordinance allowed universities to be established by local governments at prefectural and (from 1928) city level. This then marked the start of the three-way categorization of universities based on establishment body (private, national, local public) mentioned earlier. Regardless of their founders, however, all universities fell under the regulatory ambit of the national Education Ministry and a unified framework was thereby created for a state-managed university sector.

The 1918 University Ordinance was also designed to cultivate a common understanding of the social function of universities, declaring (in Article 1) that they were 'to provide instruction in the theory and practical application of learning as required by the needs of the state and to delve into the mysteries thereof'. This clearly reflected the original Meiji-era goal of designing a university system to serve the state. The new private and local public universities were in this sense required to emulate the imperial university model: critics described this as an effective 'nationalization' (*kangakuka*) in both regulatory *and* ideological terms (Narita and Terasaki 1979: 81–3). This nationalization process intensified through the late 1920s and 1930s as Japan entered its militarist phase. Throughout this period, however, private universities remained procedurally subordinate to their imperial counterparts by virtue of the continued operation of the Imperial University Ordinance and various other regulatory distinctions. These regulations in turn sustained popular perceptions of imperial universities being at the pinnacle of the education system and providing the pathway to the elite positions of power in Japanese society (Amano 1986).

The pre-war private universities provided the government with a market-based solution to the growing demand for higher education, enabling the sector to expand in line with demand for highly trained personnel without requiring large-scale government investment. This arrangement served further to entrench the existing state/private hierarchy and, as discussed below, it persisted well into the post-war era.

Post-war Reforms and Growth

As part of the education reforms conducted under the Allied Occupation after Japan's surrender, a new higher education system was established to consolidate the different types of pre-1945 institutions into a 'single track'. Under the School Education Act of 1947, universities (*daigaku*) were all to offer 4-year bachelor degrees and could optionally have graduate schools (*daigakuin*) offering doctoral and other higher degrees. The multi-track system of progression through the school education system was also simplified at this stage, with completion of secondary education stipulated as the basic eligibility criterion for admission to bachelor degree programmes, and a bachelor degree required for admission to graduate school.

In line with the dismantling of the nationalist regime which had developed in the final years of the war, the mission of universities was now re-cast as to 'disseminate knowledge broadly, conduct in-depth, specialised research and education in the arts and sciences, and develop intellectual, moral, and applied capabilities' (School Education Act, Article 52) in line with the guarantee of 'academic freedom' in the new Constitution of Japan (Article 23). The reforms did not, however, put an end to the fundamental distinction between state and private higher education. The pre-war imperial universities were reconstituted as national universities (*kokuritsu daigaku*), a label also applied to sixty-nine new universities formed across the country, mainly through amalgamation of various public professional training colleges, normal schools, and other public higher education institutions from the pre-war system (Hata 2004: 39). These universities remained strictly under the state umbrella, funded and managed by the national educational bureaucracy and focused on the task of producing elite human resources and research for national development. Under this new system it was also possible for local government authorities to establish universities, and twenty-six of these new local public universities (*kōritsu daigaku*) were in operation by 1950 (Japan Association of Public Universities 2017).

Private universities under the new system were governed by the Private Schools Act of 1949, designed to 'promote the sound development of Private Schools by taking account of their characteristic features, putting a high value on their autonomy, and enhancing their public nature' (Article 1). The statutory separation of the private education sector from the national one was originally intended to enable the sector to flourish independently from governmental control, but by enshrining a role for the national government in ensuring the 'sound development' of private institutions and emphasizing their 'public nature', the Act justified the continued application of a centralized administrative regime. It provided that each private educational institution be operated by a *gakkō hōjin* (educational corporation, as defined in the first section of this chapter). The process of establishing a new university or department within an existing one was also formalized and centralized. Initially, requirements were set by the Japan University Accreditation Association, an independent body formed in 1947 by forty-six pre-existing universities, but from 1956 the Education Ministry itself took on the role of stipulating and administering standards for establishment (*setchi kijun*) (Baba and Hayata, 1997).

Establishing these uniform structures was an important strategy at a time when a wide variety of interests in society—from religious organizations to business entities—were seeking to gain a foothold in higher education, and there was great potential for proliferation of governance models and divergence in approaches to education and research. Vast differences in origins, missions, and educational outlooks were accommodated within the single *gakkō hōjin* system, while the standards for establishment served as a set of common expectations for facilities, staffing, and curriculum. The contrast between the uniformity of these basic frameworks and the heterogeneity of institutions in qualitative terms remains one of the most distinctive features of Japanese private higher education today.

All of the private institutions which had obtained *daigaku* status under the pre-1945 system were also approved as fully-fledged universities under the new statutory regime, although in some cases they had been amalgamated and/or renamed. A much larger number of new private universities was also established, bringing the number to 105 in 1950 (JAPCU 1987: 34). Many of these new universities were created by private bodies also operating other types of institutions such as secondary schools and the professional training colleges (*senmon gakkō*) remaining from the pre-war period. For these organizations, moving into the university sector was a natural earlier in this chapter in response to Japan's growing and increasingly complex human resource needs and, for the operators of pre-war professional training colleges at least, an opportunity finally to earn the status of *daigaku* which was unattainable under the narrow pre-war system.

Nonetheless, many found it difficult immediately to muster the resources and specialized academic expertise required to establish a full university. The government saw the need for an interim system to provide such institutions with a foothold in the university sector, allowing them to contribute quickly to Japan's pressing need for skilled human resources as well as providing an alternative option for students facing economic and cultural barriers to participation in university education—notably women and those from financially disadvantaged backgrounds. The School Education Act was thus amended in 1949 to allow for the establishment of universities which would operate more vocationally oriented curricula in associate degree programmes of 2 or 3 years' duration, rather than full 4-year Bachelor degrees. This became known as the system of 'junior colleges' (*tanki daigaku*), mentioned earlier in this chapter, which was finally made a permanent fixture in Japanese higher education following a further revision of the Act in 1964.[19]

The number of these junior colleges greatly exceeded those of 4-year universities right through the 1960s, despite the fact that they were originally envisaged simply as a temporary measure in Japan's period of transition to a mass university education system. Operators of junior colleges found a willing clientele of secondary school graduates seeking high-quality post-secondary education but whose future employment prospects did not call for advanced academic credentials: a clientele which was, in short, overwhelmingly female. By the 1960s Japanese women were completing secondary school education

---

[19] For a good overview of the rise and fall of junior colleges, see Walker (2007). By the mid-2000s, junior colleges tended to be found mainly in regional areas, meeting the needs of those who did not want to leave home, where they often had better employment rates than local 4-year universities (because of the vocational nature of their courses) and were more popular than the 3-year professional training colleges (because they had better facilities) (*NKS*, 14 March 2005).

Table 2.2 Universities (*daigaku*): Number of institutions and students, 1955–75

		1955	1960	1965	1970	1975
Private		122	140	209	274	305
National		72	72	73	75	81
Local Public		34	33	35	33	34
Total		228	245	317	382	420
Percentage private		53.5%	57.1%	65.9%	71.7%	72.6%
Students	Total	523,355	626,421	937,556	1,406,521	1,734,082
	Percentage female	12.4%	13.7%	16.2%	18.0%	21.2%
	Percentage private	59.7%	64.4%	70.5%	74.4%	76.4%
	Entrance rate	7.8%	8.2%	12.8%	17.1%	27.2%

Source: Created by the authors from MEXT 2017a.

in roughly the same numbers as men, but still faced significant barriers to participation in highly skilled occupations, and many parents did not see a full university degree as a worthwhile investment for their female children. Junior colleges provided a useful middle ground. Although junior colleges had begun catering for both genders in roughly equal proportions in the 1950s, the female-to-male was skewed by four to one by 1970, while in full universities it was the opposite (Table 2.2). For private educational conglomerations (*gakkō hōjin*), junior colleges thus offered a highly viable enterprise in their own right, as well as a potential stepping stone to the establishment of a full university which, in many cases, had been their original aspiration. Meikei Gakuin University, which we look at in Chapters 3 and 4, exemplifies this pattern.

There were also some institutions which fell outside the official boundaries of the supposedly 'single-track' post-war education system, not attaining university or junior college status but nonetheless offering important educational pathways for post-secondary students. These became known as *kakushu gakkō* (miscellaneous schools) to distinguish them from the primary, secondary, and higher education institutions expressly specified in Article 1 of the School Education Act (collectively, *ichijō-kō* or 'Article 1 schools'). Many of these miscellaneous schools offered vocational training akin to the pre-war professional training college (*senmon gakkō*) system, which as noted earlier was the home of many private educational institutions pre-1945. There were several major differences between these schools and the universities/junior colleges. Firstly, classification as *kakushu gakkō* placed them largely outside the purview of government policy. Neither supported nor regulated substantively by the national government, they were largely free to develop their own curricula and were not required to provide any kind of general foundation but could instead focus directly on the skills and qualifications required for a specific occupation. Moreover, they were free to admit whatever students they wished and charge them whatever they decided. It is important to note, however, that there was often no fundamental difference between the operators of these schools and those which had moved into the private university or junior college sector. The decision to operate one type of institution or another, or both, was not necessarily based on any divergence in educational philosophy.

Although apparently disinterested in developing a fully-fledged policy on post-secondary vocational education, the government did through the 1950s and 60s impose some minimum educational standards on the miscellaneous schools sector, as well as establishing a small subsidiary category of higher technical colleges (*kōtō senmon gakkō*) straddling upper secondary and higher education. It was not, however, until an amendment of the School Education Act in 1975 that miscellaneous schools were properly systematized into a new category of *senshū gakkō* or specialized training schools. *Senshū gakkō* offering post-secondary curricula (*senmon katei*) became known as *senmon gakkō*, a revival of the term for pre-war professional training colleges.

Japan's post-war higher education system, originally envisaged as a simplified, single-track system, thus evolved into a rather diverse assortment of educational pathways and organizational profiles, each catering for different needs within the context of growing demand for post-secondary education. Even within the university sector itself, there was a mixture of old-timers and newcomers, with new labels employed to distinguish hierarchically between the two. Greater prestige was afforded to universities originally established under the pre-war ordinances (*kyūsei daigaku*) than to the new institutions (*shinsei daigaku*), while the original national universities enjoyed (and continue to enjoy to this day) a distinctive pedigree as 'former imperial universities' (*kyū-teidai*). Meanwhile, new universities in provincial locations were often referred to pejoratively as *ekiben daigaku* (a reference to the *ekiben* boxed lunches sold at local train stations): just as every station has its own *ekiben*, it was said, soon every town would have its own university.

Yonezawa (2010: Chapter 3) also points out that this was a period of increased differentiation within the private university sector, with well-established, reputable institutions able to abandon demand-absorbing expansion in favour of greater selectivity, creating an 'elite' private sector, while the newer universities tended to split into 'peripheral' institutions that continued to absorb the growing demand and 'niche' ones catering for specialized markets. The 'elite' category, however, was impeded from developing into something similar to the top private research universities in the United States by its continued reliance on revenue from student fees and resultant focus on admissions selectivity as a reputational strategy.

These distinctions are also important in terms of understanding the priorities of the private educational conglomerations (*gakkō hōjin*) which operate universities today. On the one hand there were those which had run universities in the pre-war period and were thus readily able to make the transition to the post-war university system, and others which, while unable to establish universities under the restrictive pre-war rules, had sufficient resources to launch them as soon as the new system came into effect. There were also those which aspired to university status but were forced to make do initially with a junior college, which often became a permanent, and sometimes principal, part of their operations. Then there were those which were firmly rooted in the vocational education field, and used their expertise in school management and connections with the secondary education sector subsequently to launch junior colleges and universities. Given the poor treatment afforded to vocational schools by government and the inferior status which inevitably accompanied it, one may well imagine that the owners of many of these *gakkō hōjin* saw establishing a university as a form of upward mobility: a way of imbuing their operations with some respectability even if they had little inherent interest in purely academic activities.

Mass Higher Education and the Rise of the Private Sector

The post-war reforms also created the conditions for universal participation in primary and secondary school education. It was clear that as a new generation moved through the school system, and as the demand for skilled human resources grew in line with industrialization and technological advancement, Japan would quickly require a mass higher education system. Lacking the resources to fund such a system itself, the government allowed growth in the private sector to absorb the increasing demand, thus mirroring the approach taken in the 1920s and 1930s but on a much larger scale.

As shown in the figures above (Table 2.2), there was remarkable growth in the Japanese university sector in the 1950s and 60s. The number of students in universities increased by 231 per cent between 1955 and 1975, and 192 new universities were established in the same period. Most of this growth was in the private sector, where student numbers rose by 324 per cent and 183 new universities were established (95 per cent of all new establishments).

This growth enabled the university entrance rate (i.e., the percentage of 18-year-olds entering university undergraduate degrees)[20] to climb rapidly throughout the 1960s and into the early 1970s.

It is important to view this change in the context of the specific economic conditions which prevailed in Japan at the time: i.e., elevated rates of GDP growth and high levels of household savings. It was these that enabled the government to rely so heavily on families to fund the higher education of their children in the private sector, and itself to avoid the kind of large-scale public investment which typically accompanies such dramatic growth. In one of the most in-depth analyses of this period of expansion, James and Benjamin (1988: 179) lay great emphasis on this point, and conclude that it is 'not clear that the same private demand for education would develop under normal growth and savings conditions.'

As Table 2.2 shows, the university student population was still heavily skewed in favour of males at this time. It was only in the second half of the 1970s that the proportion of women climbed above 20 per cent and not until the 2000s that anything close to parity was reached. The percentage of women in higher education *overall*, however, was higher than in universities alone, as they dominated enrolments in junior colleges (Table 2.3). The distinction between universities and junior colleges became very pronounced not only in terms of gender balance but also in curricular content. McVeigh (1997: 16–17) explains that while

Table 2.3 Junior colleges (*tanki daigaku*): Number of institutions and students, 1955–75

		1955	1960	1965	1970	1975
Private		204	214	301	414	434
National		17	27	28	22	31
Local Public		43	39	40	43	48
Total		264	280	369	479	513
	Percentage private	77.3%	76.4%	81.6%	86.4%	84.6%
Students	Total	77,885	83,457	147,563	263,219	353,782
	Percentage female	54.0%	67.5%	74.8%	82.7%	86.2%
	Percentage private	81.1%	78.7%	85.3%	90.1%	91.2%

Source: Created by the authors from MEXT 2017a.

---

[20] There are several ways of measuring university entrance rates, including university entrants as a proportion of senior high school (*kōtō gakkō*) leavers in the same year, and university entrants as a proportion of middle school (*chūgakkō*) leavers 3 years prior. The formula employed in this chapter (university entrants as a proportion of the 18-year-old population in the same year) is the one preferred by MEXT and is used here for the sake of consistency.

engineering and social sciences dominated in 4-year universities, enrolments in junior colleges were skewed overwhelmingly to what were considered 'feminine' subjects such as domestic science, humanities, and school teaching. This led to junior colleges being nicknamed *hanayome gakkō*, or 'schools to train future brides' (Fujimura-Faneslow 1985: 476).

While Japan was clearly achieving a transition from an 'elite' to a 'mass' higher education system in Martin Trow's (1973) terms, competition for access to the university echelon of this mass system remained intense. The percentage of applicants to universities and junior colleges who actually gained admission averaged around 60 per cent in the 1960s and 70 per cent in the 1970s (MEXT 2013), and the competition for admission to the most prestigious universities was so fierce it became characterized as 'examination hell' (*juken jigoku*).

The question of how best to select applicants for university admission was thus a crucial and hotly contested one. Since pre-war times, Japan's elite universities had operated a system of selection through rigorous entrance examinations; in the post-war expansion this system was simply extended on a mass scale on the basis that it offered an equal chance to all candidates. Anyone, regardless of their background, could gain admission to the University of Tokyo, provided they could prove their academic worth in the entrance examination. This promise of equality of opportunity was compromised by the palpable impact of factors such as household financial resources and geographical location on a student's capacity to perform well in the exams, making Japan an archetypal manifestation of both the functions and dysfunctions of meritocratic selection (Kariya and Dore 2006). Nonetheless, it was difficult to argue against the basic egalitarian principle which underpinned this system, especially in the absence of any more equitable alternative which could similarly be implemented on a mass scale.

The exam system was not simply a means for selecting candidates for university education and matching them with specific institutions: it also became part of selection for employment. Large firms, the preferred employment destination for university graduates owing to their superior benefits, training systems, and stability (the so-called 'lifetime' employment system), tended to prefer graduates from more selective universities, as they had already proven their intelligence and diligence through success in the university entrance examinations. Inevitably, such universities continued to attract the most applicants, driving competition to even fiercer levels (Kaneko 2004: 128–9). Selectivity, as expressed in the *hensachi* score described in Chapter 1, came to function as a default measure of university quality for both prospective students and graduate employers. High schools began to guide students in their application choices based on *hensachi*, and a huge industry sprang up to provide supplementary education for students preparing for entrance exams, as well as comparative data on the selectivity of each university and department (Goodman and Oka 2018).

Public Policy and Funding for Private Universities

As intimated above, the growth of private higher education in the 1950s and 60s was just as much a product of conscious government policy as it was pure market forces. James and Benjamin (1988: 65–7) point especially to the relaxed standards for establishing new institutions and departments in the 1960s, and the 'implicit' encouragement offered to banks to provide *gakkō hōjin* with generous loans to fund these establishments at a time when there was stringent credit-rationing. It was not until the 1970s, however, that the government manifested concrete and unequivocal support for private higher education in the form of a direct subsidy scheme.

The separation of the private sector from public financing had actually been mandated under Article 89 of the 1946 Constitution of Japan, which stated that '[n]o public money or other property shall be expended... for any charitable, educational or benevolent enterprises not under control of public authority.' This provision was a product of the post-war reformers' desire to minimize governmental interference in non-commercial private sector activity, rather than to advance a basic principle that private education should not be funded from the public coffers. Indeed, public support was expressly envisaged under the Private Schools Act—passed just three years after the Constitution—Article 59 of which reads: 'Where the State or a local public entity finds it necessary for the promotion of education, it may provide incorporated educational institutions with the necessary assistance concerning private school education, as separately provided for by law.'

Debates over constitutionality, however, were overshadowed in the late 1960s by violent student uprisings on university campuses across Japan, motivated by a variety of factors but united in their opposition to the rising cost of a university education. Meanwhile, bodies representing the private university sector had become increasingly vociferous in their demands for some sort of 'equalization' of higher education costs across the sector, especially given that private institutions, and by extension their fee-paying students, were footing the bill for Japan's shift from an elite to a mass higher education system. Private universities had borrowed heavily to raise the funds needed to acquire new land, facilities, and staff to accommodate rising enrolments in the 1960s, and with a decline in revenue resulting from a dip in university-age population at the end of that decade (in the wake of the post-war baby boom generation), this left many institutions severely stretched. When loans and subsidies were subtracted, the basic revenue/expenditure balance in the private sector was in the red by almost 20 billion yen in 1973 (Yonezawa 2010: 242). The decision to subsidize private universities was in part an acknowledgment that the state bore some responsibility for this predicament.

An ad hoc funding regime was instituted in 1970 and formalized in the Act on Subsidies for Private Schools (*shiritsu gakkō shinkō josei hō*) of 1975. A parliamentary resolution accompanying the passing of this Act stated the aim of eventually subsidizing private universities to the value of one half of their operating expenditure (Baba 2002). When ad hoc government subsidies were first introduced in 1970, they accounted for just 7.2 per cent of the operating expenditure of private universities; this figure increased significantly with the passing of the Act to over 20 per cent in the latter half of the 1970s and as high as 29.5 per cent in 1980. By 1980, subsidy rates had reached a high point; however, they have been decreasing ever since, and in the mid-2010s they stand at just under 10 per cent (MEXT 2017b). As noted earlier in this chapter, Japan has long had one of the lowest rates of government funding and highest private-to-public expenditure ratios in higher education among all the OECD countries. Calls for greater public recognition, and subsidization, continue to this day, supported by evidence that investment in private institutions generates greater social and financial returns on investment than those achieved by the heavily subsidized national ones (Tanaka 2019: 275).

There were two significant impacts of the government subsidy system launched in the 1970s. The first was the ushering in of a new era of planned higher education development. By subsidizing private universities, the national government could also require them to submit to stricter controls over student enrolments in line with its projections for growth in population and demand for skilled labour. In effect, the amount of financial assistance a university received varied according to the degree to which it conformed with Ministry objectives.[21] The funding regime included disincentives for over-quota enrolment and a system of setting aside a proportion of funds—initially

---

[21] According to Geiger (1986: 219), an institution with an operating budget of 1,000 million yen could qualify for a subsidy in the early 1980s as high as 520 million yen or as low as 200 million yen depending on the extent to which they met Ministry standards.

just a few per cent but rising to higher than 20 per cent of overall subsidies in the 2000s—for 'special subsidies' (*tokubetsu hojo*) to support universities proactively engaging in reforms and conducting projects in priority areas (MEXT 2017b). The standards for establishing new universities and expanding existing ones were tightened, with all aspects of organization and operation closely monitored to the point that, as one American researcher observed, the Ministry could control the number of students in a class, the time of day at which it could be held, and the dimensions of the building in which it was taught (Ellington 1992: 219). The growth in numbers of both universities and students slowed considerably in the second half of the 1970s as this mechanism of 'subsidization and control' (Yonezawa 2010) became entrenched.

The second impact, closely related to the first, concerned the costs of attending university. Rather than prompting a lowering of private university fees to bring them closer to public sector levels, the subsidies coincided with the start of a long-term trend to higher fees across the entire university sector. Stronger control on expansion in an era of growing demand created a 'monopolised and protected market' which enabled existing private universities to raise their fees with little fear of losing clientele (Kaneko 2004: 126). As Yonezawa (2010: 246) shows, the most dramatic rise in average private university fees, in the years from 1973 (under 300,000 yen at 2000 prices) to 1988 (almost 700,000 yen at 2000 prices) coincided precisely with the period of slowest growth in private student numbers (1.2 million to 1.4 million) since the establishment of the post-war university system. These fee increases were, however, outstripped by rises in the public higher education sector. The gap between private and national fee levels narrowed from 5:1 to 2:1 (National University Corporation Evaluation Committee 2015). University education had paradoxically become more expensive in real terms as more public funds were directed to it and more students participated in it. Nakazawa (2014) suggests that students and parents tolerated these rising fees mainly because university education was viewed primarily as a private good whose benefits accrue personally to those receiving it rather than to society at large and, moreover, a good to which access is managed through an impartial selection system—entrance examinations. As we shall see below, these notions have been called into question by the expansion of the higher education system in the context of population decline.

Yonezawa (2010) offers in-depth analysis of the effect which the new enrolment controls had on the market for private university education. He shows how manipulation of the supply/demand balance (limiting the former while the latter continued to grow) allowed private universities to leverage the already well-established link between selectivity in admissions and university quality to build their reputations and ultimately, at the upper end of the sector, attract students of a similar calibre as the national universities, despite the huge structural inequalities. Yonezawa (2010: 231–4) concludes that this degree of 'overlap' between public and private sectors would not have been possible without the combination of subsidization and control. He also highlights the adverse effect on educational and research quality, whereby private universities, as rational market actors, inevitably focused their efforts on selectivity-based reputation-building, while public funding remained limited and government controls did not extend to quality assurance. This analysis also helps explain the anomaly, noted in Chapter 1, whereby the fees a private university charges do not necessarily reflect its prestige.[22] In the controlled, high-demand environment, universities striving for 'elite' status tended to set their fees lower in the hope of attracting more applicants, which in turn allowed them to be more selective and boost their reputation further.

The net effect of the reforms of the 1970s, therefore, was a complete turnaround in the financial situation of the private universities in Japan. When an OECD team visited Japan in 1970, it concluded that Japanese private universities were, in effect, financially bankrupt and it was only the voluntary restraint of the banking community not to call in their loans which allowed them to survive (OECD 1971). By 1978, however, revenues (which had come roughly in balance with operating expenses in 1974) exceeded expenditures by 13 per cent (Geiger 1986: 48). This was due, as Geiger (1986: 48) put it, to private universities 'taking advantage of their market position to enhance revenues'. This is a trend which continued for the next decade and helps explain how many private universities were subsequently able to weather the downturn in student numbers in the 2000s.

Expansion and Diversification

The 1980s was an era of further expansion, as demand continued to grow despite a brief decline in university-age population in the first half of the

---

[22] The inverse relationship between ranking and fee levels continues to the present day, and is most pronounced in faculties of medicine. In 2017, the highest fees in the private sector—over 47 million yen (430,000 USD) for a 6-year medical degree, or around thirteen times those of national universities—were charged by a university which sat at the bottom of the *hensachi* ranking for medical faculty admissions (Shomura 2017).

decade. The Japanese economy was maturing, driving both demand and capacity to pay for university education upward. The enactment of equal employment opportunity legislation in 1986 was particularly effective in prompting more women to seek undergraduate education. This was also the year in which the second post-war baby boom generation began to reach university entrance age. The combination of heightened demand and a population bubble made competition for university places fiercer than it had been since the 1960s. The term *juken nanmin* or 'entrance examination refugee' came into vogue to describe the growing number of university applicants unable to secure admission (*AJ*, 3 November 1989). The government introduced a system of temporarily raised enrolment quotas (*rinjiteki teiin*) to cater for this population bubble, but demand continued to outstrip supply, and the ability of the government to maintain its control over the system was considerably weakened as market forces increasingly came to dominate (Amano 1997).

The years from 1986 to 1992 were particularly advantageous for private universities and became known as the 'golden seven'. The government allowed both temporary and permanent enrolment quota increases far higher than its original plans,[23] but demand remained strong, meaning that universities could fill their classrooms with greater numbers of students while still selecting rigorously from a huge pool of applicants. As many applicants hedged their bets by applying to several universities and participating in multiple entrance examination streams, the 'application processing fees' of 30,000 yen or more (charged per application rather than per applicant) became a major source of private university revenue in their own right.

This was also a time of great uncertainty, however, as dire forecasts of long-term population decline began to emerge and the government sowed the seeds of major reform in the university sector. In 1984, Prime Minister Nakasone Yasuhiro formed a Special Advisory Council on Education (*rinji kyōiku shingikai* or *rinkyōshin* for short) to chart a course for Japanese education in the post-high economic growth era (Schoppa 1991; Hood 2001). Some of the council's harshest criticism was directed at universities, which it saw as inefficient and unresponsive to increasingly diverse student needs. Developing greater variety in educational offerings and paying more attention to the

---

[23] Between 1986 and 1992, the overall increase in permanent quotas was 78,173, compared to the initial government plan of 42,000. The proportional increase in *temporary* quotas was even higher: 112,443 against a planned 44,000 (Central Council for Education 2003). Reliance on temporary quotas became extremely high in some private universities: as high as 42 per cent of total intake at Ryukoku University and 48 per cent at Osaka Sangyo University in 1992 (Morozumi 2010: 210).

quality of teaching and research were seen as essential prerequisites to keep universities in step with major currents of change such as internationalization and the rise of the 'information society'. Nakasone, like his contemporaries in the UK and North America, is said to have ushered in a long-term shift to neoliberal policymaking. The reports of both the Special Advisory Council, and the University Council which succeeded it in the 1990s, are indeed strongly coloured by the idea of universities as the powerhouse of labour force development and industrial innovation, as well as an emphasis on market competition over government micro-management of the university sector (Special Advisory Council on Education 1987; University Council 1991 and 1998; Takahashi 2017). The novelty of these developments should not be overplayed, however: the private university sector was already well-accustomed to shaping by market forces and many of the reform themes pursued in and after the Nakasone era, especially the diversification of curricular offerings and enhancement of teaching quality in a competitive environment, had been on the agenda since at least the 1970s (Amano 1988; Nagai 1971).

One of the most significant changes for private universities came in 1991, when the standards for university establishment were revised to give universities more freedom to design their own undergraduate curricula, unfettered by conventional disciplinary designations and previously strict distinctions between education for general purposes (*ippan/kyōyō kyōiku*) in the first years of undergraduate education and specialist education (*senmon kyōiku*) in the later years. After the 1991 reforms, establishment of new curricular offerings still required governmental approval, but the approval process was streamlined, and required applicants mainly to demonstrate compliance with formal requirements such as overall adequacy of physical infrastructure and number of qualified teaching staff, rather than conformity with conventional disciplinary frameworks. The quality and efficacy of the new offerings was to be adjudicated by a combination of market forces (i.e., whether or not students would be willing to enrol in them) and an emerging emphasis on self-assessment and evaluation, which would eventually (from 2004) be enshrined in a mandatory third-party evaluation and accreditation system.

New undergraduate degree titles proliferated after 1991, to such an extent that by the mid-2000s there were 580 different types of undergraduate majors operating in Japan; around 60 per cent of these were offered by only one university (Central Council for Education 2008). Creating new courses allowed private universities not only to adjust to changing labour market demands and wider trends such as the onset of the information age, but also appeal to school leavers previously uninterested in or unqualified for undergraduate education. Universities looking to rationalize their offerings also benefited from the new scope for employing contemporary themes, as opposed to conventional disciplines, as the basis for curriculum design. By incorporating existing curricula and teaching staff spread across a number of disciplines under a single, topical umbrella, universities could re-brand themselves while avoiding the kinds of substantive changes to personnel and degree structure which often held up the granting of ministerial approval.[24] By the 2000s, this kind of cosmetic renovation had become standard practice in struggling private universities—as we shall see in later chapters.[25]

The period from 1990 to the mid-2000s saw the most dramatic growth in university numbers and entrance rates since the initial post-war boom of the 1960s (see Figure 2.5). Between 1996 and 2005, 167 new 4-year universities opened, most of them private, raising the total nationwide number to 710. The entrance rate, which had stood at just under 25 per cent (male 33.4 per cent, female 15.2 per cent) at the start of the 1990s, was 39.7 per cent (47.5 per cent, 31.5 per cent) by 2000 (MEXT 2017a). The 2000 entrance rate was close to 50 per cent when junior college enrolments were added, and almost 70 per cent for higher education overall, when one added the professional training colleges and higher colleges of technology. For private universities, the rising entrance rates more than compensated for the drop in population after the 'golden seven' years. The temporary enrolment quota increases introduced in the boom period were not immediately removed, and ultimately universities could apply to have up to half of their temporary increase rolled in to their official enrolment quotas. These quotas were not strictly enforced, either: only private universities enrolling more than 130 per cent were penalized in the form of a temporary suspension of government subsidies. In practice, therefore, over-enrolment was habitual. This combination of more relaxed enrolment controls and a laissez-faire approach to the establishment of new

---

[24] This process was facilitated in 2004 with the introduction of a 'reporting' (todokede) system for many changes which, even under the 1991 relaxation, were previously subject to formal ministerial approval. Private universities used this system creatively to establish brand-new offerings through a series of incremental changes requiring only todokede. Watanabe (2017: 89ff.) describes the mechanics of this process in some detail, concluding that it provided a loophole (nukemichi) for some private universities to reinvent their disciplinary identity without any quality control.

[25] The 1991 relaxation of establishment standards also served as a new point of distinction within the aforementioned category of universities established under the post-war system, as distinct from those first established in the pre-1947 era. The new universities could from this point be divided into three types: those established prior to the original ministerial standards being put in place in 1956; those complying with the strict 1956 standards; and those established after the 1991 relaxation. The latter two categories each account for around two-fifths of all private universities today, evidencing the immense growth of the sector since the late 1950s. The popular perception is that the pre-1991 institutions are the more respectable.

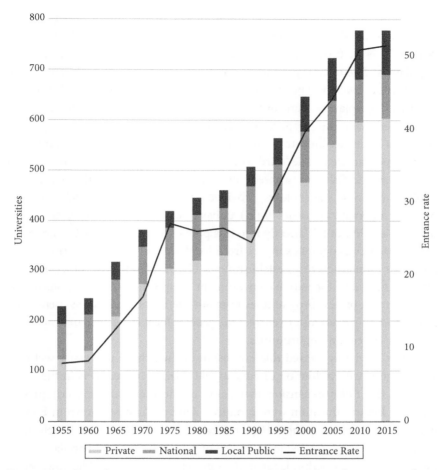

Figure 2.5. Growth in university entrance rates and number of universities by type, 1955–2015.
Source: Created by the authors from MEXT (2018a).

programmes in the 1990s is identified by Amano (1997) as the key point in Japan's shift from a 'planning' to a 'market' model for higher education, a shift which took place in the context of a trend to deregulation and privatization across many other areas of society.

This era was thus one of diversification not only in terms of curricular offerings but also institutional identities. Many of the new private universities created in the 1990s were junior colleges taking advantage of the relaxed establishment standards to 'upgrade' (*shōkaku*) to full university status or be absorbed into existing universities, often within the same *gakkō hōjin*. No fewer than 161 junior colleges were closed between 1990 and 2010 as a result of such moves, and overall student numbers in the junior college sector dropped from 479,389 to 155,273 in the same period (Kida 2012; MEXT 2017c). This in turn affected the gender balance of the university student population. The overall proportion of female university students grew from 24 per cent in 1985 to 37 per cent in 2000 to 43 per cent in 2015 (MEXT 2018a).[26]

Other new players were private universities in rural and regional areas established with the support of local government authorities, as part of strategies to attract industrial investment and halt the outflow of population to metropolitan areas. The 'third sector' approach employed in industries such as tourism and fisheries, whereby new enterprises were jointly financed by public and private stakeholders, provided a model for these publicly founded, privately operated (*kōsetsu min'ei*) universities. A number of other private universities did not fall directly into this public/private category but nonetheless enjoyed considerable support from local authorities in the form of land and other infrastructure for establishment. The proliferation of rural campuses was also fuelled by the national government's imposition of restrictions on the establishment of new programmes in major metropolitan areas as mentioned in Chapter 1—an attempt to correct the geographical imbalance in availability of higher education opportunities.

Critics inevitably viewed this expansion of the private university sector as synonymous with a dilution of educational quality. Indeed, it is in the aftermath of the 1990s expansion that some of the most scathing critiques of Japanese higher education were produced. One of the best known in English is Brian McVeigh's *Japanese Higher Education as Myth* (2002), which in its introductory chapter provides a review of some of the more popular critical literature emerging within Japan in the same era. It is also possible, however, to think of the changes which took place in the 1990s less in terms of a dilution of quality and more as an inevitable blurring of some of the previously strict boundaries between different kinds of institutions in Japanese higher education. The phenomenon of junior colleges converting or being absorbed into universities, for example, was a natural product of the breaking down of the gender-based distinction between 2-year associate degrees (traditionally for women) and 4-year undergraduate degrees (for men). Private universities established with the support of local government, meanwhile, are evidence

---

[26] Japan still, however, has the lowest proportion of women entering tertiary-level science, technology, engineering, and mathematics fields among all OECD countries (OECD 2017: 1). The greatest imbalance is in engineering, where just 15 per cent of undergraduate students are female. Meanwhile, women account for close to two in every three enrolments in the humanities, and almost as high a proportion in education and teacher training.

of the difficulty, noted earlier, of pursuing a strict differentiation between the 'private' and the 'public' in higher education.

Despite this blurring, however, the formal distinctions of the post-war system remained in place, giving rise to a number of paradoxes. Local governments which bankrolled the establishment of new private universities, for example, sometimes found that the *gakkō hōjin* governance structure often afforded them very little say in the actual management of those universities, and thus struggled to ensure that such universities developed with the interests of the local community at heart. Another example is the persistence of the distinction between universities and junior colleges. Despite the gradual breakdown of the gender hierarchy, junior colleges retained a very distinct organizational identity, which often worked against collaboration and resource-sharing with universities whose offerings might otherwise have been highly complementary. The Meikei Gakuin University case, discussed in following chapters, provides a vivid example of this divide in operation even within the same educational conglomerate.

Some of the most important changes in the Japanese educational landscape were actually occurring beyond the university and junior college sector. As noted earlier, post-secondary vocational education providers had long operated outside the formal system of schools and universities established in the post-war period, but from 1975 had the opportunity to acquire formal status as professional training colleges (*senmon gakkō*) (Yoshimoto, K. 2003). Table 2.4 shows that enrolments in these colleges, which were overwhelmingly private, soon equalled and then outstripped those in junior colleges, and by the 1990s

Table 2.4 Professional training colleges (*senmon gakkō*): Number of institutions and students, 1980–90

		1980	1985	1990
Private	Colleges	2,187	2,664	2,952
	Students	396,443	496,036	746,193
National	Colleges	187	178	166
	Students	15,843	18,070	17,433
Local	Colleges	146	173	182
	Students	20,628	24,069	27,805
TOTAL	Colleges	2,520	3,015	3,300
	Percentage private	86.8%	88.4%	89.5%
	Students	432,914	538,175	791,431
	Percentage female	66.5%	58.0%	51.9%
	Percentage private	91.6%	92.2%	94.3%

Source: Created by the authors from MEXT 2017a.

accounted for more than 30 per cent of all students entering higher education in Japan. More managerial and less collegial in their operating structures, and free from the same degree of regulation as junior colleges and universities, professional training colleges could be much more agile in responding to changes in both student preferences and the needs of the job market (Goodman, Hatakenaka, and Kim 2009).

From Golden Years to Recruitment Hell

By the mid-1990s, the tide had begun to turn. As noted in Chapter 1, the 18-year-old population was dropping sharply: from a peak of over 2 million in 1992 to around 1.2 million just 15 years later. University entrance rates continued to climb, but not quickly enough to keep pace with the combination of population decline and ongoing growth in university enrolment capacity. It may seem counter-intuitive that universities would be expanding their capacity while their pool of applicants was shrinking, but this was in fact a strategic response to the drop in enrolments: universities established more and more new departments in the hope of attracting new types of applicants and differentiating themselves from competitors. The number of applicants gaining admission had topped 80 per cent by the end of the 1990s, and it would not be long, pundits warned, before there would be more places available in universities than students to fill them. Universities would be happy to take anyone who applied, and the 'examination hell' of earlier times would be replaced by a 'recruitment hell' for universities themselves (Kinmonth, 2005).

Private universities began to adopt new approaches to admitting students. Most of these involved the concept of 'recommendation' (*suisen*), which had previously been used in relation to the admission of students from affiliated high schools, was now appropriated in new terminology such as *jiko suisen* ('self-recommendation') and *kōbo suisen* ('open recommendation'), to describe processes whereby students could apply and be selected not on the results of a written exam, but by demonstrating their individual talents and aptitude through interviews and other means. By 2000, almost 40 per cent of new students in private universities—and 34.2 percent across the entire university sector—were enrolled through non-standard admissions processes (MEXT 2013). Such was the significance of this development that a report of the University Council on the university entrance exam system in 2000 devoted a whole section to such 'Admissions Office' methods, both endorsing their capacity for more accurate 'matching' of student abilities to curricular priorities and urging 'proper' implementation to maintain high academic standards and communicate expectations clearly to applicants (University Council 2000).

At the same time, the government was preparing a major shake-up in the traditional order of the university sector, with a number of reforms in the same spirit of deregulation (*kisei kanwa*) vigorously pursued in many other policy realms in early 2000s Japan. National universities were to be transformed into independent administrative corporations (*dokuritsu gyōsei hōjin*) in 2004, freed from direct ministerial control and, ultimately, their reliance on conventional per-capita government subsidies.[27] It was thought that as national universities pursued their self-sufficiency goals, they would became active market players, bringing new competitive challenges to the private university sector, especially as the previously discussed 'dual-layered' inequality (a radically low proportion of government funding directed to private institutions, in the context of a low level of public expenditure on higher education overall) persisted.[28] Meanwhile, the corporatization process itself came in for extensive criticism from within the national university community as being pushed through as a political showpiece of deregulation and downsizing, with insufficient attention given to the original goal of creating the best possible system of university governance (Amano 2006: 102–3; see also Goldfinch 2006; Yamamoto 2005; Yamamoto 2004).

Alongside corporatization, a number of other changes were planned in the same spirit of deregulation and market competition.[29] One was to open the door to new players in the university sector. From 2003, a system was instituted to allow private for-profit companies to establish universities (*kabushikigaisha-ritsu daigaku*) in certain areas. A new category of institution, the professional graduate school (*senmonshoku daigakuin*), was also introduced in 2003, extending postgraduate education beyond its traditionally heavy focus on pure research and coinciding with other reforms to highly skilled professions in Japan. The law schools introduced in Chapter 4 were

---

[27] Local public universities were also given the option of corporatizing as a way of pursuing more efficient operations with greater autonomy from their municipal governments, but the uptake was relatively slow initially: only one (out of seventy-three) local public universities was corporatized in 2004, seven in 2005, and twenty-one in 2006 (MEXT 2018d). Even at the time of writing in 2018, almost twenty local public universities remain uncorporatized.

[28] This sense of apprehension is best encapsulated in the title of Nakamura's 2001 book *Kokuritsu daigaku min'eika de 300 no shidai ga tsubureru* (National university corporatization will lead to 300 private universities going bankrupt]).

[29] For a list of key words (and explanation of their significance) in higher education in the early 2000s, see Osako and Shirakawa (2003: 162–9).

part of this category. Another important change was a shift from ex ante to ex post evaluation and quality assurance. A new regime of 'accreditation evaluation' (*ninshō hyōka*) was introduced, under which all universities—not only national universities—submit to a 7-yearly cycle of evaluation by a government-approved independent accreditation agency. Detailed evaluation reports, including performance assessments and recommendations, were to be published regardless of the accreditation outcome. Deferral or rejection did not lead directly to disbarment, but would clearly have significant reputational impact as well as jeopardizing future funding applications.

Viewed from the standpoint of ordinary students and households, one of the most significant changes of the 1990s and 2000s was the decline in affordability of university education. These decades saw a rise in insecure employment and growing disparity in household incomes which stood in stark contrast—especially given the shift in the supply demand balance—to the continuing upward trend in university fees. The average private university tuition fee doubled between 1990 and 2010, while the average wage in Japan declined by close to one-fifth (JASSO 2017).

One factor which enabled private universities to continue to charge high fees and attract a wider variety of school-leavers, despite the economic slowdown, was the expansion of the public system of financial aid for low-income students in higher education. This system was administered from the national budget by the Japan Scholarship Foundation until 2004 and by its successor, the Japan Student Services Organization (JASSO). Despite the use of the term 'scholarship' (*shōgakukin*), what the scheme offered was not grants[30] but loans, both interest-bearing and (for students from low-income households) zero-interest, repayable after graduation. Universities keen to attract new clientele began presenting JASSO loans as a solution for prospective students whose household's financial resources would otherwise have put private university entrance beyond their reach. This strategy was tacitly supported by the government, which approved major increases in the JASSO loan budget throughout the late 1990s and early 2000s. The total number of students accessing these loans rose rapidly, from 380,000 in 1998 to 840,000 in 2004, and topping 1

---

[30] Data on the provision of grant-based scholarships by private universities is rather limited, but a 2001 survey by the Association of Private Universities of Japan shows that the average proportion of students in receipt of grant-based scholarships was just over 1 per cent; averages for university-administered loans and tuition fee reductions were both well under 1 per cent. There was also, however, huge variation from university to university, with rates for grant-based schemes ranging from zero to 13 per cent, and between zero to as high as 63 per cent for loans. Detailed analysis of these data by Hōzawa and Shirakawa (2006) found a positive correlation between rate of students receiving scholarships and the selectivity of the university, but not with the level of tuition fees charged.

million in 2007 (JASSO 2017). The role of the expansion of the JASSO loan system in sustaining private universities through the period of demographic decline is a contentious topic and one to which we shall return in Chapter 5.

Looking Back: The Planned and Unplanned Development of Private Universities

The foregoing could be described as a brief history of the development of Japanese private universities in the modern era, except that the word 'development' suggests some degree of coordination or at least premeditation, which is notably absent from this narrative. Yet it is also difficult to conclude that the haphazard evolution was solely a product of private institutions of higher education being left to their own devices. Many of the decisive changes did not stem from neglect, but rather from policymakers' active cultivation of a market-based solution to changes in demand for higher education. Private institutions were expected to absorb the impact of declines in demand but were also allowed to reap the benefits of growth, thanks to flexible enrolment quotas and lax establishment requirements. Private universities were assisted indirectly by policies such as rural revitalization, which furnished public sector support for many new private establishments, and the cultivation of a friendly credit environment, which gave private institutions access to the funds needed to grow apace with burgeoning demand. Even the tightening of government controls often worked to the benefit of the private sector. The introduction of government subsidies in the 1970s, for example, was accompanied by stricter controls on expansion, but this created a sellers' market, allowing private universities to be more selective and to charge higher fees. In these conditions, it is not difficult to imagine private university establishment being viewed as a lucrative and relatively low-risk venture, notwithstanding the lack of direct government funding.

Despite the absence of a long-term vision and reluctance to offer direct financial support, the government has, ever since the Meiji period, struggled almost constantly to balance its reliance on private demand as a means of financing the growth of a modern higher education system with the temptation to micro-manage private institutions and keep them tied to the same regulatory framework as national/public ones. Ichikawa (2004) summarizes this history as a progression from 'regulation' (*tōsei*) in the pre-war period, to 'non-intervention' (*hōnin*) in the post-war, to 'nurturing' (*ikusei*) in the 1970s, and to a combination of nurturing and non-intervention since the 1990s.

Ogata (1978) uses the terms 'non-support, full control' (pre-war), 'non-support, non-control' (post-war), and 'support and control' (1970s). This laissez-faire yet interventionist attitude has in turn made private universities proud and staunchly protective of their independence but also highly attuned to changes in the regulatory regime, eager to please the national educational bureaucracy, and still prepared to take the lead from their national university counterparts.

A final conclusion which can be drawn from this historical account—and a theme that we develop in the subsequent chapters—is that private universities are highly experienced in dealing with fluctuations in consumer demand and levels of government regulation. Contrary to the tone of much of the literature produced around the turn of the millennium, it is difficult to paint the situation facing private universities around that time as completely unprecedented, or the private universities themselves as entirely without resources to weather what was to come.

In the next chapter we turn to examine how these changes were experienced on the ground through an ethnographic portrait of a private university which we call MGU. Like many other private universities, MGU suffered a serious crisis of under-enrolment in the early 2000s. An examination of how different actors within the university perceived and responded to the crisis underlines many of the features of private universities identified in this chapter and how they were challenged and sometimes reinforced. It also sheds light on one important feature of private universities which does not appear in the account above, nor, with a very few exceptions, in the scholarly or administrative discourse on private higher education in Japan generally. This is the kinship relationships which often exist among key actors in the governance of universities and the educational corporations (*gakkō hōjin*) which operate them.

3

A University Under Fire

A Short Ethnography of MGU 1992–2007

There have been very few anthropological studies of the academic world since the 1970s when Van den Berghe (1973) published his detailed account of a thinly disguised university in Nigeria under the title, *Power and Privilege at an African University* and F. G. Bailey (1977) published his equally thinly fictionalized account of university committee politics with the title *Morality and Expediency: The folklore of academic politics*. This lack of ethnographies of higher education institutions might be thought surprising given that most professional ethnographers work in such institutions themselves. There have been a number of ethnographic studies of college students (see for example, Moffatt [1989] and, more recently, Nathan [2005]) and the plethora of works on the history and organization of higher education institutions. It is the shortage of studies of professors, trustees, administrators, and how they interact with each other and with students which he finds particularly conspicuous. Wisniewski (2008) puts this down to a combination of a sense of superiority ('we know who we are') and sensitivity about lifting too many rocks among your own community when careers may be at stake.

In the case of Japan, as we have seen, there is a large body of work on the history and political economy of higher education in Japan, both in English and Japanese. There is a substantial literature in Japanese on the student experience in Japan, although almost all of this is quantitative in nature. Lee-Cunin (2004) provides a good example of survey work in English in this field. There are also a number of generally critical 'insider' exposés of university life. Based on his 17 years at a private university in Tokyo and calling himself 'Professor S of the department of literature', Suzuki (2001) writes an account of the lives and views of the students in his university and sheds light on what conditions are like for the academics. Other accounts from the same era include books by one of the few foreign presidents of a Japanese university, Gregory Clark (2003), Fujii (1997), Kitamura (2002), Kusaka et al. (2003), and Yoshimoto, Y. (2003) the titles of which—respectively *Why Can't Japanese*

Family-Run Universities in Japan: Sources of Inbuilt Resilience in the Face of Demographic Pressure, 1992–2030.
Jeremy Breaden and Roger Goodman, Oxford University Press (2020). © Jeremy Breaden and Roger Goodman.
DOI: 10.1093/oso/9780198863496.001.0001

Education Change, The Truth and Fallacies of the University's Ivory Tower, Can Universities Be Reborn, What Is to Be Done With Our Current Universities?, You Have Gone to University, But... ?—convey that they are more complaints about the current system than ethnographic descriptions of it.

That there is almost no ethnographic work in Japanese on Japanese higher education institutions can also be put down, in part, to the fact that Japanese anthropologists rarely study their own society. One of the few examples of an ethnographic study of a Japanese university by a trained anthropologist is Funabiki Takeo's *Daigaku no ethnograffiti* (2005). This is a set of slightly whimsical observations on academic life and culture at the University of Tokyo by one of Japan's leading anthropologists (a specialist on South East Asia) reminiscent of, though not as structured, as Bailey's account of academic politics.[1]

There have been a number of ethnographies of Japanese universities written by non-Japanese anthropologists in the past two decades. Brian McVeigh (1997, 2002, 2006) has written a series of highly polemical critiques of Japanese universities and junior colleges based on his many years teaching in a variety of lower level institutions. The titles and subtitles of his books give a strong sense of the position he takes: *Learning to Be Ladylike* (1997); *Japanese Higher Education as Myth* (2002); *Deception and Disaffection in Japanese Higher Education* (2006). Somewhat like Sacks (1996) in his critique of US colleges, *Generation X Goes to University*, McVeigh does not engage with or reflect the views of those charged with running and overseeing higher education institutions.

Gregory Poole (2010), on the other hand, presents a more neutral analysis of roles of the different actors in Japanese universities. He gives a fascinating account of the response of faculty staff at the institution which he calls Edo University of Commerce (EUC) when it was under pressure to reform its programmes to recruit and retain students in the midst of fierce competition in the late 1990s. He describes a divide between reformers and traditionalists and he shows how each group developed their own narratives. Those who Poole dubs the '*sotomuki*' (outward-oriented) group emphasized the need to move away from the past and, instead, saw universities more like a business which provided a professional service to students. 'Quality' and 'efficiency' were two of their buzzwords, as was the notion of individual faculty and staff being rewarded by results. A *sotomuki* professor spent as little time as possible

---

[1] There are also a number of 'insider stories' by university presidents which contain the same kinds of observations on academic and administrative culture, see Kuroki (2009), Sugiyama (2004).

on the campus, was outside the inner circle of power, and was more concerned with establishing a publication and research record which would enable him or her to transfer to a higher-ranking university. The *'uchimuki'* (inward-oriented) group preferred to emphasize the community nature of universities with their familial roots and reliance on consensus decision-making. Loyalty and equity of workloads were two of their core principles and they believed rewards should be given to those who supported the group rather than those who sought personal advancement through academic publications or positive student assessments of their teaching. An *uchimuki* professor showed full commitment to the EUC mission, spent long hours on campus (especially on committee meetings), and privileged the 'notions of cooperation, effort and form over results and content' (Poole 2010: 123). Both the *sotomuki* and the *uchimuki* professors are, of course, as Poole is at pains to point out, Weberian 'ideal types' and, as such, they provide useful insights for understanding how institutions respond to crises.

In this chapter we provide a detailed ethnographic account of a Japanese private university which in the early 2000s was facing exactly the sort of challenges that were discussed in the introduction to this book. This account is based on 12 months of fieldwork in 2003–4 and it sets out not only to explain the background to the situation that then pertained in the university itself but also to present the perceptions of the key actors about how the crisis was being faced. We have called this university Meikei Gakuin University (MGU).

MGU: A Short History

MGU's origins can be found in an Institute of Accounting founded in the early 1940s (the first professional accounting school in the Kansai) to which a College of Business was added.[2] It was officially classified as a *senmon gakkō*, a 2-year professional training college. According to Han (1996), *senmon gakkō* in Japan have always been distinguished by their strong focus on the employ-ability of their graduates and their emphasis on preparing students for voca-tional qualifications. These same attributes in many ways have always been part of the DNA of MGU.

---

[2] According to a survey by Chen (2003), of all the 654 corporations (*gakkō hōjin*) which had private universities in 2001, only in 18.2 per cent of cases had a university been the founding institution. The largest proportion had started out as senior high schools (26 per cent), followed by junior high schools (22.5 per cent). 7.2 per cent (47) had started as a *senmon gakkō* as in the case of MGU.

As the demand for secondary education grew with the first post-war baby boom reaching their teenage years, Meikei Gakuin High School was founded. The founding family had always enjoyed good relations with the ruling Liberal Democratic Party and, through this, was able to buy land cheaply in a prime site not far outside Osaka. In time for the cohort who had entered the high school 3 years earlier, Meikei Gakuin Tanki Daigaku (a 2-year junior college, with a department of Business Administration) was established. In the early 1960s, MGU itself was founded with a Faculty of Commerce to which Departments of Business Administration and Economics were added the following year. The University's founder announced that MGU's founding principles were to 'develop individuals of both practical ability and broad vision (*shiya no hiroi jissentekina jinzai*), who can serve society at large and contribute to the peace and welfare of humankind'. MGU's first master's programme was set up in the Graduate School of Commerce followed by its first doctoral programme, in the same school. Other schools and programmes, at undergraduate and graduate level, were added over the next four decades.

When MGU moved to its current site, there would have been just farmland in the area. By the early 2000s, it was surrounded on all sides by urban residential buildings. The boundaries of the campus were marked by metal fences and gates manned by smartly dressed security staff (*shuei-san*) who kept a close watch on all who came and went. They knew the names and faces of all the academic staff in front of whom they stopped and saluted as they came across them on campus. When still in uniform, they would even salute academic staff beyond the campus, demonstrating the extent to which they saw themselves as representatives of the institution.

Since the neighbourhood had grown up around the university rather than the other way around, it was interesting by the early 2000s to note the extent to which the institution went to ensure good relations with the local community. There were numerous signs reminding students to keep their noise down and pick up their rubbish out of respect for the residential nature of the environment and, in particular, not to cause problems with car parking (*meiwaku chūsha*) in the surrounding streets. MGU welcomed members of the local community to sign up for non-accredited courses. The impressive Christmas lights which the university put up on the campus in December were much enjoyed by those who lived nearby. Local members of the community could also attend free music concerts which were put on at MGU. The extent to which MGU was felt to be vulnerable to bad neighbourly relations was evident in a still-remembered incident from the 1980s when the Kansai branch of the professors' union had gone around the neighbourhood in cars with loudspeakers denouncing the university's employment practices in relation to a (foreign) part-time teacher who had not had her contract renewed.

By the early 1990s, MGU was generally described as having 10,000 students, 200 full-time teaching staff, and 200 part-time teaching staff. While it could not be described as an elite institution, it was considered a favourite second choice and entry was competitive. In 1991, 42,000 applicants competed for 2,750 places in its undergraduate programmes, a ratio of almost seventeen applicants for each place. With so many applicants paying application fees; with many students paying large non-refundable deposits to secure places which they would often give up if they subsequently got into academically stronger universities; and with some of the highest tuition fees in the Kansai region, the general view of MGU in that period was that financially it was doing very well and that it had found a lucrative and successful niche for itself in an increasingly crowded and competitive market of private, urban-based, 4-year and 2-year liberal arts universities and junior colleges.

MGU's 'Distinctive Features' (*tokuchō*)

MGU was known by the mid-1990s for a number of distinguishing features. Its geographical position was considered very advantageous. Almost equidistantly 5 minutes' walk between the stations of two railway lines running between two of the biggest metropolises in the Kansai area, it was extremely easy to access. This was an attraction since, as with many Japanese universities, most students commuted on a daily basis from their family homes. Moreover, it meant that students could combine attending classes with holding down part-time jobs, sometimes far from the campus, which for many of them was another crucial consideration when looking for an institution. It was also appreciated by both full-time professors who taught at other institutions and the part-time professors who came to MGU.

By the 1980s, MGU's buildings and facilities were considered some of the finest in the region. It had a campus tower clock jokingly said to be built by Rolex—though more reliable sources suggested it was actually made by the Japanese firm Seiko—and the possible cost of which was much discussed. Unusually, it had an escalator which took students up just a couple of floors as well as multiple and efficient lifts and was one of the best-designed campuses for students with physical disabilities in Japan, though one rarely saw such students there. One of the newest buildings with faculty offices was so well appointed that it was joked that, if the university got into financial trouble, it could be turned into an old people's home or hotel overnight. Buildings were not only well and imaginatively constructed and decorated but also meticulously maintained, such that many of them still looked brand new years after their construction. A president of another university in the Kansai area said of the MGU facilities that when they had been built it would have been on the basis that a high investment would lead to a high return.

In some ways, the campus was also distinctive for what could not be seen: there was no graffiti, there were no flyers or advertising posters hanging off walls, there were no student protests (at the time the Second Iraq War was waging and many campuses in Japan as elsewhere saw protest movements). The only time a visitor would have been fully aware of student activity on the campus, other than academic study, was at the annual cultural festival (*bunkasai*), some lunch-time student concerts, and when the tennis club was playing.

MGU was well known for its early investment in technology to support learning. Its multimedia facility, opened in the late 1990s, was equipped with hardware and software that covered a wide range of fields and functions. It organized multiple activities to teach multimedia skills to any students who thought this would help their career development long before this was fashionable across Japanese campuses. It had a drop-in centre to help students enhance their communication skills in foreign languages and 'broaden their awareness of cultures around the world' which was supported by foreign staff and volunteers. The library was an 'information centre' which encouraged online independent learning, and benefited from the rapid development of access to electronic resources. There was a focus on information and communication from the early days in MGU; first, with newspapers being made available across campus and latterly with computer terminals being set up in public spaces. Its Extension Centre offered practical training programmes, largely related to computer use, on campus in the evenings and on Saturdays both for students and non-students.

MGU had a reputation for non-curricular activities, especially sport. It was strong in American football, which was not common in Japanese universities at the time, but also had a history of success in soccer, baseball, volleyball, golf, and athletics. In a list of the forty-two best-known alumni of MGU, eleven were professional soccer players (one of whom had played for Japan). By far the best known alumnus of MGU, however, was a former Olympic gold medallist; for the 4 years after her victory she was used in almost all of the university's promotional literature. It was a huge blow to the university—and also something of a national controversy—when, having struggled with injury, she was not selected to represent Japan at the following Olympics to defend her crown.

MGU was, from the early 1980s, an avid collector of links with overseas higher education institutions. This was seen as important both for recruitment and for the development of 'global citizens'. Some of those relationships were born out of personal links between MGU staff and individuals overseas. MGU had particularly strong links with the birthplace of the president's wife in the US. It had a long-standing relationship with a college in the UK where for many years it ran an English-language programme each summer for MGU students. MGU also had links in Australia, Austria, China, Finland, France, Germany, Iceland, Lithuania, Mexico, Netherlands, New Zealand, Philippines, South Africa, Sweden, Taiwan, and Thailand, though the origins of many of these seem to have been lost in time and, by the early 2000s, seemed to be rarely mobilized.

While all of the above features made MGU attractive, especially to parents insisting on Campus Open Days, they also made it expensive. Indeed, by the 1990s, MGU seemed to revel in being considered the most expensive university in the Kansai area of Japan, roughly 30 per cent more expensive than most other private universities. The high price was seen to go with offering a form of cultural capital that came from being able to pay such fees and this was thought to be attractive to a certain kind of parent who had not themselves gone to university (or at least not a 4-year university) but who had made money, often through their business dealings in the bubble economy of the 1980s. The Kansai area in Japan is particularly well known for its interest in business and capital accumulation as well as a down-to-earth attitude towards money, and it is possible to see why MGU might particularly have appealed. The children of such parents are often tagged in Japan with the titles 'o-botchan' (little princes) and 'o-jōsama' (little princesses) and staff at MGU would often describe their students as such—children from nouveau-riche families who were the first of their family to go to formal higher education—and would ascribe their failings, such as non-attendance in class, to their indulged background. Even if the students were not always described as hard-working, they were generally described as relatively easy to work with or even docile (otonashii) and were compared favourably with students of some universities in the southern part of Osaka which were known for taking in students from more working-class families. One reason given by staff that parents were keen for their children to come to MGU, despite the cost, was that it would enable them to meet others from a similar class background as potential marriage or business partners.

The business backgrounds of many of the parents of the students who studied at MGU meant that they were particularly interested in job prospects for their children. As the labour market tightened up after the economic slowdown in Japan in the early 1990s, so universities invested more in career support and were increasingly judged by their ability to help their students find jobs on graduation. The image which MGU enjoyed of being close to business (and indeed of being run like a business itself) was seen as a major advantage in helping its graduates find jobs and was given as one reason why some parents were prepared to pay such high fees.[3] Many graduates from MGU did indeed go on to work in small businesses, sometimes those set up by their families. For many years, MGU had been in the top seventy universities in Japan in terms of how many company bosses (*shachō*) had graduated from it; a point which was much touted in its careers office advertising. It scored particularly strongly among bosses in their 20s and 30s, presumably because many of these had taken over family firms. Many others went into professional jobs and joining the police force or the fire service were quite common career tracks.

As fees went up, so did the ability to pay higher academic salaries, and MGU was able to pay some of the highest in the Kansai area. The biggest packages were generally received not by those who had been at MGU for a long time but those who transferred to MGU when they retired from leading national universities in the Kansai region. In 2004, the retirement age at national universities had gone down to around 62 years. At MGU it was 70 for most academics and 75 for those in the graduate school which, combined with the high salaries and low teaching loads, made it very attractive for those who could no longer work in the national universities. Some of the senior professors who came to MGU after working in national universities had been hired by MGU specifically to fulfil ministry requirements to have staff with their background and qualifications on the payroll before the university could open new departments, especially graduate schools. MGU actually only had to meet 60–70 per cent of the salary costs of many of these professors since if they were employed as *tokunin* (*tokubetsu ninyō kyōju*)—a specially designed category which existed only in private universities—the remaining 30–40 per cent was

---

[3] A report by the Japan Association of Private Colleges and Universities (JAPCU 1987: 144) expressly stated that private universities have stronger alumni groups than do public ones and that these can be of considerable assistance to graduates from that institution when looking for a job.

covered by the pensions received from their former institutions. In the minds of at least some of these professors, they were doing MGU a favour by allowing it to use their names in applications to open new departments. MGU had a particularly distinguished set of professors who had retired from Osaka University, and they would regularly hold Osaka University alumni events (*dōsōkai*) on the MGU campus. When these professors published articles, they still tended to describe themselves as '*moto Osaka daigaku*' (formerly Osaka University) rather than use the designation of MGU.

Some of the most conspicuous symbols of the image that MGU wanted to present to the students, parents, and visitors could be seen in the institutions it had invited to set up facilities on its campus. Its book shop was outsourced to Kinokuniya and its general store was a branch of Takashimaya. Just as Kinokuniya could be described as a top brand book store, then Takashimaya was a luxury Japanese department store and an unusual one to find on a Japanese university campus. Kinokuniya seemed to have embraced its opportunity and had a wide selection of books which went far beyond the courses taught on campus.[4] The branch of Takashimaya was less obviously successful. It might have been because it had less flexibility than a book shop, but the high cost of its offerings and the lack of relevance to a student group meant that the shop was almost always empty. Instead, the branch was said to make its money through having a monopoly over furniture orders on the campus. University staff could also get a 10 per cent discount if they placed their domestic orders through the shop. At the same time, it was said that the Takashimaya parent company preferentially employed graduates from MGU.

Another example of the importance of brand was the belief that all overseas trips had to be arranged through JTB, Japan's national tourist agency, and flights with JAL, at that time Japan's national carrier, both known for being much more expensive than other options. Finally, MGU was unusual in having a branch of McDonalds on the campus; in the early 2000s, this still carried a certain amount of cultural prestige, especially with younger members of the public.

MGU used not only symbols such as the brand of their support services to present the desired image but also performed numerous rituals designed to

---

[4] Ironically, most of its income probably came from the books bought by academics with their research allowances and which technically remained part of the university library collection even on the academic's departure, something which some academics only fully realized when they wanted to take their collections with them when they moved to other universities and found that they were not allowed to do so.

serve the same purpose. New members of staff were introduced to these rituals from the moment they arrived on campus at the *jirei* ceremony, which involved being introduced one-by-one to the President following a set of carefully prescribed actions in an extremely serious atmosphere. The second occasion was the entrance ceremony (*nyūgakushiki*), when all members of staff were required to wear formal academic gowns and to process and sit behind the President and the members of the governing board (*rijikai*). Both ceremonies, along with the end-of-year graduation ceremony (*sotsugyōshiki*), where academic gowns were also worn, were all apparent attempts to imitate the practices of medieval European universities.

The Crisis of 2003–4

It may have been due to its success in the early 1990s that MGU did not appear to be prepared for the crisis it faced only 10 years later. It was only in early 2003 that the university leadership set in train a number of reform and review groups and initiatives. The President established a central reform committee with around ten members, including the heads of the General Affairs and the Academic Affairs offices and a number of academics. The document which the reform committee produced and sent to the faculties for consultation set out the difficult situation that the university was confronting. It used the word *kiki* (crisis) for the first time.

The 'crisis' was explained under four points: (a) the decrease in applicants (by nearly 90 per cent); (b) the increase in students dropping out (*taigaku*) before graduation (to nearly 20 per cent); (c) the increase (to 20 per cent) in the proportion of the entry cohort who could not graduate in 4 years and had to stay on (*ryūnen*) to do a fifth year (i.e. in effect, b and c combined meant that only 60 per cent of all those who entered were leaving MGU with their degrees in the planned 4 years); and (d) only 30 per cent of those who graduated in March (i.e. only 20 per cent of those who entered MGU in that cohort) being in full-time jobs by the end of the calendar year, 9 months later.[5]

Each of these points needs some expansion. Table 3.1 shows the decline in the number of applications to MGU between 1991 (when applications peaked, and 1 year before the peak of 18-year-olds in the population) and 2003 (when

---

[5] According to Daigaku Mirai Mondai Kenkyūkai (2001: 104–5), in 2000 across all Japanese universities around 10 per cent of students were dropping out during their 4 years and a further 10 per cent were doing at least 1 extra year (*ryūnen*), which was roughly half the rate at MGU in 2004.

Table 3.1 Decline in applications and total enrolments at MGU, 1991-2003

Year	Applications to MGU University	Quota (*teiin*)	Newly Enrolled	Newly Enrolled/ *teiin* (%)	Total Enrolment
1991	41,344	2,250			
1992	35,319	2,250			
1993	33,254	2,250			
1994	37,229	2,250			
1995	33,389	2,250			
1996	27,702	2,250			
1997	23,172	2,250	2,818	125.24	
1998	23,949	2,250	2,842	126.31	
1999	13,491	2,350	2,803	119.28	11,381
2000	8,561	2,750	2,786	101.30	11,276
2001	5,828	2,475	2,329	94.10	11,118
2002	5,044	2,400	2,289	95.37	10,498
2003	4,442	2,325	2,124	91.35	9,901

the MGU reform committee produced its report). It is unlikely that even those pushing the 'crisis' agenda in 2003 could have foreseen how much further applications would fall over the next 3 years and the extent that this would impact on the *total* enrolment in the university which almost halved over the 8-year period.

If the inability to recruit students was seen by some as the major issue facing MGU in 2003, retention was seen by others as even more important. The university was still able to fill over 90 per cent of its places with fee-paying students, but it was at the financial mercy of students dropping out while on course as it was not permitted to refill their places to over-recruit in successive years with other fee-paying students to cover the shortfall. Some of this shortfall was made up by students taking a fifth fee-paying year but there were also potential penalties to this for the university. The reasons for doing a fifth year in a 4-year university were complex. Sometimes students were held back because they had not taken or had not passed enough credit-bearing courses; sometimes students held themselves back because they had not found a job and wished to apply the following year while still at university since they believed this would look better on their CVs than having a blank year. While this could be a source of extra income to the institution (students paid full fees for this extra year) it was also potentially damaging to the university's reputation. Finally, in relation to the 'crisis document' of 2003, universities were aware that they were increasingly being ranked on the basis of the proportion of students in full-time employment six or nine months after graduation.

Stakeholders to the Crisis

There was much discussion as to who were the key stakeholders responsible for—both in the sense of getting in to and getting out of—the crisis which the reform committee report had outlined. Four groups could be identified: the owners, the academics, the support staff and the students.

The Owners

MGU, along with its junior college, high school and attached *senmon gakkō*, was part of a family-run educational corporation (*dōzoku keiei gakkō hōjin*). The President was also the head of the whole corporation and chaired the board of trustees and hence was always referred to as *sōchō* rather than just as head of the university (*gakuchō*). *Sōchō* was the second son of the original founder, the oldest son having been passed over as not suitable for the job. His immediate younger brother was head of the *senmon gakkō* which was part of the MGU *hōjin* and many other members of his immediate and extended family (the founder had seven children in total) were, or had been, employed within MGU. One of the President's younger brothers was a professor of international accounting in the economics department from where he had earned his PhD; a sister had been a lecturer specializing in the economics of social welfare law before her death, although many had not realized she was the daughter of the founder because she had taken her husband's name; her widowed husband, the President's brother-in-law, was head of a faculty at the junior college; another sister ran a cafeteria on the campus; the President's oldest son, who had also got his graduate degree from MGU, was an associate professor; and the President's wife was heavily involved in the English language outreach educational programme.

The President's mother was considered to be one of the most powerful voices in the governance of the University right up to her death. There had been a brief 3-year period after her husband, the founder, died, when MGU was run by a law professor, and there was the possibility of the institution continuing to be run by someone from outside the family. The founder's widow, however was widely credited for securing her son's position as President, when still in his 30s, and restoring the family to the head of the institution. When she died, all full-time academic and non-academic MGU staff attended her funeral in Osaka.

In terms of the family's role in the institution, it was significant that sometimes being a direct member of the President's family trumped other forms of hierarchy on the campus. At an end-of-year party for the foreign faculty, for example, it was the President's brother—who was a member, but not the chair, of the committee which had organized the event—who stood by the door to thank all the staff as they left for all they had done for the institution that year.

The President had an office on the campus, but the two floors on which his office was based in the large and impressive administration block (nicknamed the 'White House') were not marked on the elevator buttons. Many staff at the university said that they had never had a meeting or even a personal conversation with the President even though some of them had been there for over 20 years. One said she had resorted to posting a letter via the regular mail system in order to get a message to him; she never received an answer, though subsequent actions suggested that he had received it.

While the President had a master's degree from the United States, staff sometimes said that he considered himself a businessman rather than an academic. His school board (*riji*) included the maximum-permitted number of family members plus other personal contacts of the extended family, but it was not perceived to be closely involved in the management of the institution and allowed the President (and when she had been alive, his mother) to run the institution as he saw best. The membership of the board was not published, so few knew who sat on it or even that it was possible for the President to also be chairman of his own board. Several members of staff described MGU as a 'one-man university' and that the professors were his 'guests'—the opposite to national universities where the President was elected by, and expected to provide support to, the professors.[6]

As the crisis in recruitment was being debated, staff complained about the lack of transparency in the running of MGU. Very few financial details were published beyond those which were minimally required by the Ministry of Education and even those were hard to find. In the past, the Ministry had been reluctant to push private universities too hard on their finances.[7] However, the new culture of accountability for taxpayers' money which started in Japan

---

[6] For an overview of different modes of election and expectations of presidents in Japanese universities, see Ushiogi (2002), Kobayashi (2008).

[7] As Kinmonth (2005: 110) pointed out in this period: 'Despite receiving public money and being tax-exempt, private educational institutions are not required to publish detailed accounts or submit to public audit.' In 2007, only 55.4 per cent of universities and junior colleges disclosed their financial reports (*NKS*, 12 January 2008).

during the late 1990s and early 2000s meant that the authorities were beginning to demand more in terms of transparency. This may explain why MGU found itself during the 2000s in trouble several times with the Ministry of Education and the tax authorities over the way it used its public money and set expenses against tax. The university argued that these were misunderstandings and indeed many other institutions with a similar status to MGU had similar issues. MGU was also one of an increasing number of universities in Japan not publishing transparent data on student admissions (total number of applicants, students admitted, pass rates) because of concerns over their market sensitivity (*NKS*, 10 November 2005). This omission was perhaps most visible in the annual *Asahi Daigaku Ranking*, where the lack of data sat conspicuously alongside the returns of other institutions. This added to the sense of uncertainty, with student numbers plummeting and retired staff not being replaced.

The President was believed by some of the academic staff to be surrounded by a small clique of senior managers, few of whom were academics. They said that he would select members of the academic staff to advise on certain issues, but they could find themselves out of favour as quickly as they were in favour. Many within the institution described this form of management as a 'court culture' and worried about the lack of transparency or opportunity for critical feedback. Staff felt that it was difficult to raise issues directly with the President. When he attended meetings where faculty were also present, these were always described as being highly choreographed, with little room for spontaneous discussion or feedback from the staff.

When the President entered the main administration offices, everyone stood up to bow. As he walked around the campus, he was often attended by a group of staff in what one jokingly described as a '*daimyō gyōretsu*' (a feudal lord's procession). He handed out the seasonal bonus payments (actually only a symbolic portion of the bonus with the majority going straight into individuals' bank accounts) in person to staff. Some, particularly non-academic, staff said they liked this system as it meant the President got to see who worked at MGU at least three times a year, but others described this ritual, and the *jirei* ceremony for new academic staff, as feudalistic (*hōkenteki*).

The Full-time Academics

Despite the physical attractiveness of the MGU campus for both academic staff and students, one of the most conspicuous features was how little used it was for much of the time. The academic week was clearly defined as 09.00 to 18.00

from Monday to Friday. This was marked in many ways, but the most obvious was the fact that the centrally controlled heating and air conditioning were turned off at all other times. Apart from a few weeks in spring and autumn, this made it impossible for academics to start early or to stay late in their offices since the Kansai area is cold in winter and extremely hot and humid in summer. It was unusual to see either staff or students on campus at all during long periods between the academic terms when the university was officially 'shut'. Outside those times, most services were not available; for example, the photocopying rooms were closed, which meant that those who were teaching a class at 09.00 on Monday morning had to prepare their materials the week before or else get it done, as many did, at local convenience stores over the weekend.

Most academics came to the campus only to teach and did not stay long afterwards. Very few appeared to hold office hours, even though the campus was equipped with electronic signboards which technically allowed any academic to let any student know in real time when they were available for consultation. In a corridor with forty or so offices, there would rarely be more than ten academics present, unless there was a staff meeting to attend. The campus had an attractive staff dining room (*shokuin shokudō*), franchised to an external partner, with high-quality food, but it was rarely even busy let alone full. The large and impressive senior common room next door was almost always virtually deserted, with seldom more than a couple of people, despite the good collections of newspapers and magazines available, at any one time.

The academics at MGU did not feel that the university provided as much an intellectual community as a place to teach. As with most non-elite private universities, there were very few academic seminars or workshops on campus and the rare conferences which were run at the weekends were generally organized by external agencies. The lack of seminars was sometimes mentioned by those who had moved from research-intensive institutions, especially in the US and Europe, and one academic referred to feeling 'brain dead' when on campus. The annual occasion when there were academic presentations was the *gakkai* (academic meetings) which provided material for each faculty's academic journal (*kiyō*). MGU academics were encouraged and incentivized (they were paid ¥10,000 for each piece they published) to submit articles to their faculty *kiyō*. These were generally one-off pieces and rarely, if ever, articulated with other papers in the same issue. As a result, *kiyō* had a huge variety of content and ranged in quality from some serious research outputs—they were generous in terms of the number of off-prints they supplied which was attractive to some academic staff—to little more than fieldwork notes or what Cummings (1994) has described as 'knowledge seeking' rather than 'knowledge creation' research.

Another notable feature of the full-time academic staff at MGU was that many of them taught in other institutions. The origins of this common practice in Japan, known as *kakemochi*, lie in the idea that professors should teach only in their immediate areas of expertise (for example, the sociology of work but not the sociology of religion) and it makes more sense for colleagues to swap teaching than to expand their teaching range. According to a large-scale survey by Morgan (1999: 17–18) from the 1990s, 69 per cent of full professors and 49 per cent of associate professors taught on a regular basis at other institutions as well as their own. This practice was so widespread at MGU that some of the more senior academics informed the administration at the beginning of the academic year when they would be available to teach. In 2003, there was some consternation among these faculty when a message came down from the central administration that, from the following year, they would be required to prioritize their teaching at MGU over their teaching elsewhere. Most academic staff reported that when they were not teaching at other institutions or at MGU, they preferred to stay at home to do their research and teaching preparation rather than commute to the campus.

Permanent employees enjoyed annual wage rises which were not linked to performance reviews; they received substantial seasonal fixed-value bonuses (up to 5 months' worth of salary or 5/17th of the total of their annual pay); very generous annual support for research, either in the form of covering the costs of conference attendance or buying equipment (most staff had top-of-the-range computers and cameras bought from their research funds); the possibility of applying for paid sabbatical leave (sometimes given for up to 2 years); their own offices; free annual health checks; administrative and IT support; automatic outlets for publishing their research; freedom to teach what they wanted, when they wanted, and how they wanted; and, most importantly, job security. In theory, they also had support from the MGU Professors' Union, though this was extremely weak by the early 2000s when only about fifteen out of the 220 or so academic staff at MGU were thought to be members of the union and very few knew who it was who put the occasional note from the union in their letter boxes.

These benefits for the permanent academic staff need a little unpacking. While the overall pay of the permanent staff at MGU was believed to be among the highest in the Kansai region, individual pay was closely linked to age and years of service as, indeed, was academic title. It was possible, for example, for a visiting academic to be a full professor at a leading global university but only an associate professor at MGU because they had not reached the magic age of 44 to hold the title. On the other hand, they did not have to go through any form of tenure or performance review once they had taken up their role and could reasonably expect that the seniority promotion system would eventually lead to them being a professor.[8] Junior academics did not negotiate their salaries on appointment. Indeed, many said they did not know exactly what it would be until they received their first payslip. On the other hand, senior academics who moved to MGU on retirement from national universities seem, in some cases, to have negotiated quite hard for salaries on the basis that they were bringing lustre to the institution. Some of these high-profile names who came on retirement to MGU in the 1990s and early 2000s were believed to be among the best paid academics in the whole of Japan.

In most cases, permanent staff at MGU were appointed through personal recommendations, from staff who were already employed by the institution. Before the 2000s, jobs were very rarely if ever advertised and, even when reforms in 2004 meant that they needed to be advertised, it was assumed that the successful candidate would have been encouraged to apply by someone already inside MGU. This pattern of employment was not unusual in Japan at the time and it was based on the belief that it would ensure a conducive working environment; the supporter of the successful candidate would be made to feel responsible for their behaviour and the successful candidate him or herself would feel responsible to their guarantor. It is probable that this form of appointment was also responsible for another element of the staff profile at MGU, namely the high proportion of relatives among the permanent teaching staff, especially father–daughter pairs.

A paramount principle for all permanent academics at MGU was their freedom to research and teach what they chose. In terms of research, MGU had no laboratory-based subjects (although it did have one professor each in chemistry, biology, and physics who offered options in each of these subjects).[9]

---

[8] In a typically whimsical explanation, Funabiki (2005: 104–5) compares a Japanese professor with a *shusse-uo* (a fish which changes its name as it advances through life): 'If a young yellowtail (*hamachi*) lives long enough, it will become an adult yellowtail (*buri*); likewise if one stays long enough one can become a professor (*kyōju*). The first post is crucial for an academic, but once he becomes a lecturer (*kōshi*) or assistant professor (*junkyōju*), as long as he does not do anything terrible or politically provocative, he does not need to worry about his professorship.'

[9] The absence of medicine and science is one of the key identifying features of lower-tier private universities. The high cost of laboratory-based teaching and research was much less attractive than the low cost of social science and humanities teaching. Indeed, it was in part the fact that teaching numbers in these subjects could be expanded almost infinitely with the same cost base which led to the student protests in the 1960s and the introduction of stricter government controls over class size and faculty: student ratios in private universities in return for state subsidies (Kitamura and Cummings 1972: 316).

Very few academics held external research grants of any kind and there was no expectation that they should do so or, indeed, a support structure for them if they did. Doing research, though, was an important part of the self-identity of permanent academic staff, almost all of whom were members of external study groups (*kenkyūkai* or *benkyōkai*) related to the work of their graduate supervisors. They would attend meetings of these groups, often at weekends, several times a year.[10] Most academics would publish articles, though very rarely in peer review journals, and present papers at conferences in their subject areas.[11] What an individual undertook research into was very much a matter of personal choice and generally an extension of what they had studied at graduate school.

Permanent academics at MGU would also not expect to receive pressure as to what they taught. This could sometimes lead to a very disjointed learning experience for students. For example, a programme could be numbered sequentially as students went through their university course—English 1, English 2, English 3, . . . —and students might reasonably have expected that the content reflected the skills they had mastered in previous courses. But, while professors might be asked to teach a course with a particular title (say English 3), they would not be expected to consult with the teachers of English 1 or English 2 about what they had covered. Indeed, many professors appeared to teach exactly the same course whatever its title and for whichever cohort of students it was offered. Very often this was also based on the professor's own graduate speciality. English students who were struggling to say in English what they had done the previous weekend might find themselves working on two short stories by Elizabeth Gaskell, *The Heart of John Middleton* (published in 1850), and *The Manchester Marriage* (published in 1858) in their reading class. As a result, it was perfectly possible for English 2 to be much more difficult than English 3. Indeed sometimes, due to a timetable clash, students would take a higher-level course before they could take the lower one. As long as they had credits for all the courses by the time they graduated, this did not seem to be a problem for the university. As for the teachers, the main way that they could discover the level of what was being taught in other classes was through asking the students themselves.

---

[10] According to Yamamoto (1999: 316), 'On average, academic staff are members of three or four academic associations. There were more than 1500 associations in 1995, with about 3.2 million members, though not all members are university staff.'

[11] Birnbaum (2005), in an interesting comparison of Japanese and US professors, comments that peer reviewing is not common in Japan and that Japanese professors tend to write much more for audiences outside academia than do US professors.

As in most other universities in Japan, professors not only enjoyed great autonomy in what they taught but also in how they taught. Teaching in effect was a closed circle. Professors set the curriculum; taught the course; set the exams; marked the papers themselves; submitted the marks to the administrative office of academic affairs (*kyōmuka*); handed out and collected the student feedback papers, normally at the end of the last class in the course; and received the results of the completed feedback forms directly from the *kyōmuka*. As long as students turned up to enough classes, it was very rare to fail them, in part because there were serious disincentives in place for staff who wished to do so. Students who received less than a C grade for any course were offered the chance of an immediate re-sit, which meant professors setting an extra paper and turning up on campus to invigilate it on one of the three days set aside for this after the end of normal term. Some experienced staff simply avoided this problem by not offering formal exams but instead grading students on the basis of in-class tests.

In 2004, there was no process for reviewing what colleagues did in their classes and little attempt to exchange information about teaching. Student accounts of their experience of teaching suggested that it was highly variable, ranging from some very well-crafted classes to sessions where the professor spent the whole time writing on and talking to the whiteboard, sometimes while students turned around and talked to each other, what might be described as 'back-to-back teaching'. In general, there was little interaction between academic staff and students at MGU. Students did not feel they had a chance to get to know their professors well, in part because they themselves were so busy. Teichler (2019: 15–16) has called the relationship between teacher, students, and prospective employers as a 'marriage of convenience':

Employers trust the good basis of the school system and their freedom to train the graduates, whom they recruit as 'raw material', whereby the low quality of teaching and learning in higher education even increases their freedom to shape initial training on the job. The low interest in study on the part of students helped professors to concentrate most of their time on research as their preferred activity. Under these circumstances, the students could be more or less certain that they would graduate successfully, even if the energy put into study was limited.[12]

---

[12] Abe et al. (1998: 77–8) apply economic theory to this situation which they ascribed to a problem of the 'commons': market signals to students that they do not need to study once they are at university mean that professors lose interest in teaching.

A common complaint from teachers was that, although class sizes had reduced dramatically in some faculties, students were more difficult to teach. They complained that students thought of the internet as their main source of information, rather than the library, and rarely checked information or cited sources. They felt that students were much lower ability than they had been only a few years earlier.[13] Many of them blamed the recommendation entrance system which meant that students had not had to study for entrance exams. Such complaints were a common theme of conversation among those professors who did eat in the staff canteen at lunch times.[14]

Another common topic of conversation, especially among older professors, was the decline in the politeness of students and their untidy appearance (a key exception being members of the baseball club who were always immaculately turned out in their club uniform). Not only would students regularly fall asleep in class (which was widely tolerated) but they would also engage in private conversations (*shigo*) while professors were talking and often gave their main concentration to their mobile phones. When challenged, students would generally say they were discussing the class or looking up key words on their phones, but the reality and prevalence of such behaviour was perhaps best attested to by the publication a number of manuals, mentioned in Chapter 1, on how to manage disruptive students in class.

The one exception to the weak relationship which generally existed between permanent academics and students was the final-year seminar (*zemi*) class with a chosen professor who was supervising their graduation thesis (*sotsugyō ronbun*). These class groups formed close bonds, both between the students and with their professor, and sometimes would provide the best memories and learning experiences of their whole time at university. The value that MGU placed on the *zemi* class could be seen in the extra financial contribution that the university made to enable professors to take students on activities off campus as part of the bonding experience.

---

[13] According to Ogata (2015: 82–3) and Yamasaki (2015) there was fairly universal agreement among academics in Japan in the early 2000s that the quality of students had declined over the previous decade. A survey in 2008 revealed that 68 per cent of managers, 61 per cent of labour union leaders, and 87 per cent of academics perceived students to be below the level of those 10 years earlier (*YS*, 25 January 2008).

[14] The Daigaku Mirai Mondai Kenkyūkai (2001: 102) list five main reasons why professors in the early 2000s might have thought that student ability had declined: the increase in the number of students going to university; changes in the school curriculum; the fact that entrance examinations were becoming easier and students had to take fewer of them; the lower ability of school teachers; changes in social structure. The first two of these were by far the most commonly referenced at MGU.

Professors who came to MGU from national or public (but also some private) institutions were struck by just how top-down and centralized its operations were, especially for an institution of over 11,000 students. Many were clearly happy to go along with the President's view that he was protecting their research time by taking on the responsibility for the management of the university. There was a lack of engagement in issues of either financial or academic planning on the part of the vast majority of professors within the institution. Most professors simply turned up to undertake their teaching and then left the campus as quickly as possible. Many of them liked it this way: they were well paid, received very generous research allowances, they had comparatively low teaching obligations, and there was little administrative burden on their shoulders. It was not unknown for professors who had left MGU to go to supposedly academically stronger universities to want to come back when they realized how good the overall conditions were there.

Part-time Teachers

The experience of part-time teachers at MGU—who in 2004 already totalled more than 50 per cent of all teaching staff—was very different from that of the permanent staff. Indeed, the two groups hardly ever met or had a conversation, even if they were teaching the same students on the same course. Part-time staff were not invited to staff meetings or staff parties. They had one point of contact with the permanent staff which was through a member of the administrative office who would pass on the timetable of classes for which they were responsible. Many part-time staff had had their annual contracts renewed many times and the total number of hours they spent in the classroom was comparable to the full-time staff, but they had almost none of the benefits of the full-time staff. Their salary was fixed each year regardless of how many years they had taught; they were rarely given a contract that lasted more than a year; they received no union support; they were not eligible for bonuses or research funding; they were not paid during the vacations; they did not have their own offices, only a locker in a shared space next to the administrative headquarters. Most part-time staff, especially the foreign language teachers, taught in a large number of institutions across the Kansai area, often travelling long distances from one job to another. Not unreasonably, few of them felt any sense of allegiance to MGU. They were often high-quality teachers, though, and could engage students better than some of the full-time staff for whom teaching was often seen as something they were fitting around their research which was their main concern and from which they got their primary sense of identity and status (Yamasaki 2015).

The Full-time Administrative Staff

The one group at MGU who were consistently on campus were the full-time staff who were part of the administrative office. They, in many ways, provided the continuity in the institution. Indeed, quite a large proportion of the administrative staff were graduates of the university. According to a report by the Japan Association of Private Colleges and Universities (JAPCU 1987: 142), this was a common pattern at private universities: 'the workplace is their beloved alma mater to whom they are only too happy to devote their careers ... [T]hey are especially attentive to the students, whom they regard as younger members of the school family.'

The full-time administrative staff were themselves divided into two groups, generalists and specialists. Some of the generalists had been at MGU for many years.[15] They would expect to change roles, generally every 3 years, at the beginning of the new academic year. Through this system they were not only being promoted but also developing a broad overview of how the institution operated. This could lead to some apparently counter-intuitive appointments: a head of the library who had no training in librarianship, a senior member responsible for IT who was not an IT specialist, even a senior member of the international office who was not comfortable speaking a foreign language. In most cases, however, senior generalist support staff had specialists who worked under them and knew about libraries, IT, or could speak English, but the hierarchical system within which they all worked—as contributors to Bachnik's edited volume, *Roadblocks on the Information Highway*, 2003, suggested in the specific case of IT—could, in theory at least, make it difficult for the voice of the specialists to be heard.

Job transfers took place at the beginning of April every year and meant that there were occasionally problems of continuity in the daily operation of administrative departments at that time of year. In April 2004, for example, the head of the library service and the head of the admissions office swapped jobs. Staff were sometimes given only a few days of warning and hence could

---

[15] According to Yamamoto (2002: 108), administrative non-academic staff in private universities keep working for the same institution far longer than those who work for national and local universities.

never be sure if they would or would not be moved at the beginning of the new academic year. One member of staff said she had been moved five times in the 8 years since she had joined MGU while two colleagues who had joined at the same time had never been moved at all. Despite this system, it was conspicuous how few complaints there were among the academics about the support they received from the administrative staff.

A further way in which the administrative staff was divided was by gender. In 2004, female staff had to wear uniforms, but this was not required of their male counterparts. This added to the rather conservative atmosphere of the institution, which may have appealed to some of those local parents who had not themselves been to university and had concerns that universities could be sites of student radicalization.

A professor who had moved from a national university to MGU felt that the MGU academic staff and administrative staff were two branches of equal status. In terms of governance, in theory it was the academics who were in charge of the major committees and committee decisions at MGU. However, the fact that they were not experts in the field, especially when it came to technical projects, and also that the committee chairs were frequently rotated, often on a 2- or 3-year cycle, meant that it was frequently the senior members of the administration who actually became responsible for decisions as well as their implementation.[16]

The Part-time Support Staff

Just as a very large proportion of the teaching staff at MGU were part-time, so many of the support staff functions had been outsourced as a way of relieving some of the burden of employment overhead costs. The *shuei-san* (security staff), for example, were not direct employees of MGU even though many of them had been working there for a long time. They were instead the employees (known in Japanese as *haken shain*) of a despatch company which specialized in temporary agency work of which, it was believed, the MGU corporation was actually the major shareholder. The existence of *haken shain* allows institutions to have much greater flexibility and control over its wage bill than having to deal with directly employed staff (Fu 2012).

---

[16] The results of a survey sent to the chief administrative officers of 400 private universities in Japan in the early 2000s suggested that they felt they were generally involved, at least to some degree, in the decision-making process of their institutions (Fukudome 2004). As explained in Chapter 2, lines of decision-making in a private university are often more closely aligned with the *gakkō hōjin* corporate structure than with the university's academic structure.

A second large group of *haken shain* on the campus were the so-called Office Ladies (OLs) who supported the work of the academics. At the end of each corridor of offices, there was an open desk area staffed always by a young woman who was available to help with photocopying and give directions. As they were despatch workers, these staff would change regularly, which meant there was no continuity of practice and they would often need to refer to their handbooks when asked something. In total, there were twelve of these OLs on campus in 2004 and they were rotated between different office corridors, the library, and the main reception of the university. They often said they felt underworked and several that they used their time to develop other skills, such as English.

A third group of staff at MGU who were not directly on the payroll were the IT staff, all but two of whom were employed by a subsidiary of Fujitsu which had a contract to support the university.

A fourth, and by far the largest, group of *haken shain* on the campus were the cleaning staff (all women) and maintenance staff (all men). At all times during the working day, large groups of these uniformed staff could be seen moving across the campus. They would bow to academic members of staff and would never enter the lifts if academics were already using them, or about to use them, rather like maintenance and cleaning staff in five-star hotels. Like many private universities, MGU was extremely well maintained.[17] The MGU campus had no litter, no fallen leaves (in the autumn they were swept up three or four times a day to stop them settling), no dust in the corridors. Staff would not even let students sleeping in chairs in the common areas get in the way of their cleaning. A member of cleaning staff would stand outside every classroom ready to clean the whiteboard as soon as a class was finished. Such was their enthusiasm that on occasions when a professor had two consecutive classes and wished to retain the material on the white board for the next class, they could only do so by staying in the class during the break between lessons. The full scale of the cleaning staff at MGU was made most manifest during the preparations for a final journey around the campus that the President's mother was given on the way to her funeral; the railings around the whole campus were each individually cleaned by hand and the campus was immaculate.

---

[17] The most visible difference between national and private universities in Japan in the early 2000s was in the quality and maintenance of their buildings. National universities often had extremely shoddy and run-down buildings, which is related to the financial categories under which they received government funding.

The Students

Time spent in class, especially for students in their first year, could be extensive with up to twenty-two *koma* (90-minute sessions) a week. Physical attendance at class was often considered as important as exam and test results in order to secure credits courses (see Usami 2000 for an account of this process). Two questions which students often asked their teachers at the beginning of courses were: how many attendances (*shusseki*) do I need to have on this course to be able to graduate and how late (*chikoku*) can I turn up for it to be considered an attendance? The formal response from the central administration to these questions was that students needed to be signed in as present for 66 per cent of classes and could not turn up more than 30 minutes late to be counted as present. Faculty were told that it was important to keep this attendance information in part in case it was requested by parents. Many students were still under 20 (the age at which young Japanese were considered adult) and the administration seemed quite relaxed about giving information about students to any parents who asked and indeed would often talk to parents directly about students who were struggling. Students would regularly check their running percentage of absences (*kesseki*) at the end of classes; they would also quite often turn up for the class just under 30 minutes late. If they turned up later, they would sometimes bring chits from the local railway company to say the train was running late or from their sports club that they had been training.

When students were on campus, they were mostly in class. The other times when students were on campus were mainly during major events, such as the matriculation and graduation ceremonies which were organized by the institution to welcome and despatch them. The one big event on campus each year which was run by the students themselves was the 3-day cultural festival (*bunkasai*) in the autumn. This festival mirrored similar festivals which the students would have organized in their elementary, middle, and senior high schools before they came to university and was mainly a demonstration of the activities of the separate university clubs rather than a demonstration of collective MGU student identity. The President and his wife paid several visits during the 3 days of the festival—during which all classes were cancelled—but very few other academic staff could be seen.

Apart from above events and classes, there was not much to keep students on campus. Other than a student cafeteria (*gakusei shokudō*), there was no student common room, and no lockers for students to leave their possessions. More importantly, there were a lot of attractions off campus. For many, this included a part-time job (*arubaito*). It was very common, if not an expectation, that university students took a part-time job, which they held down both during term and vacation time. Most of these were in fast food outlets, convenience stores, and in video shops and could offer anything between 10 to 40 hours a week of paid employment. In a sample class of twenty students in 2004, only two were not doing any part-time work at all; the average was 15 hours a week.[18] One student was working at least 40 hours a week in a video store, another was sorting letters in the post office for 36 hours, and a third waitressing for around 34 hours. The combination of part-time work and class attendance meant that many students were burning the candle at both ends and hence it was common for them to fall asleep in class.

Recruitment of Students

The above account provides a context for a more detailed analysis of the students who were recruited to come and study at MGU in 2003/4 and why it was so difficult for the institution to respond quickly in the face of rapidly falling applications in subsequent years. An excellent example of how the activities of the academic and administrative staff of the university appeared to be out of line with changing external realities was the work of the entrance examination committee (*nyūshi iinkai*). This had been a crucial committee back in the early 1990s. At that time MGU was getting over 42,000 applications for 2,250 places a year—each paying about ¥30,000 just to apply—and there was a media spotlight on how universities ensured transparency and equity in their processes. By 2003, as we have shown, while the quota of places had risen to 2,325, applications were down to well under 4,500 (see Table 3.1) The major loss of revenue that this entailed was compounded by a new requirement to refund prepaid tuition fees in case of non-enrolment (universities had previously banked these on the basis that they were a form of non-refundable deposit) following a series of court cases under a new consumer law enacted in 2000 (see Kinmonth 2005: 109).

In 1992, in line with practice in private universities in general (*AS*, 19 June 2007), almost all students who were enrolled at MGU came through the

---

[18] Teichler (1997) reported that fifteen hours per week of part-time work seemed to be average for Japanese students across the sector, combined with an average of twenty-five hours per week of study. Lee-Cunin (2004: 165–71), in her survey of students at Shiga University, found around 75 per cent were doing part-time work of whom around 40 per cent gave the reason as 'economic-based'; 40 per cent 'for pocket money'; and 20 per cent for 'work experience and personal development'.

entrance examination system. By 2004, roughly half of the students (the maximum allowed at the time by the Ministry of Education), however, who were gaining places at MGU by 2004 were entering through alternative systems. These alternative systems included demonstrating strengths in art or sport, or on the basis of their school reports, or on the recommendation of particular high schools which were designated as *shiteikō* (schools with a quota of places which they could directly allocate to students to study at MGU).

The largest *shiteikō* by far was MGU's own attached senior high school. MGU Senior High School had capacity for over 2,000 students across its 3 years, but its enrolment had shrunk in recent years in line with the nation-wide demographic decline in children between 15 and 18. It was mainly to counter this drop in numbers that the school had admitted girls for the first time in the late 1990s. In the past, a very large number, up to 500, of the students who went to MGU each year came from its attached high school, constituting 20 per cent of the total intake at the university. However, the number and proportion had decreased very significantly in more recent years as the academic status of the high school had gone up and that of the university had declined. Put simply, if a student had a place in the high school, they could be guaranteed a place in the university, but if they could get in somewhere academically stronger, then they were increasingly likely to go there.[19]

In the case of applicants from *shiteikō* such as MGU Senior High School, there was no need for any kind of entrance test or interview and hence some of the students may have been selected because they would not get into academically higher-level institutions. Students who were recommended by schools which were not designated *shiteikō* would also not need to take an examination but instead write an essay (of no more than 800 characters) on why they wanted to go to MGU and have an interview with a staff member of the Admissions Centre (*Nyūshi Centre*). As application numbers dropped, so interviews became increasingly perfunctory: one student could only remember being asked about his school trip (*shūgaku ryokō*) and several said that being accepted on the basis of such an interview did not leave a very great 'sense of accomplishment' (*tasseikan*).

Whereas, in 1992, MGU was in the happy position of being able to choose students, by 2004, the number of applicants would soon be equal to, or indeed

---

[19] The Daigaku Mirai Mondai Kenkyūkai (2001: 47) lists the proportion of students from some of the schools attached to high-level private universities who went on to those universities in the early 2000s. Some of these were still very high: for example, one of Keio's attached schools (99 per cent); two of Hosei's attached schools (91 and 90 per cent); one of Waseda's attached schools (89 per cent); Aoyama Gakuin (85 per cent); two at Gakushuin (78 per cent and 73 per cent).

less than, the number of places it needed to fill its Ministry-approved quota. The pressure on recruitment was partly fired by the fear that if the university did fall below the quota of places allocated to it by the Ministry, it would be in danger of losing the government subsidy that all private universities had received since the 1970s and which still constituted around 13 per cent of its total income. This was an important source of funding when around 85 per cent of income came directly from student fees and less than 2 per cent in total from other sources. Going 'below quota' was also reputationally damaging and held the risk of getting into a downward spiral. It was vital, therefore, to provide opportunities for as many students to apply as possible.

MGU began to substantially step up its recruitment efforts from the early 2000s in the face of falling applications.[20] Along with all other private universities in the Kansai region, it developed an aggressive advertising campaign each year from mid-summer onwards, most visibly in the form of posters in trains. The Admissions Office staff, together with designated academics, visited schools across the region to advertise the university. It held an Open Campus event on about six Sundays a year which provided an opportunity for potential students, and their parents, to attend a sample lecture and visit and meet administrative and academic staff in order to ask questions about coming to MGU. The campus would be even better presented than normal on such days and students often admitted that seeing its buildings and facilities were a major reason for their application.[21] At that time, there was a general belief at MGU that for prospective students and their parents the quality of the facilities would be felt to be worth the high cost of attendance. As a result, in 2003/4, MGU did nothing to lower its fees in the face of falling enrolments or to increase its scholarship provision: for the whole incoming cohort, it offered only two full-time and two part-time scholarships. The expectation was still that parents would pay or take out loans to cover the cost of university education and that the high-cost, high-return model that MGU offered would be sustainable on the same scale that it had been practised over the previous two decades.

While only half of the students coming to MGU in 2004 were taking entrance examinations, it was felt important for those who wanted to use

---

[20] For an example of some of the new marketing theory which was beginning to be discussed in Japanese higher education circles at this time, see Imai and Imai (2001).

[21] For a list of some of the strategies which universities used to attract students on Open Days in the mid-2000s, see NKS, 27 July 2005. These included magical mystery bus tours, free iPods, dessert buffets, and a fortune-telling corner.

that route that there be examinations at a time and place which suited the students rather than, as in the past, which suited the university.[22] This was the context in which the entrance examination committee (*nyūshi iinkai*) was operating in 2004: how to maintain the tricky balance between keeping standards at a level to maintain MGU's reputation as an academically mid-level university (which, once lost, would be very hard to win back) and, at the same time, take in enough students to be able to continue to receive financial support from the government.

Examining the work of the entrance examination committee is a good insight into how much of professors' time at MGU was taken up in detailed administrative tasks in which their ability to innovate was extremely limited. It is significant that, while being a member of almost any committee at MGU triggered an extra payment, being a member of the committee for the English entrance examinations was particularly well rewarded. Each member of the committee received, in total, around ¥600,000 (about £3,000) extra in pay. Even so, it was an unpopular committee and it was hard, for example, for the chair and the administrative lead to fill the eleven slots that were needed to write the English entrance examinations. A number of people who had been on the committee the previous year, for example, declined to serve again. One calculated he had spent almost a hundred hours the previous year in the entrance examination meetings. Another blamed his bad back on sitting in those same meetings for too long. This created a problem of continuity.

The committee was tasked with setting a total of eighteen different English entrance examinations, all of the same level, in order to make sure that there were enough for all the different dates and methods through which potential students could apply, as well as a few spare. It was recognized that some of these papers might be taken by very few, or possibly even no, students at all. The system was clearly a legacy of the early 1990s and a very expensive one at that: with eleven exam setters each being paid ¥600,000, it would need 190 applicants each paying around ¥36,000 to cover just their direct costs and, of course, English was only one of the exams which applicants would need to take. There would, of course, also be administrative costs associated with running the exams themselves. Perhaps more importantly, many universities were beginning to waive fees for taking their examinations altogether in order to encourage applications. As the Daigaku Mirai Mondai Kenkyūkai (2001: 74) pointed out, it would actually have been much more logical—in terms of cost, expertise,

---

[22] In 2007, 69 per cent of private universities provided examination locations beyond their region (*YS*, 13 January 2007).

and use of time—to ask the professional university entrance cram schools (*yobikō*) to prepare these exams for them. In fact, it was reported that over 10 per cent of universities were doing this by the mid-2000s, in part to protect themselves from criticism if there were mistakes in the papers (*YS*, 4 January 2008). This was frowned upon by the Ministry. MGU had not gone down that route in 2003/4.

Much of the work of the entrance examination committee was highly ritualistic, as indeed is much to do with the entrance examination system itself and the teaching of English more generally in Japan (see Aspinall 2013). As with almost all other entrance examinations, most of the English examination was presented in a multiple-choice format which allowed students to fill in a computer card choosing one out of four options for each question or placing words from a preselected list in gaps in a piece of English prose. In practice, therefore, it should be possible for any applicant to score 25 per cent just by guessing, and indeed many students admitted that random guessing (*atezuppō*) had been their main technique when they had taken such an exam to enter MGU. Students were also all aware of a few examination techniques which should help them do better than 25 per cent. They would always see if there was any answer which was so out of line with the others that they could eliminate it from the four on offer and thereby increased their chances of guessing correctly from 1 in 4 to 1 in 3. It was widely believed that the middle columns (2 and 3) were more popular than the outer columns (1 and 4) and students would disproportionately select these. If an answer was either longer or shorter than the other answers then it could generally be discounted. These techniques alone could often be enough to get student scores up to 30 per cent, which was considered a pass mark.[23]

Given that in some faculties at MGU, in 2004, there were already fewer applicants than places available, it was widely accepted that any student would be admitted—even without getting 30 per cent. In the exams which were taken at the end of 2003 for the junior college, only one out of sixty-five applicants was turned down and that was because their total score of 50 out of 200 was so far behind any other student. In the Faculty of Foreign Languages only one out of forty had been turned down; faculty members clearly felt that they were

---

[23] For a pastiche on such examination techniques, in this case in Japanese language exams, which basically demand that the student does not waste time reading the actual questions, see Shimizu Yoshinori's *Kokugo nyūshi mondai hisshōhō* (Japanese entrance exams for earnest young men) translated in Alfred Birnbaum (ed.), 1991. For a less sanguine account, see Miller (1982: 244) who suggests in the case of the English entrance examinations that 'a practical working knowledge of English can only get in the way of solving (such tests).'

under pressure by the academic affairs section of the university only to turn down students in the last resort.

The top priority of the *nyūshi iinkai*, therefore, was not to weed out students or even set exams which gave an indication of the level of knowledge of applicants in either a relative (i.e., compared to other students) or absolute (i.e., how much English they really knew) sense. Instead it was to produce examinations which reflected well on the ability of the committee to set an entrance examination within the parameters expected of such exams in Japan. The brief was orthodoxy and consistency not innovation and, as the chair of the committee put it, 'in order ultimately not to find ourselves the object of public derision'. Many entrance examinations end up becoming public documents made available each May by the publishing company Kyōgakusha in a relatively cheap format (known as *akahon*) for use as practice papers by students who might consider applying in the following year.[24] All members of the committee would be aware of cases where institutions, at all levels from junior high school onwards, had been held up to public ridicule by newspapers because their examinations contained mistakes or did not fit within the required parameters. At the same time, the examinations needed to demonstrate the high quality of the admitting institution and the erudition of the professors who set them. No allowance could be made for the fact that the ability of those applying was declining. Indeed, the committee never once stopped to consider the ability level of the students.[25] The net effect of these variables was that the entrance exams, certainly in English, were set at a level which meant that students were virtually forced to resort to guesswork.

The committee's jurisdiction, however, was not over the exam per se, only over the questions contained within it, and the rules and precedents for the English examination were very restrictive indeed. These were largely dictated by the expectations of the high schools and the supplementary education institutions (*juku* and *yobikō*) which were preparing the students and would not take kindly to any deviation from precedent. MGU would not want to upset these key stakeholders as they had great influence on students' and parents' application choices (or at least the capacity to influence those choices negatively). It would be a dangerous game for a university which was already

---

[24] For a good account of the slightly controversial role, particularly in relation to copyright abuse, of these examination compilations in Japanese society, see Wheeler (2012).

[25] In theory, the 'level' of the students was the school leaving certificate. Since there are no final examinations in Japanese senior high schools, however, this was only an indication of what, in theory, they should have been taught and not at all what they might have actually learned.

struggling to attract enough applicants to consider any reform of its examination process.

The primary concern of the entrance examination committee, as the chair kept reminding it, was to ensure that the material in the exam was within the approved parameters of the government-regulated high school syllabus. For example, the committee had to constantly refer to the list of English words approved for teaching on the senior high school curriculum. It discovered that neither 'suitably' nor 'turtle' were included but that 'strychnine' and 'turpitude' were.[26] It also discovered that the phrase 'that's a shame' could not be used; the approved expression was 'that's a pity'. Where the syllabus did not provide a decisive answer, the committee spent a long time in speculative discussion over students' relative familiarity with different terms: 'mobile' or 'cell' phone? Would they know what a 'fitness club' was? Much of the discussion around grammar and other linguistic conventions was too esoteric for an average native speaker to join in. It concerned dangling modifiers or collocations or entailed a long discussion over the acceptability of the structure 'be not' because John Donne had used it. The ability of the professors on the committee was tested to make fine distinctions between different complex structures, such as between 'what he said cannot be true' and 'he said what cannot be true'. All of this for an examination being set for students, some of whom would not yet have mastered the Roman alphabet and few of whom would be able to understand or produce more than the most rudimentary level of English prose.

Along with attention to detail, the other most conspicuous feature of the entrance examination committee was its concentration on reputational risk management. Preventing any information about the examinations from leaking was a key concern of the committee. The dates and location and the membership of the committee was kept secret, even from other members of the faculty. The use of email to discuss the committee's work was heavily discouraged; the focus was on everything being done through face-to-face meetings. All versions of the exams were distributed in hard copy and kept under lock and key between meetings. The committee spent as many sessions on collectively proofreading the papers as preparing them and any proposals for changes at the proofreading stage were approached in the most cautious terms for fear that editing would produce further mistakes.

---

[26] Words could only be taken from the easiest levels into which the Taishukan Genius English-Japanese dictionary divided all its entries.

The eighteen entrance exams which the committee produced required clearing 8 days from 9.00 in the morning until 5.00 in the afternoon, always at weekends, in the diaries of the eleven members of the committee. Although members of the committee complained about how much work was involved, none questioned the process itself and entrance exams were seen as an important rite of passage between high school and university. Universities like MGU, to some extent, had to compensate for the decline in the competitiveness of its entrance process by placing even greater weight on cementing their *formal* rigour through adherence to the rituals (of secrecy, procedural uniformity, and accuracy). In other words, the less selective a university was, not only the higher its fees (*YS*, 20 December 2007) but the more the 'performance' of entrance exams mattered.

This dynamic was also reflected in the implementation of recommendation 'entrance exams' which at places like MGU were clearly intended as pathways for students to get in without being tested. These systems were nonetheless operated through the same formal channels as written exams. They were contained in the same overall schedule (*nyūshi nittei*) of application deadlines, exam dates, and results announcements. The 'exams', even if only a short interview in this case, were conducted under the same conditions of secrecy and procedural uniformity as written exams. Their 'results' (interviewers' notes and numerical marks) were scrutinized, reviewed, and ranked in the same way by the entrance exam board and their results announced through the same formal channels. It was intended that students who came to MGU felt that however they got there, they had been through some kind of formal selection process.

Admissions from the Student Point of View

As described above, students arrived at MGU via multiple routes. Students calculated from talking amongst themselves that roughly half of all MGU students had aimed for a higher-level university and hence saw MGU as a back-up (*suberidome*) institution. It would be possible for a group of six students, though, to have arrived via six different routes, as with the following group of six students in their fourth and final year discussing their experiences in 2003.

Yusuke arrived through the *naibu suisen* (internal recommendation) system from the MGU-attached high school. He calculated that around half of his cohort of 450 who graduated from the high school in his year had come to

MGU, constituting nearly 10 per cent of all the new entrants. As part of the entrance process, he had had to write an essay on his club activities at the high school and had an interview with a non-academic member of staff from the admissions office who had asked him why there were so many baseball players at his school.

Masanao came to MGU through the *kōbō suisen* system. His headmaster had written a letter to say that the school recommended him to MGU. He was not required to submit his school academic record (*seiseki*) but had to come to the campus to do a one hour test which consisted of ten multiple choice questions which he said were very easy and which he was confident that he had got all correct.

Eiichiro said that his route was via the *shiteikō suisen* as his school had a quota of two places which they could give to students to go to MGU. He believed that there were ten in his year who had applied, but he did not know how or why he was selected.

Tetsu took the MGU entrance examinations in the March of his final year at school (*kōki futsū nyūshi*) which was administered by members of the MGU academic affairs office (*kyōmuka*) at the supplementary education school (*yobikō*) in Hiroshima where he was taking extra courses. He had decided that he wanted to study in the Kansai region and had looked at universities with *hensachi* entrance scores that averaged around 60, 55, and 50 in his subject area. For the first group he had chosen Ritsumeikan, for the second group Kansai Gaidai, and he claimed that for the third group he had put all the universities in the area with a *hensachi* of around 50 into a list, shut his eyes, and ended up with MGU. He described his place at MGU as *suberidome* in that he had wanted to get into a better institution. He said his *yobikō* teachers were disappointed when they discovered where he was going. The exam was his last chance to start the new academic year in the April. At the same time, MGU was looking to fill its places and, as a result, he was only required to take a single paper.

Hitomi took the national university examination (*centre nyūshi shiken*) and MGU decided to offer her a place on the basis of those results without asking her to take any of their own exams. The *centre shiken* system was set up mainly to support students who wanted to go to national universities, but over 80 per cent of private universities also took students though this system by the mid-2000s (*YS*, 20 January 2007). It was both efficient and cheap. Hitomi had paid only a fee to take the exams which had gained her a place at MGU. Even so, like all the other students who came to MGU, and regardless of how they got there, she also had to pay the MGU 'entrance examination fee' of ¥35,000.

The students were interested in comparing their experiences but were agreed that the overall *hensachi* for MGU had dropped by as much as five points to close to forty since they had applied 4 years earlier. Now there was virtually one applicant for each place, although the drop in the number of applicants and in the *hensachi* scores varied greatly across faculties. The foreign languages department was still competitive and had a *hensachi* which placed it close to the top 200 of Japan's 700 universities, while the *hensachi* in some of the other faculties placed them in the bottom 200. It was easy to see why these final year students worried that any real or perceived drop in the overall quality in the MGU intake might affect their own job prospects on graduation.

First Reactions to the 'Crisis of 2003'

The initial response to the pressure of declining student admissions varied greatly across the institution. The response from the academic community was very muted. McVeigh (2002: 246), writing in the same period, argued that the word 'crisis' had become so 'hackneyed' in Japanese higher education that it failed to carry any meaning any more. Overall, it was conspicuous how little open discussion there was on the matter among the academics on the MGU campus.

Some academic staff did not appear to believe that reform was really necessary because there were so few signs of panic on the campus; there were no obvious cutbacks in salaries and bonuses or discounting of fees. Others clearly did not feel empowered to engage in such debates and said they felt nervous about even discussing potential reforms in public in case this was seen as disloyalty to the institution and loss of confidence in the President.[27] Instead,

---

[27] Staff at MGU sometimes said they did not feel able to speak freely about reforms because they were not sure which of their colleagues were related to the family who owned the university. The idea that staff in an institution cannot work out which of their colleagues are related to the founding family may seem puzzling on first gloss, but the situation at Chubu University in Nagoya in the mid-2000s provides a good example of the problem. Chubu was originally founded as an institute of technology in the late 1930s by an individual called Miura Kohei. Miura had three children, two sons and a daughter. The oldest son was adopted by his wife's family and took her family name of Yamada. In 1975 he succeed his father and became President of the university, a position he held until 1999. He had one daughter, in her mid-thirties in 2004, who worked in the university's international exchange centre after having been a student at the university. The second son kept the name Miura. He was now in his seventies and was still working as a dean (*gakkan*) in the university. He was expected to take over the role as head of the *rijikai*. His son was currently working at (sometimes described as 'loaned to') another university and was expected to return to Chubu at some point in the relatively near future as a professor. The daughter of the founder had married a man called Onishi, whose family ran an architectural business. Onishi was the current *rijichō* but, because he was in his 80s, was expected to stand down in the near future. He also had a son who was currently the head of the administration (*somubuchō*) of the university and the son's wife was a professor of biology in the university. This son, as well as the son of Miura and the daughter of Yamada, were all spoken of as potential future

they arranged private meetings—with no great conclusions and no obvious outcomes—off campus. When reforms were mooted among the academic community, for example around the curriculum or assessment, it was conspicuous how little if any progress was made on them. It was often said that while younger academics were keen to try out some new ideas, older ones were very reluctant to support them and, in effect, blocked such reforms. Many of these older faculty were either long-term MGU academics who had benefited the most from the traditional high-salary, hands-off management style and appeared to have no desire to disrupt this at the end of their careers, or high-profile recruits who (as we saw earlier) were already semi-retired, engaged on a limited-term basis, and had less interest in MGU as an institution.

Even attempts to discuss reforms were sometimes rejected outright. One example related specifically to the junior college on campus where applications had dropped from 5,871 to 144 (an astonishing 97.5 per cent) over the 11 years between 1992 and 2003 (see Table 3.2). A recently arrived professor with considerable academic and practical experience of higher education management and reform was invited by the President to propose a reform strategy

Table 3.2 Decline in applications at MGU Junior College, 1992–2003

Year	Applications to MGU Junior College
1992	5,871
1993	5,179
1994	5,099
1995	3,767
1996	2,750
1997	1,784
1998	1,353
1999	891
2000	449
2001	238
2002	187
2003	144

presidents of the university. It can easily be seen how people with the surname Miura, Yamada, and Onishi (all common surnames in Japan) might be thought to all be related to the founding family, and if there were three surnames which were known, how many others might there be which were not? In the meanwhile, the university President was an external who had been brought in to succeed President Yamada in 1999. He had been recruited from Keio and was a popular figure but aware that the expectation was that after him, or possibly after his successor, the headship of the family would revert to someone from the founding family. The fact that the *rijikai* was still controlled by the family was what would make this possible.

to the faculty. He undertook extensive consultations, a SWOT analysis, looked at other institutions facing similar threats, and made a number of suggestions, in particular the idea that MGU was already a regional leader in the use of digital technology in education and that this could be pursued as a corporate aim. He was very clear on the principle that piecemeal or departmental changes which did not contribute to a whole institution reform would be unlikely to be successful. His appointment was met with considerable suspicion by the faculty in the junior college; one professor indeed brought a tape recorder to all the meetings as a sign of lack of trust and staff were reluctant to be involved in his surveys or focus groups with their students to find out what they thought about their current courses. After several months of meetings and the distribution of numerous papers, the President asked the professor to give up on the process. In the professor's view, the problem was that the faculty members were not prepared to contemplate retooling themselves and offering courses outside their own specialisms; in the view of the faculty in the junior college, he failed because he did not understand the local culture.

After the circulation of the aforementioned crisis document in 2003, applications and enrolment continued to fall at the university until it hit what, in hindsight, can be seen as the bottom. In both 2006 and 2007 only 850 or so students (less than 40 per cent of the quota of 2,175) enrolled (Table 3.3) and no department met its quota. MGU began to appear in rankings of universities which had the largest total decreases in student enrolment. In 2009, as the small 2006 and 2007 intakes moved through together and the larger 2004 intake graduated, it topped the national list for the biggest decline in total enrolment, with a figure which was almost twice that of the next institution.

MGU was the subject of an extremely critical report by the Japanese Universities Accreditation Association (JUAA) in 2010. The JUAA was the first of the bodies authorized by the Ministry of Education following the introduction of the Certified Evaluation and Accreditation System in 2002 which obliged all higher education institutions to undergo an evaluation once every

Table 3.3 Decline in applications and total enrolments at MGU, 2004–7

Year	Applications to MGU University	Quota (*teiin*)	Newly Enrolled	Newly Enrolled/ *teiin* (%)	Total Enrolment
2004	3,636	2,250	1,740	77.33	9,126
2005	3,038	2,175	1,396	64.18	8,090
2006	*Unavailable*	2,175	845	38.85	7,143
2007	*Unavailable*	2,175	854	39.26	5,791

7 years. In 2010, the JUAA accepted applications for accreditation from sixty-three universities and seven junior colleges. Of the sixty-three universities, fifty-six were accredited, one was denied accreditation, and the decision for six other universities was suspended in order for improvements to be made and continuously observed until re-review in 2013. MGU was in this last category. Similarly, while six of the seven junior colleges were awarded accreditation, the decision on MGU Junior College was suspended for re-review in 2012. The categories under which the institutions failed were: student admissions, financial affairs, and accountability. These failings were detailed at length in a thirty-page report. Student admissions referred to the mismatch between quota and intake over the previous 5 years; financial affairs related to concerns about money not being spent directly on educational matters; accountability related to the need for greater transparency around finance but also improved consultation in decision-making.

The head of the almost completely inactive union at MGU was clear as to why there was not more concern among the academic staff at the university about the rapidly falling application rates; it was very hard to get any figures relating to the finances of the institution. Even when these were available, it was hard to separate the finances of the university from the rest of the *hōjin* which included the *senmon gakkō* and the senior high school which were allowed to make a profit. According to the union's own newsletter, the university had been making annual profits of around ¥10 billion yen (£6.5 million) in the early 1990s and it was believed that these had been invested—since the university technically was a non-profit (*hi-eiri*) institution—and that the institution had built up a big land bank and put away major savings from that period which would see it through any crisis. It was hard also to get clarity on the staffing costs of the university when so many of the services were outsourced.

Overall, it was felt that only a tiny number of people at the very centre of the university understood its finances ('like Enron', the head of the union suggested, using a then-topical comparison). He felt that in this, MGU was typical of private universities, especially in the Kansai region where ideas from business dominated. In the Kanto area, where he had come from, he felt that there was a slightly stronger commitment to transparency among private universities. One reason, therefore, why the professors at MGU could not react to the crisis they were potentially facing and which had been gradually getting worse year by year—despite the union having warned about it in its newsletters some 10 years earlier—was that they all had such partial views of the situation. He described them as like 'frogs in boiling water' (*yude kaeru*) though it might have been better to have described them as like 'frogs in a well' who could only see what was directly above them. Ultimately, though, the union head felt that the main reason for the lack of academic interest in the current situation was because the union had secured them such good working conditions—in effect making itself redundant—and they had come to expect the university leadership under the President to guide them in a typical example of what he called, echoing the typology introduced in Chapter 2, a '*rijikai shihai* (board-led)' as opposed to *kyōjukai shihai* (faculty-led)' institution.

As we shall see in Chapter 4, the vast majority of the ideas for reform in the early 2000s did indeed seem to come from the President's office. He did seem to feel that was his and his team's role and he had little faith in the academics' ability to reform their own institution. Academic faculty, he felt, should be protected from management concerns. Their self-image was as *gakusha* or *kenkyūsha* (scholars, interested in research) rather than *kyōikusha* (education-alists, interested in teaching) and this made it difficult for them to empathize with making reforms that would be attractive to students.[28]

Conclusion

The above account highlights the key features of MGU in 2004 and, in particular, two points: that MGU was a family-run institution which was part of a conglomeration of family-run institutions and that there was a general level of dissatisfaction among academic staff towards management as the institution faced an increasingly insecure future and frustration of man-agement towards staff who would not change their practices to confront some of the realities of the problems they faced. In many ways these two features were perceived to be linked. Staff claimed that they had no information about the real situation because of a tendency of management towards secrecy and hence felt powerless to do anything to change the institution. Management claimed to feel—reflecting ideas from the classic kinship system in Japan—that it was their personal responsibility to sort out the problems of the institution,

---

[28] Academics at MGU were not out of line with academics elsewhere in Japan if they did primarily think of themselves as researchers rather than teachers. Surveys from the early 1990s through to the mid-2000s showed consistently higher satisfaction levels among those with a research orientation than those with a teaching orientation (Aichinger, Fankhauser, and Goodman 2017: 166–8).

in part because of the sense of duty they felt towards those family members who had founded MGU, those running linked institutions, and those who would inherit it in the future. Overall, these differing perceptions led to a divided community, and it was hard to see how MGU would be able to rescue itself. In Chapter 4, we will look at some of the ways in which it attempted to do so. These strategies were similar to most other private universities in Japan at the time facing the same challenges (see Kinmonth 2005: 113) and could be classed in three broad categories: reduce costs; cultivate new markets; introduce new recruitment practices.

4

MGU 2008–18

The Law School and Other Reforms

In the mid 2010s, the following notice—without warning as far as most of the MGU staff were concerned—appeared on the MGU website: 'Meikei Gakuin University Law School has recently taken the decision to stop enrolling students (including transferring students) from the next academic year onwards.'

The notice then set out the background to the law school, both its founding philosophy and the way it was designed to operate:

> With the launch of the Law School system in April 2004 and basing its approach on the founding philosophy of our university 'to serve society at large through education and research, and to nurture individuals with practical ability and broad vision who can contribute to the welfare and peace of humankind', this law school opened with the aim of implementing the idea for reform of the legal system that involved 'introducing many people from diverse backgrounds to the legal profession'.

> To this end, adopting the night and day course system, of which there are few examples to be found across the country, we have offered classes from 7:30 pm to 9 pm from Tuesdays to Fridays, and from 9 am to 9 pm on Saturdays and Sundays. In addition, we have made available a dedicated library-cum-study room 24 hours a day, and introduced an on-demand support system whereby even people from outside the school can attend lectures. In these and other ways we have endeavoured to maintain a learning environment which enables even mature students with jobs (*yūshoku shakaijin*) to receive a law school education without having to give up their employment.

> This approach, as well as being highly praised for providing a 'learn-while-you-work law school', has won the backing of mature students. Indeed, the majority of our enrolment has come to be made up of company employees, civil servants, and those with highly specialised professions such as doctors, teachers, judicial scriveners, chartered accountants, tax accountants, chartered surveyors, and patent attorneys. Indeed, it is a matter of pride that

Family-Run Universities in Japan: Sources of Inbuilt Resilience in the Face of Demographic Pressure, 1992–2030.
Jeremy Breaden and Roger Goodman, Oxford University Press (2020). © Jeremy Breaden and Roger Goodman.
DOI: 10.1093/oso/9780198863496.001.0001

these mature students with jobs, while fostering interdisciplinary exchange have also provided a stimulus to the student body as a whole, such that our school has become the epitome of the ideal law school, brimming with 'diversity' (*tayōsei*).

Despite the initial positive reception that the law school had received, for a number of reasons which were beyond its control it had run in to trouble:

The national target of having approximately 3,000 candidates a year pass the Bar Examination by around 2010 ran into trouble and, as the pass rate actually fell, applications to law schools all over the country continued to decline, such that by 2012 the number of applicants had dropped dramatically to just one quarter of the number in 2004, and the proportion of mature students amongst the 2012 intake fell to less than half that seen in 2004.

For a law school such as ours, which has been very positive about taking in mature students with jobs, this trend has proved to be a particularly severe blow. Also, the public perception of what is important when it comes to evaluating law schools has gradually shifted away from diversity and openness (based on, for example, the proportion of mature students and non-law faculty graduates enrolled) and towards the pass rate for the Bar Examination. This law school's public reputation has, therefore, suffered due to its continuing difficulties regarding the new Bar Examination in terms of the number of successful candidates and the pass rate achieved, a situation partly attributable to the special circumstance of having the bulk of its enrolment made up of mature students in employment, who find it hard to set aside enough time for exam preparation.

In this harsh climate, we put great effort into implementing a number of measures, such as reducing the intake (from 50 students to 30) over a period of two years, starting an extended course system (lasting 4 years) to give mature working students more study flexibility, and introducing a transferred-enrolment system to take in students who, for financial reasons, were unable to continue studying on daytime law school courses at other universities. Unfortunately, however, these countermeasures did not have the desired effects, such that in 2013 we had 7 candidates sit the entrance exam, and just 2 new students enrolling. As we can see no possibility in the future of maintaining student numbers at a level sufficient to continue offering an effective education, we have taken the painful decision to stop accepting new students. (Unofficial translation by the authors.)

The notice, which faculty at MGU jokingly referred to as 'an obituary', marked the beginning of the end of what was one of the most ambitious projects initiated following the 'crisis report' of 2003. The story of the establishment—and in some cases, such as MGU, the dismantling—of the new law schools in the 2000s in Japan is relatively well known,[1] but it is worth rehearsing at some length here as it crystallizes many of the broader challenges facing Japanese higher education in the first two decades of the twenty-first century and in particular shows the very complex decisions that a university like MGU had to make. It is a complicated story which requires considerable background.

The History of Law Education in Japan

Before we look at the establishment of the new law schools themselves, it is important to consider a brief history of the development of law education more generally in Japan. In the early years of the Meiji period, the pattern was for government ministries to establish their own training schools to educate their personnel. The Justice Ministry, for example, established its own law school, teaching French law, in 1871 for which it gave scholarships to students in return for them committing to work for the Ministry for a number of years. In 1877, the Ministry of Education established Tokyo University with faculties of Letters, Science, Medicine, and a Faculty of Law teaching Anglo-American law. Graduates of the University of Tokyo Law Faculty were allowed to practise as attorneys (*daigennin*) on behalf of third parties without the need to take any further legal training or qualifications (Flaherty 2013).

In 1880, a number of private law schools were set up for the first time: Senshū School (now Senshū University, teaching Anglo-American law); Tokyo Law School (now Hōsei University, teaching French law); and Meiji Law School (now Meiji University, teaching French law). In 1882, Tokyo Professional School (now Waseda University) and in 1885 the English Law School (now Chūō University) were established—both taught Anglo-American law. In 1886, Kansai Law School (now Kansai University) was established. The rapid development of these private law schools (all of which went on to become leading private universities in Japan) was unprecedented. In part, this reflected a struggle for dominance between supporters of the French and

---

[1] The literature on the establishment of the new law schools in Japan was sufficiently large, and covered the issues from such a range of angles, that already by 2013 it was possible to publish an English language bibliography of works on the topic (see Levin and Mackie 2013).

Anglo-American legal systems, which led to a tuition price war between institutions that almost bankrupted some of them in their attempts to attract students (see Amano 1990 and Miyazawa 2000).

It was to counter the growing influence of the largely unregulated private sector that when University of Tokyo was renamed Tokyo Imperial University in 1886, all private law schools in Japan were placed under the supervision of its President—a government official (Watanabe Koki) who proclaimed the University's educational function to be the training of bureaucrats for the state (Motoyama and McMullen 1997: 327). This control over the private law schools that was given to the Imperial University led to a double structure of legal education with national university law faculties producing judicial officers and administrators and private schools, which were not formally given university status until 1918, producing attorneys.

From the beginning, anyone, regardless of whether they had studied law formally or not, could take the examinations to become qualified as lawyers, and indeed many students prepared for them while working. As Amano (1990: 108) points out, this meant that the examination system to become an attorney, however hard, was a highly meritocratic one. It is also important to note, given the subsequent history of legal qualifications in Japan, just how difficult it was to pass these examinations from the very beginning. During the five years between 1881 and 1885, only 4.7 per cent (371) of 7,968 candidates for the attorney examination were successful.

The Imperial Universities generally did not get involved in professional education, and this pattern became solidified in the post-war period when universities which taught teachers, doctors, vets, dentists, librarians, pharmacists, nurses, and other specialist programmes were generally kept separate from mainstream universities and given different titles (such as *kyōiku daigaku* and *ika daigaku* for education and medicine). The training of lawyers became the responsibility of an independent body completely outside the university system. From the late 1990s, however, many of these specialist institutions of professional education merged with mainstream universities, in part to achieve economies of scale but also as a move away from the purely generalist education model (which was blamed by many for Japan's economic problems) towards a more specialist model in Japan's top universities.

In 2004, 6 years after the idea was originally proposed by the Ministry of Education, a new system of professional graduate schools (*senmonshoku daigakuin*) were inaugurated, which saw the establishment of schools of business (teaching MBAs), public policy (*kōkyō seisaku*), management of technology

(MoT, *gijutsu keiei*), accounting, and finance in universities. These schools were designed for students who wished to 'bridge theory and practice ... in a variety of fields, coming from a broad range of backgrounds, including former company employees' (Kano 2015: 36). They were required to recruit 'expert teachers' who could teach the practice of each of the subjects. Universities responded well to these opportunities, preferring, despite the higher costs, to establish professional schools rather than masters programmes because of the associated brand value and attractiveness for business and industry with which universities were keen to make links (see *YS*, 18 March 2005). The Ministry recommended that law schools should be included in this new system of professional graduate schools with the 'expert teachers' being lawyers and judges (Saegusa 2009: 387).

The Supply/Demand Conundrum in Relation to Japanese Lawyers and the Decision to Establish Law Schools

Murakami (2003) gives a good account of the key reasons behind the establishment of new graduate law schools (*hōka daigakuin*) in the 2000s. Most of those who became lawyers before 2004 first did a law degree at a university and then took a National Legal Examination to enter the Supreme Court's Legal Training and Research Institute in Saitama which provided a practical legal training over 2 years (reduced to 18 months in 1999) and required a final examination to qualify. At face value, this system did not look very different to the system for becoming a lawyer in many other countries. In practice though it had some very distinctive elements. Most distinctive was the very high number of applicants for the National Legal Examination and the very low pass rate. Each year, tens of thousands of students would take the annual exam which was often called the 'modern *keju*', the term used for the exam that was taken to become a bureaucrat in Imperial China.[2] The pass rate never exceeded 5 per cent after 1952 and generally fewer than 3 per cent ever passed; at its peak, in terms of numbers and competition, there were 45,622 candidates in 2002 of whom only 2.5 per cent passed (Foote 2006). The reason for the low success rate was due to the cap which was imposed every year by the administrative committee which reported to the Ministry of Justice. Until 1991, the cap was set at 500 passes per year; from 1991, it gradually increased to 1,000 in

---

[2] For a full account of the introduction and perception in Japan of the *keju* (known as *kakyo* in Japanese) see Amano 1990: 3–20.

1999; 1,200 in 2002; and 1,500 in 2004 (Foote 2013: 382; Watson 2016, 5). Even so, competition remained ferocious.

There was no limit on how many times candidates could try the National Legal Examination. The average number of attempts was between six and seven and the average age for passing over 28; in 1986, of 24,000 people who took the bar exam, only one passed on the first attempt and thirty-seven on the second (Ramseyer and Rasmusen 2015: 115). Three per cent of those who passed had taken the exam fifteen times or more and the vast majority, of course, never passed at all, however many attempts they made. Sixty per cent of those who passed described themselves as 'unemployed', meaning they were only working on taking the exam. Perhaps most unkind of all, employers of lawyers clearly had a preference for those who had passed at the least attempts (Ramseyer and Rasmusen 2015: 134). In effect, the bar exam was a competition rather than a qualifying test. The main financial beneficiaries of the process were the supplementary education institutions (*yobikō*) which specialized in training applicants for the exam; tuition for preparing for each year's exam was on average around ¥1 million (£5,000 at the then current exchange rate) per person (Watson 2016: 5). In a survey of those who had taken the bar exam in 1999, virtually all had been to *yobikō*, two-thirds for at least 3 years and a quarter for more than 5 years. While 50 per cent had attended a few days a week, 10 per cent had gone on a daily basis (Foote 2006: 217). For such applicants, the cost of the *yobikō* was on top of any foregone income for those who gave up work in order to concentrate on the examinations, plus the tuition fees and other costs invested in obtaining their initial university degree.

In 1999, the government set up a Judicial Reform Council to review a wide range of issues relating to the legal system, including expanding the number of legal professionals and revamping the system of legal education. The report emanated from earlier reports by both Keidanren (the Japan Business Federation) and a committee established by the ruling Liberal Democratic Party which were both highly critical of the current system of legal education and in particular of the National Legal Examination. Criticism included the waste of time, talent, and money involved in taking the exams. Equally importantly, it was felt that those who did pass the exams might have demonstrated good exam technique and memory for legal detail but no obvious critical understanding of law in either theory or practice (Wilson 2014). The exam was essentially a sorting device which restricted the number of lawyers rather than a contribution to the training of better lawyers. Even once they were in the Legal Training and Research Institute, they received fewer than 12 months of practical training before they graduated.

Another factor which led the Reform Council to recommend change was the sense in the late 1990s that Japan was simply not producing enough lawyers to deal with the increasing demand for legal services both domestically and globally. According to Foote (2013: 384–5), similar calls for increasing the number of lawyers in Japan can be traced back to the 1960s. However, while the population of Japan grew by 25 per cent between 1966 and 1990 and nominal GDP rose more than eleven times, the quota for those able to pass the bar exam stayed almost constant around the 500 a year level. It was commonly cited that, while there was one lawyer in the United States for every 300 citizens, one in England for every 670, one in Germany for every 900, and one in France for every 2,000, in Japan there was only one lawyer for every 7,500 citizens (around 17,000 in total in 2001).[3] The shortage of lawyers in the countryside was said to be particularly problematic (Arakaki 2004: 142). Almost half of all the lawyers in Japan in 1998 were based in Tokyo Prefecture, while there were only twenty-two lawyers in Shimane Prefecture and twenty-six in Tottori Prefecture. Even in Shimane and Tottori, lawyers would be located only in the largest cities so that, according to the Reform Council report, in 2000, out of 3,371 registered cities and towns in Japan, nearly 90 per cent either had no or only one lawyer (Foote 2013: 391).

The solution to all these concerns, it was concluded in the late 1990s, was the establishment of American-style graduate level professional law schools based in universities which would teach critical legal thinking and prepare lawyers who could deal with the situations that would face Japan in the new century (Saito 2006).

Outline of the New Graduate Law Schools

According to Saegusa (2006: 71), law professors in the elite universities anticipated that no more than thirty universities would be permitted to set up law schools. This number in conjunction with setting an annual pass figure of 3,000 per year would lead to an annual pass rate of between 70 and 80 per cent once the system was fully in operation. Instead, the Ministry received

---

[3] As many have pointed out (see, for example, Henderson 1997) these comparisons are somewhat misleading in that those who passed the law exams and became *bengoshi* (lawyers in the narrow sense in Japan) were only part of the community who provided legal services. *Bengoshi* generally only did litigation-related work, while para-legals did commercial, corporate, intellectual property, employment, bankruptcy, probate, and other work that was normally handled by lawyers in western countries.

seventy-two applications from universities in the first round, fifty of them from private universities. Once the decision to establish law schools had been taken nationally, it was very hard for universities like MGU that already had an undergraduate programme in law to avoid applying to set up one of their own. Not to do so would, it was widely believed, send a negative message about how MGU viewed its law faculty, which was actually, at the time, one of the strongest in the institution, taking in 350 students a year. Not to open a law school, therefore, when one had a law faculty, would lead to losing not only students but also faculty staff to other universities which did. In the spirit of deregulation (*kisei kanwa*) which then prevailed in Japan, the Ministry eventually approved sixty-eight of the seventy-two applications for accreditation.[4]

As Anderson and Ryan (2010) have pointed out, the new law schools were actually a paradoxical combination of state-imposed caps and free market deregulation. Almost as soon as the law schools were established, it was clear that there was going to be severe competition between them. In the second year of student applications, a third of the new schools received less than half the number of the previous year and several saw a 90 per cent reduction. Something which added even greater pressure on the new law schools, however, was the continuing existence of what became known as the 'law school bypass' system which allowed candidates—at the same time as students in the law schools were preparing to take the new bar exam—to continue to take the old bar exam without going to law school. In 2006, when the first graduates from the new law schools sat the bar exam, 35 per cent of all those who passed came through the 'bypass' system.[5] In 2011, just when it became no longer possible to take the old bar exam, a new system was introduced called the 'preliminary examination for the bar exam' which allowed those who passed it to take the bar exams, also without being enrolled in a law school at all. The argument for introducing this new preliminary examination was there had to be some system which allowed those who could

---

[4] It is interesting to note that when South Korea followed the Japanese example in setting up law schools in 2009, it limited the number of accredited law schools to twenty-five and the total number of law students who could be enrolled to 2,000 (Tanikawa, *NYT*, 10 July 2011). This was to try to ensure that around 75 per cent of students passed the bar exam. The result was that the competition simply shifted from the bar exam itself to the entrance exam to get in to the law schools.

[5] The 549 who passed the old exam in 2006 were of course still competing against much bigger fields: while 48.25 per cent of those who took the new bar exam were successful, only 1.81 per cent of those who took the old bar exam passed. Ramseyer and Rasmusen (2015: 116–18) point out the calculations which each individual might have made in choosing which of these routes to go down.

not afford to go to the law schools to apply to become lawyers. By 2016, over 15 per cent of all those who passed the bar exam came through this system.

The figures in Table 4.1 tell much of the tale of what has happened over the 13 years after the first students arrived at the new law schools. The schools collectively accepted 5,800 students in the first cohort, but when those on the shortened 2-year course (for those with an undergraduate degree in law) came to take the bar exams 2 years later, the pass rate was slightly under 50 per cent. When the following year the first cohort of 3-year students joined them, the absolute numbers increased from 1,009 to 1,851, but the percentage pass rate reduced to around 40 per cent. If one added the applicants who were success-ful taking the old bar exam, the total number in 2008 was over 2,200, so the target of 3,000 candidates successfully passing the exam seemed eminently achievable. The number of those passing the exam, however, plateaued over the 4 years after 2008 and then fell below 2000 in 2014, settling around the 25 per cent mark. In 2015, the government removed its official goal of qualifying 3,000 new lawyers a year and proposed a new target of 1,500, which was exactly the same number of lawyers who had been allowed to qualify in 2004, the year before the new law schools were opened (*JT*, 22 May 2015).

As Table 4.1 graphically shows, student applications to law schools also dropped rapidly from around 40,000 in the early years—if one ignores the 72,000 who applied in the first year of the law schools when there was presumably unusual pent-up demand—to around 8,000 in 2016 and 2017 (column 3). The two reasons given for the decline in applications were the low pass rate for those who went to law schools and increasing concerns about the job market for those who did qualify as lawyers. The total number of qualified lawyers in Japan had doubled from around 20,000 in 2004 to almost 40,000 in 2017 due to the higher numbers passing the bar exam than in the 1990s.[6] The impact on the job prospects of new lawyers was dramatic. According to a survey carried out by the Japan Federation of Bar Associations on the employ-ment situation of those who had just received their National Licence for Legal Practice, those who had *not* received 'assurances of employment' rose from 7 per cent in 2007 to 17 per cent in 2008, 24 per cent in 2009, 35 per cent in 2010, and 43 per cent in 2011 (Tanaka 2016: 45). Average starting salaries for new lawyers were reported to have dropped by as much as 27 per cent between 2007 and 2010 (Itō 2013: 103).

---

[6] While the reforms appear to have had a marginal impact on the gender balance of lawyers in Japan (Table 4.1: column 8), they had none on the age of those qualifying to work in legal practice. In 2012, the average age of successful candidates was 28–9 years old, almost exactly the same as the average age in the 1980s and 1990s (Steele and Petridis 2014: 105).

Table 4.1 Applicants, enrolments, bar examinees, number of passes, and pass rates in Japanese law schools, 2004–17

Year	Number of law schools accepting students	Total number of applications to law schools	Total quota for places in law schools	Total number of enrolments in law schools (% quota)	Total passing new bar exam (+old exam) [+new preliminary examination candidates]	National average new bar exam pass rate	Number of attorneys in Japan (female %)
2004	68	72,800	5,590	5,767 (103.2%)	(+1,483)	n/a	20,224 (12.1)
2005	74	41,756	5,825	5,544 (95.2%)	(+1,464)	n/a	21,185 (12.5)
2006	74	40,341	5,825	5,784 (99.3%)	1,009(+549)	48.3	22,021 (13.0)
2007	74	45,207	5,825	5,713 (98.1%)	1,851(+248)	40.2	23,119 (13.6)
2008	74	39,555	5,795	5,397 (93.1%)	2,065(+144)	33.0	25,041 (14.4)
2009	74	29,714	5,765	4,844 (84.0%)	2,043(+92)	27.6	29,930 (15.3)
2010	74	24,014	4,909	4,122 (84.0%)	2,074(+59)	25.4	28,789 (16.2)
2011	73	22,927	4,571	3,620 (79.2%)	2,063(+6) [+58]	23.5	30,485 (16.8)
2012	73	18,446	4,484	3,150 (70.2%)	2,102[+120]	25.1	32,088 (17.4)
2013	69	13,924	4,421	2,698 (61.0%)	2,049[+163]	26.8	33,624 (17.7)
2014	53	11,450	3,809	2,272 (59.6%)	1,810[+186]	22.6	35,045 (18.1)
2015	50	10,370	3,169	2,201 (70.0%)	1,850[+235]	23.1	36,415 (18.2)
2016	43	8,278	2,724	1,857 (68.1%)	1,583[+290]	22.9	37,680 (18.3)
2017	39	8,058	2,566	1,704 (66.4%)	1,543	25.9	38,980 (18.4)

Sources: Sato (2016), Tanaka (2016), Japan Federation of Bar Associations (2017), Ramseyer and Rasmusen (2015).

At the same time, the downturn in the global economy in 2008 also meant a major depression in the market for lawyers in Japan.[7] Many potential applicants could see that it was no longer such a good bet to enter law school. Those who came from a non-law background, however, consistently did at least 20 per cent worse in terms of their overall examination pass rate compared to those who were graduates from undergraduate law faculties. By 2014, their overall success rates were over 30 per cent lower (JFBA 2017: 12).[8] It is not surprising, therefore, that the reduction in applications from those who were not from a legal background[9] or were more mature applicants (*shakaijin gakusei*) was particularly conspicuous. As we shall see, this was particularly serious for MGU.

Statistics which look at the total number of students going to and graduating from the law schools do not show the situation in individual schools. Here the picture was even starker and reflected again the pattern in the wider higher education system.[10] In 2007, the second year of the new bar exams, three universities had no successful candidates at all. By 2009, a major differentiation between the results of schools began to appear when, although every law school had at least one successful candidate, fourteen had a pass rate of under 10 per cent. In 2010, two law schools had no successful applicants and eighteen had fewer than five. In 2011, twenty law schools enrolled fewer than ten new students and for the first time one law school (Himeji Dokkyō) stopped taking students altogether. In 2012, 60 per cent of all successful bar exam applicants came from the top ten law schools. By 2015, a further twenty law schools had announced that they would no longer be recruiting new students and would

---

[7] Law schools in the US were going through equally challenging times after 2008 (*JT*, 1 February 2015). Applications to US law schools fell by almost half between 2008 and 2014 (Gunderman and Mutz 2014). Even so, the difference between the number of those who graduate from law school in the US (around 50,000) and in Japan (fewer than 5,000) is still huge, given that the US population is roughly twice that of Japan and that the pass rate of those who graduate in the US on the bar exam is over 50 per cent rather than 25 per cent in Japan (*JT*, Gardner, 2 November 2014).

[8] For an account of those who went through the law schools from a non-legal background (*mishūsha*) compared to those who had graduated from an undergraduate law degree or gained legal experience in other ways before going to law school (*kishūsha*), see Lawley (2005: 88ff) and Foote (2013: 413).

[9] Ramseyer and Rasmusen (2015: 118) also point out that as students began to rank law schools by their success in the new bar exam and as students from non-law backgrounds did worse than those who had done their first degree in law, the law schools themselves began to favour those with law degrees when it came to admissions.

[10] Most accounts of the law schools concentrate on the failing schools, but it is important to point out that at the other end of the hierarchy, the top schools were getting very high pass rates. For example, the University of Tokyo was taking in around 240 students each year, of whom around 87 per cent on average were passing the new bar exam within the allowed three attempts within five years, even if the pass rate within any one year was closer to 50 per cent. At Hitotsubashi, with a much smaller intake of around eighty-five students, the eventual pass rate was over 90 per cent; Kobe 88 per cent, Tohoku 74 per cent, Keio 72 per cent, Kyoto 63 per cent (Ramseyer and Rasmusen 2015: 133–4).

close once their current students had graduated. A further nine schools announced in 2015 that they would not be recruiting for 2016. The following year, a further four universities, including such prestigious institutions as Aoyama Gakuin and Rikkyō, both based in Tokyo, announced that they would not be recruiting for 2017, leaving only thirty-nine of the seventy-four law schools which had existed in 2005 still recruiting new students.[11]

When the new schools were established in 2004, the government offered them all generous subsidies on the basis that they were performing a public service.[12] In 2010, however, the Ministry of Education began linking the subsidies to pass rates in the new bar exams and, from 2014, to enrolment rates. While a small number of institutions saw their subsidises rise as a result of this assessment process, 80 per cent of the law schools still accepting students in 2015 saw them reduced, by over 50 per cent in the case of seven schools (Watson 2016: 32). These cuts were the final nail in the coffin for the MGU Law School.

MGU Law School

In hindsight, it is easy to question why MGU set up a law school in 2004, but at the time it seemed the logical step to take. As we have seen, the fact that MGU already had an undergraduate law faculty was a strong determining factor. Not to do so would almost certainly doom the faculty to a slow and unpleasant death. On a more positive note, however, establishing a law school was believed by some faculty to have been seen by the administration as an opportunity for MGU to regain its status among private institutions in the Kansai region, back to the position it felt it had once had in its heyday of the 1980s and early 1990s when it attracted over 40,000 undergraduate applicants each year. Not many universities would have law schools, and it would distinguish MGU in an increasingly competitive market. MGU already had a good record for producing accountants and tax lawyers (*zeirishi*) through

---

[11] Ironically, these closures, combined with the regulations which stipulate that graduates of the law schools can only sit the bar exam for up to 5 years after graduation, may mean that by around 2020 or 2021, the pass rate for the new bar exam at those law schools which are still open will rise to an average of 70 per cent, the original target of the reform council, even if the total number of new lawyers is half of the original target of 3,000 (Sato 2016: 221).

[12] According to Tanaka (2016: 46), the full subsidy which law schools received *per student* over 3 years was just over ¥2 million. This was slightly less than half the fees law schools in national universities were allowed to charge students (the figure being set by the Ministry of Education) and around a third of the average fees in the case of students in law schools in private universities which had greater freedom to set their own fees.

professional graduate training courses, and the law school would complement those programmes well. The institution also seems to have been confident that it had the financial resources as well as the connections through its law faculty to make the project work. Importantly also, when the call for law schools went out from the Ministry of Education, it was widely believed that it might not be repeated.

The new law school had to be independent from the old law faculty but, to some extent, as it was being established, they found themselves in competition. One of the criteria for the academic staff of the new law school was that they had to have had more than 5 years of teaching experience. This meant that some of the most senior teachers in the law faculty found themselves 'moved up' as it was seen (Nottage 2007: 248) to the new law school and their positions in the law faculty were often taken by less experienced and younger staff.[13] At the same time, the new law school had to recruit, as professors of practice, 20 per cent of staff who had at least 10 years of practical experience of the law in roles such as lawyers, judges, and prosecutors.[14] The fact that so many of these new appointments were retirees meant that the average age of the staff in the new law school was considerably higher than in the law faculty[15] and that, in turn, meant that they also enjoyed higher salaries. Finally, the new law school—as was the case with most of the new law schools in private, though not necessarily the national, universities (Nottage 2007: 243)—was given refurbished facilities on the MGU campus, considerably nicer than those of the law faculty, in a building which had housed some of the university administration. The building was refitted with more than a hundred study carrels for the law students' exclusive use on the ground floor; a major hall on the second floor was fitted with sliding partitions and furnishings which could be arranged into a mock court room with an hour's notice; the third floor was renovated to become small seminar rooms that law school students could use

[13] Tanaka (2007: 201–2) describes a 'great migration' of staff from law faculties to law schools in 2004 when the new law schools were opened and argues that one reason the new law schools were supported by law academics was because of the new positions they potentially opened up and that for many of them this might mean moving to a higher status university. Saegusa (2006: 118) quotes a professor involved in the process of recruiting faculty for the new law schools describing it as '*jingi naki tatakai*' (a 'battle without either honour or humanity') after a scene in a famous *yakuza* film.

[14] As Arakaki (2004: 109–11) pointed out at the time the law schools were being set up, the recruitment of senior professors from law faculties plus retired professors of practice meant that many of the former might have little knowledge of practising law, and the knowledge of many of the latter might already be out of date.

[15] At Doshisha University, for example, the average age of faculty in the new law school was 58 (Nottage 2007: 249).

for small classes and for study sessions. The whole building was a given new carpets, new furniture, and a new coat of paint.

Institutions like MGU faced two major disadvantages in the competition to attract students to their law schools. The first was that all private universities were having to compete with the national and public universities which were massively better subsidized overall and hence could charge much lower fees.[16] The President of Keio University, among others, ran a vigorous but unsuccessful campaign throughout 2003–4 before the new law schools came into place, lobbying MEXT to create a special fund for law schools at private universities so that they could compete with the national institutions (*DY*, 2 July 2003). Others proposed that national universities should instead be forced to charge the full costs of their programmes to create a level playing field. The second disadvantage was that MGU's reputational pull was relatively weak compared to more established, first-tier institutions.

MGU found imaginative ways to create a distinctive niche for itself to try and get around the disadvantages which it knew it faced both in terms of having to charge higher fees than national universities and having lower brand status than its private university competitors. The essence of this niche was to establish a law school for those who wanted to continue to work while studying, by providing the majority of the education in the evenings and at weekends. This, as we saw in the 'obituary', was argued to be in line with the founding philosophy of the university. MGU was indeed the only school in western Japan with night-classes and a weekend class schedule which meant that students could take the course while also holding down a full-time job.[17] Students who wanted that combination would come from as far away as Nagoya, which involved at least an hour-long commute in each direction, often after a day at work. The early indications from the law school at MGU were promising. When the first cohort for entry in 2004 was being recruited, around 2,000 applications packs were sent out. A thousand or so people expressed an interest in applying, of whom 381 took the formal entrance examination (for which they had to pay an application fee) and fifty-five were selected, 10 per cent above the formal quota of fifty which had been set by the Ministry. The disappointing results its students achieved in the bar exams—which, from

---

[16] Tuition fees were around ¥2.6 million over 3 years in national universities and just over ¥4.0 million for 3 years in private universities (Tanaka 2016: 46). Many universities offered generous scholarships and even free places to attract the strongest students, a practice which was widely described by institutions, such as MGU, which did not follow suit, as 'dumping', an English term well known from US–Japan trade battles.

[17] The institution which embraced this night-class model most completely was Omiya Law School, founded in 2004 and closed in 2015.

Table 4.2 MGU Law School applicants, enrolments, bar examinees, number of passes, pass rates, 2004–17

Year	Applicants to MGU Law School	Enrolments in MGU Law School*	MGU bar exam applicants including retakes	MGU bar exam passes	MGU new bar exam pass rate (national average)
2004	381	55	n/a	n/a	n/a
2005	199	49	n/a	n/a	n/a
2006	137	45	n/a	n/a	n/a(48.3%)
2007	161	51	14	2	14.3%(40.2%)
2008	121	42	28	1	3.6%(33.0%)
2009	91	33	36	2	5.6%(27.6%)
2010	43	15	55	3	5.5%(25.4%)
2011	24	5	72	2	2.8%(23.5%)
2012	21	7	54	3	5.6%(25.1%)
2013	8	2	37	2	5.4%(26.8%)
2014	–	–	46	5	10.9%(22.6%)
2015	–	–	39	2	5.1%(23.1%)
2016	–	–	26	2	7.7%(22.9%)
2017	–	–	16	2	12.5%(25.9%)
Total/ Average		304	407	24	5.9%(24.5%)

* Original quota = 50; reduced to 30 in 2010

the very beginning, often placed MGU in the bottom five of all the law schools in Japan—quickly undermined that early optimism (see Table 4.2).

What was the actual experience of students at MGU Law School? For faculty and students, the fact that the law school catered primarily for those who wanted to work while doing their law study was quickly discovered to be double-edged. By the time they came to class after a day at work, students would often be tired and unable to concentrate. Further, the fact that they were holding down jobs meant that they did not have enough time at home to review their studies and to complete their homework. This is not surprising when it was estimated that they needed to study between 60 and 70 hours a week, including classes, if they had any realistic chance of being successful in the bar exam. In reality, therefore, most students found that they could not hold down a full-time job for all of the time they were doing the course, even if that had been the original attraction of the MGU course, and converted to become full-time students. Those who failed to pass the bar exam particularly resented the restriction on how many times and in what time period they could re-take after they had graduated. They believed that it should be a matter for the individual to decide, as it had been before the law schools were established.

There were many debates in the MGU Law School about how to deal with the low pass rate in the bar exam. Some professors thought that the students who were working should be allowed to take longer, perhaps as long as 5 years, but this was deemed impractical as it would take too long before MGU had any results from the bar exams to show to potential new recruits. Another idea was that the school move to a traditional daytime programme, but it was thought unlikely that MGU would be able to recruit against bigger brand names in that field, given that it was believed that its undergraduate law faculty had produced only one student who had passed the bar exam in the whole of its history before 2004.

Why MGU continued to recruit students when the results in the early bar exams were so disappointing is not completely clear. There was doubtless an element of pride involved. There was also the fact that in every year there were some students who did pass the bar exam, so clearly it was possible to do so after studying at the MGU Law School. There may have been an element of not wanting to blink first; those universities which survived the major culling of law schools in the 2010s would benefit from the closures and would probably manage to survive for some time.

A slightly bigger mystery might appear to be why did students continue to apply to MGU Law School when the pass rate in the bar exam was so low? In part this was because, with the ability to re-take the exam three times in 5 years, it could be up to 8 years after a cohort entered the law school before there was clear evidence of how many of that cohort actually passed the bar exam. From the perspective of the individual student, their chance of becoming a lawyer, still a widely sought-after and high-status role in Japan, was on average at least twice as good through the law school at MGU than it would have been before 2004 through the previous system (when the percentage of those who passed was generally under 3 per cent). The chances were also twice as good as for those who were attempting to be allowed to take the bar exam through the preliminary examination system. The students at MGU all accepted that becoming a lawyer in Japan was going to be hard—it was part of the reason that lawyers enjoyed the status that they did—and so improving one's chances by 100 per cent was not an unimaginable gamble even when they looked at the statistics from MGU in the years before it closed.

In 2018, the law school building stands more or less empty. There are one or two carrels for the use of students who graduated and have not used up all of their examination attempts, but most of the ground floor is given over to the storage of furniture. The hall is occasionally used for large events and gatherings by other parts of the university. The third floor does not appear to be being used at all. As for the teachers, as the law school wound down, some of them returned to the law faculty from which they had originally come. Others retired, since many had not been far off retirement age when they were hired.

The rise and fall of the law school at MGU encapsulates very well the wider challenges which have faced Japanese higher education in general and MGU in particular over the past two decades. In many ways, the fact that MEXT allowed almost all those who applied to open law schools to do so meant that it was an almost perfect natural experiment in how different universities responded to the same external challenges. It was also one of the first times that the Ministry has stepped back from micro-managing and allowed the principles of the free market to operate and institutions to actually fail. In order to comprehend the story in full, therefore, it is indeed necessary to understand the broader issues confronting higher education: deregulation, liberalization, vocationalization ,and the changing economic, political, and demographic situation in Japan which we examined in earlier chapters. MGU, like most universities which had undergraduate law faculties, had had almost no choice other than to apply to set up a law school. As Saegusa (2006: 147) graphically put it, for non-elite universities without a law school like MGU, the decision to open a law school was viewed as a 'matter of life and death' because it so clearly reflected a shift in legal education 'from undergraduate law faculties to graduate-level professional law schools'.

Even though the MGU Law School had to shut down, it is important to consider what would have happened if it had not been opened in the first place. It would certainly have led to many of its best staff being actively recruited to work in new law schools elsewhere. There would have been a knock-on impact on the law faculty which would have seen the quality, and probably also the quantity, of student applicants decline. It may even had led to the closure of the law faculty, which was, in 2004, the most successful faculty, in terms of both the quantity and the quality of applicants, in the university and which, to some extent, distinguished MGU from other private universities in its sector of the market. The fact that so many other law schools closed at roughly the same time as the MGU Law School meant that there was actually no impact on its undergraduate law faculty. Although its reputation had not been enhanced by the brief existence of the law school, at the same time, it does not seem to have been damaged by it. In many ways, therefore, the establishment of the MGU Law School can be seen, in hindsight, as a successful damage limitation exercise.[18]

---

[18] In terms of the overall position of the law schools in Japan at the end of the 2010s, there is a curious symmetry with the situation when the first legal training schools were established in the 1880s.

How MGU Recovered from the 'Crisis of 2003'

The 2003 'crisis report' proposed that the academic strategy of the university should be the development of projects to produce 'graduates with practical skills who were useful to society' (to be taken forward by the academic staff) and the 'development of initiatives which could help students with their study' (to be the responsibility of the support staff). All academics and administrative staff were asked to send their responses to these initiatives by a certain date.

Most of the reform proposals, however, in reality came out of the President's office, not from the academic staff. Many of these were indeed related to the introduction of training projects in practical skills, reflecting the origins of MGU, which could run alongside the academic programmes on the campus. The idea was that the latter conferred academic credibility on the former which, in turn, could make money to subsidize the institution as a whole. The President's office introduced, for example, projects on distance learning, extension learning, computer skills training, and international exchanges.

The extension learning centre was a good example of the type of practical skills project in which MGU began investing. The extension centre courses were available not only for students on the campus, but also those in the wider community and indeed for students from other universities. They focused on practical skills and in some ways mirrored the offerings of *senmon gakkō* except that they were much cheaper.[19] Courses cost on average only about ¥2,000 to ¥2,500 per class and, unlike university courses, students did not have to pay a registration fee (*nyūgakukin*). The courses took place in the evenings and on Saturdays to avoid clashing with normal MGU classes. They were generally not taught by staff from the university but external agencies. The English conversation classes, for example, were provided through major companies such as ECC and YMCA.

In 2018, 43 per cent of the total quota for places in law schools is owned by just five institutions—two national universities (Tokyo and Kyoto) and three private universities (Keio, Waseda, and Chuo). Since these institutions recruit closer to quota than other institutions, they admit close to half of all new students. Among the other surviving law schools are Senshu, Meiji, Hosei, and Kansai, all of which can trace their origins back to the beginnings of legal education. Although their quotas are modest (between twenty-eight and forty new students each year) all four recruited healthy numbers in 2018. The total number of law schools looks likely to continue to atrophy in the coming years: in 2018, six out of thirty-nine law schools failed to recruit even ten students and eleven recruited less than 50 per cent of their quota.

[19] Courses included training for English TOIEC practical tests; IT skills; job applications; public civil service examinations; estate agency work; travel industry; mental health management; design; marketing; finance and accounting; business skills; and, self-development.

MGU students who took these courses were part of a phenomenon which had become recognized in the 1990s known as 'double-schooling'. The courses provided students which practical skills which would help them in the employment market alongside the formal degree they needed to get an interview in the first place. It was felt by many students that 'double schooling' was better than simply attending a *senmon gakkō* because there was still a preference among employers for university graduate generalists than for specialists from other forms of higher education. Students could be, and were, very selective in choosing these courses and made sure they got good value from them. One of the conspicuous features of the extension centre activities, however, was how little the academic staff at MGU knew about it. It was almost as if there were two universities running on the same campus.

Other early reforms included the closing of a number of courses which were particularly struggling to recruit, such as German (this became possible when the last full-time professor retired and was not replaced), and opening new courses with supposedly attractive titles such as 'hospitality studies' and 'sports administration'. An Educational Reform Centre (*Kyōiku Kaihatsu Shien Centre*), staffed by some of the more forward-looking staff, was established. A programme of monthly faculty development (FD) talks given by outside speakers was set up. An 'Open Class' month was started in which teachers were expected to observe at least three other classes and write reports on them. A new director for the International Office was appointed from Hawaii, who developed programmes for MGU students wanting to study abroad as well as plans to double the very low number of foreign students at MGU. The counselling service was considerably enlarged and professionalized with quali-fied psychologists and therapists. A new learning centre where students could get help with skills such as report writing, mostly from retired professors, was opened.

The most significant changes, however, can be seen in Table 4.3. The overall government-approved quota for new students at MGU was reduced in 2009 by 16 per cent, continuing a process which saw it reduce by almost exactly half between 2000 and 2015. Even more dramatically, MGU reduced its annual student fee overnight in 2009 by over 27 per cent from the year before, and it stayed at exactly the same level for the following 8 years. Coterminous with these changes, the number of full-time academic staff reduced by almost 30 per cent between 2003 and 2016.

The reduction in fees had an almost instantaneous impact on student enrolments (see Table 4.4) which doubled between 2006 and 2008, and the

Table 4.3 Change in enrolment quotas, full-time academic staff, and student fees, 2000–18

Year	Quota (*teiin*)	Full-time academic staff numbers	Fees (¥million)
2000	2,750	189	1.720
2001	2,475	218	1.726
2002	2,400	218	1.732
2003	2,325	225	1.738
2004	2,250	219	1.738
2005	2,175	208	1.738
2006	2,175	211	1.722
2007	2,175	210	1.722
2008	2,175	190	1.722
2009	1,825	202	1.248
2010	1,825	193	1.248
2011	1,825	188	1.248
2012	1,825	171	1.248
2013	1,825	179	1.248
2014	1,825	189	1.248
2015	1,380	168	1.248
2016	1,380	160	1.248
2017	1,380	unavail	unavail
2018	1,380	165	1.266

lowering of the intake quota meant that the university went from meeting under 40 per cent of its quota to meeting over 90 per cent.

The easiest way to demonstrate how much MGU reformed its practices is probably to compare the situation in 2018 with the situation in 2004. The students still come from the same sector of the *hensachi* distribution curve—in the 2018 *hensachi* league tables, MGU has an overall average of just under 39 and was ranked in the 40th percentile of Japan's 751 universities—but the experience that they were offered as students had changed considerably for the better.

The university, for example, puts more effort into recruitment even though the quota of places has dropped to 1,380, almost half of what it was in 2000. Whereas in the 1990s all students had to come to MGU to take entrance exams, the university now runs exams at twelve different sites across western Honshu, Kyushu, and Shikoku; it has six Open Campus days and a further six 'entrance examination advice meetings' (*nyūshi sōdan kai*).

The senior high school is being rebuilt next to the university after being knocked down because it no longer meets modern earthquake-proof standards. It is hoped this will lead to an increase in applications from the

Table 4.4 Quota, new enrolments, quota fulfilment, and total enrolments at MGU, 1999–2018

Year	Enrolment quota (*teiin*)	Newly enrolled students	Newly enrolled /*teiin* (%)	Total enrolment
1999	2,350	2,803	119.28	11,381
2000	2,750	2,786	101.30	11,276
2001	2,475	2,329	94.10	11,118
2002	2,400	2,289	95.37	10,498
2003	2,325	2,124	91.35	9,901
2004	2,250	1,740	77.33	9,126
2005	2,175	1,396	64.18	8.090
2006	2,175	845	38.85	7,143
2007	2,175	854	39.26	5,791
2008	2,175	1,438	66.11	4,639
2009	1,825	1,654	90.63	4,467
2010	1,825	1,753	96.05	4,718
2011	1,825	1,684	92.27	5,436
2012	1,825	1,311	71.84	6,073
2013	1,825	1,420	77.80	5,868
2014	1,825	1,220	66.85	5,660
2015	1,380	1,282	92.90	5,202
2016	1,380	1,336	96.81	4,893
2017	1,380	1,536	111.30	unavailable
2018	1,380	1,572	115.36	5,423

school to the university. The independent junior college has been absorbed into the four-year university as a department (*gakubu*) taking students on two-year courses. This makes the quota of fifty places—smaller than any other department—look less conspicuous than when it was a stand-alone institution.

The number of students in receipt of a JASSO loan has increased from about 2 per cent in 2004 to over 50 per cent in 2018. There are two types of loans available: one which has no interest but is only available for those who are from lower-income households and have a 3.5 GPA or higher, and one that incurs interest and needs to be repaid within 20 years but where interest is stopped if it is repaid in the first 4 years. Repayments must start within 7 months from graduation.

There are now around a hundred foreign students on the campus—including twenty or so who are doing full 4-year degrees—whereas in 2004 there were fewer than twenty in total. The students mainly come from China, Taiwan, and Korea, which means they can manage reading and writing Japanese much easier than students from elsewhere. The international office has also expanded its efforts to arrange overseas trips and exchanges for the

MGU students. There is a campaign to encourage students to take 2-week or 3-week small group 'learn and do' breaks overseas in the hope that this will increase confidence and lead to longer study abroad. MGU now has exchange agreements with fifty-nine different institutions in twenty-three countries and, while many of them still appear to be dormant or rarely activated, each year around 35 students spend a year abroad at one or other of these sister universities.

There is also a greater support for non-curricular activity. Sports teams are going from strength to strength and indeed one of the most popular—and successful in terms of student completion rates—new degree programmes is a course in Sports Economics (*Sports Keizai*).

MGU no longer has the highest salaries of academic staff in the Kansai area. Retirement age which had for most academics been 70, is now 65. Very few professors have, in recent years, been recruited on retiring from prestigious national universities. Instead, most appointments of full-time staff have been much younger (and cheaper) academics. Bonuses which constitute a substantial part of the pay packages of permanent staff were cut by over 10 per cent in the early 2010s and are now paid only twice (July and December) rather than three times a year. Professors no longer are paid for publishing in the departmental *kiyō* (which are now only produced digitally).

The fact that there are more younger academic staff without families means that there are more professors on campus, even occasionally at weekends. It may also be a reason for what is perceived as more and better communication with students. The big increase in part-time professors means that greater use is made of the senior common room, which they have come to use as their base (they still do not have their own offices despite the decrease in full-time staff). Many of the new full-time professors are on short-term contracts for 3 to 5 years, though it is possible sometimes for them to be made permanent after a number of years at MGU.

There is no longer an army of cleaners and the campus is no longer as spotlessly clean as it once was. The number of security staff is also much lower than previously. The number of 'office ladies' despatched by an external company to sit at the end of corridors and help visitors and professors is much reduced and many of those who are there are part-time. The cutback in support staff overall is highly conspicuous to anyone who had not been to the campus for some time. Equally conspicuous, the female administrative staff who work in the offices are no longer required to wear a uniform.

The Takashimaya shop which had doubled up as an expensive student supply store is no longer there. The McDonalds store has also gone, but a bespoke soba restaurant for students is about to open as part of a campaign to improve the quality of food on campus and make it more attractive for the students to spend time there. Staff and students who book overseas trips are no longer expected to go through JTB or fly with JAL. The campus Christmas light display, which had been much enjoyed by the local community as well as those in the university, no longer happens.

As Table 4.4 shows, MGU is now able to meet its much-reduced quota. Indeed, in 2018, MGU over-recruited against its quota by almost exactly the same proportion as it had done 20 years ago. The total number of students on campus, though, is half the total number in the early 2000s. Importantly, the number of applications is moving in the right direction. In late 2018, it had over 1,600 visitors to an Open Campus student recruitment weekend, the first time more than 1,000 had attended such an event. In the 2019 edition of the *Asahi Daigaku Ranking*, MGU is listed in the top one hundred universities that have seen an *increase* in applications for the period 2013–17. In 2018, it achieved its new 7-year accreditation on the first application.

MGU is a very different university in 2018 than it had been in 2004 or in 1992 in terms of both its size and shape. There was a sense among those who had been through the whole journey and had come through the other side that the university had found a niche where it could survive. According to one professor at MGU, who had been in another institution facing similar issues, the response at MGU followed the classic pattern of response to an enrolment crisis by academics elsewhere. At first, they ignored it, in the belief that it was a blip. Then they made a number of cosmetic changes, such as changing departmental names. Then a number of piecemeal ideas (new courses, more open campuses, different forms of admissions) were introduced to try and attract more students, but, since they did not constitute a comprehensive strategy, all they achieved was academics getting busier and busier with little to show for their efforts, leading to some staff quitting. Finally, the staff who remained became increasingly motivated to think of ways to reform the institution and improve the student experience while accepting pay cuts and reductions in student numbers.

There is no doubt, for example, that there is a greater emphasis on teaching at MGU in 2018 than there was in 2003. There is a greater focus on student attendance. Fewer students are late for class or miss class than before; on some courses, if students are absent a certain number of times without a good explanation then they may be kicked off the programme altogether. Classes (*koma*) are now 105 minutes long, rather than 90, without a break. The change was introduced to meet the requirements for minimum contact hours set down by the Ministry while reducing the number of weeks of teaching from 15 to 13 weeks per semester. This is partly to allow students more time to look for post-university jobs.

Perhaps the most significant change is the increased focus on students' learning experience. They are increasingly streamed by ability in at least some of their subjects; for example, in English classes taught outside the foreign languages faculty, all students are given placement tests and taught in ability groups. There is a new focus on what is called 'Project/Problem-Based Learning' (PBL, for short) and the university has a webpage where examples of such PBL teaching is shared across the community. These include a workshop on sustainable development goals and a project making a radio commercial to promote MGU.

Individual professors have also posted their own PBL teaching on their personal webpages. Some are clearly more active than others and there is great variation across faculties, but a particularly energetic professor's page has multiple examples of such activities, mostly undertaken with his final-year *zemi* class. He has students using software to make advertising flyers for existing businesses; undertaking a project for a local city zoo in which they make English translations for the signage; undertaking volunteer work to help raise money for a conservation charity; taking a trip to see the after-effects of the 2011 tsunami in Tohoku; and writing a joint report on the local tourist facilities and how they might be improved. Some of the projects involve exchange students from other countries and other faculties; some even involve students from other universities. Professors themselves say about these new forms of teaching that they are, in part, the result of more direction from the university, which has itself received direction from the Ministry of Education to adopt more active learning methods. Many of them also admit, however, that they felt that they had to do something to make the teaching more attractive and effective in the light of the decreasing number of applications and students.

According to Kitamura and Cummings (1972: 307), historically the only way that university reform in Japan had been successful in the past had been in conjunction with 'a "Big Bang" instigated from outside the university usually from abroad such as a war or an international political or economic crisis'. The examples they give are the Meiji era and the post–First World War and post–Second World War periods. Their prediction (1972: 322–4) that university reform would fail in the 1970s because, while universities had problems, Japan as a society generally did not, was largely proven to be correct. Only when there is a 'big bang', they argued, would the academic body move into overdrive. In some ways, it can be argued that the combination of the demographic decline, plus the government shift towards neoliberalization and the stagnation of the Japanese economy, all combined in the first decade of the twenty-first century to create such a 'big bang'. We argue, however, that one other key motivator in MGU's survival was the fact that it is a family-run business. This fight for survival, in turn, has led to an improved experience for the students who attend MGU.

Contrary to expectations in the literature which we will explore in Chapter 6 that the direct involvement of family members in the family business will have dwindled considerably by the third generation, in the case of MGU it has actually become stronger. Not only is the President's younger brother a professor in the university and a key member of the Board of Trustees, but all three of the President's children are now also well-qualified and highly respected professors in the university. The youngest of the President's three children, a daughter, has returned from an undergraduate programme at a top US university and is teaching—alongside three other teachers who are also graduates of the same university—a new one-year programme delivered only in English for the best thirty students studying foreign languages. This has proven so popular that there are plans to extend it to a second year. The younger son is a professor in the economics faculty. The President's oldest son is a professor in the marketing faculty and the vice president (*fuku gakuchō*), in place to take over as the third generation of family leadership.

5

The Resilience of Japan's Private Universities

As we have seen in the previous two chapters, MGU, after many twists and turns, was able to recover from a major crisis in the 2000s. Not all private universities weathered the storm as successfully. To begin this chapter we examine an example of a university faced with a similar scenario of under-enrolment and financial stress, but one which did live up to the millennial predictions and ultimately closed its doors.

Private University Failure: The Case of St Thomas' University

St Thomas' University was established in 1963 by Eichi Gakuin, a *gakkō hōjin* founded by the Roman Catholic Archdiocese of Osaka. The university, which originally operated under the name of Eichi University, had grown steadily through the 1970s and 1980s but, by the early 2000s, it was struggling to attract sufficient students to fill its classrooms. A departmental downsizing exercise was undertaken in 2004, reducing the undergraduate enrolment quota from 360 to 250, but even this proved insufficiently ambitious: new enrolments had dropped to just 78 by 2008 (J-CAST 2009). Eichi Gakuin engaged an external educational consulting firm to draw up a reform plan, which saw the university's three existing undergraduate departments being rolled into a single unit named the Faculty of Interpersonal and Cross-cultural Understanding (*ningen bunka kyōsei gakubu*). This followed the popular trend of eschewing traditional disciplinary titles in favour of those incorporating popular themes, thus allowing disparate curricula and teaching expertise to be brought together under a single banner which was likely to gain government approval and hopefully appeal to prospective students.

This restructuring and rebranding was also designed to work in concert with new opportunities for international exchange which derived from the

Family-Run Universities in Japan: Sources of Inbuilt Resilience in the Face of Demographic Pressure, 1992–2030.
Jeremy Breaden and Roger Goodman, Oxford University Press (2020). © Jeremy Breaden and Roger Goodman.
DOI: 10.1093/oso/9780198863496.001.0001

university becoming a member of the International Council of Universities of Saint Thomas Aquinas, a global network of Catholic universities. Membership of the International Council in turn occasioned the change of name from Eichi University to St Thomas' University for the 2007 academic year (*SS*, 31 March 2007). The university also established an entirely new department in the field of early childhood education, which the consultants advised—rather counter-intuitively given Japan's declining birthrate—would be a growth area in the coming years.

This bold change of direction required considerable investment in new staff and facilities, and drove Eichi Gakuin into significant debt for the first time. It did not, however, prove effective in attracting students back to the university. With only 110 new enrolments in 2009, the viability of the university was in serious doubt. On the advice of another external consultant with a successful record of resuscitating failing institutions, Eichi Gakuin briefly entertained the idea of a further major restructuring, involving a gradual winding-down of existing offerings and the launch of four new departments, beginning with an elite tourism and hospitality programme, over the course of almost a decade. Ultimately it was decided, however, that this plan would require an injection of funds impossible to justify on top of an already unserviceable debt. With accrued losses of 2.8 billion yen (*AS*, 23 January 2010), the Eichi Gakuin *gakkō hōjin* made the decision in 2009 to cease accepting new applications to the university from the following year, with a view to closing once all current students had graduated or transferred elsewhere.

It was shortly after this closure announcement that Eichi Gakuin attracted the attention of Laureate Education, a US corporation operating for-profit universities and other institutions in twenty countries across the world. Despite the predicament of Eichi Gakuin, the university represented to Laureate a rare opportunity to gain a foothold in the Japanese educational market while avoiding the capital outlay and regulatory hurdles required to establish a brand-new institution. Laureate entered into negotiations to take over Eichi Gakuin's operations together with all its assets and liabilities. *Gakkō hōjin* cannot technically be bought or sold in the way that ownership of commercial entities changes hands so, for control to be ceded to Laureate, the existing membership of the corporation's governing organs needed to be replaced by Laureate representatives. This transfer of personnel was achieved through a series of eleven meetings, all held in the same place, as cross-appointments were made between the two organizations until all Laureate's nominees were installed.

The new Laureate-controlled Eichi Gakuin drew up yet another reform plan for the university, this time involving the establishment of two new undergraduate departments, in international liberal arts and in healthcare services, together with another name change, to Japan International University. An application for approval of these changes was lodged with the Japanese Ministry of Education in mid-2011. At the same time, around one quarter of the university's land was sold off in order to facilitate the teach-out of the old curriculum and establishment of the new departments without adding to the existing debt.

Laureate's plans for rejuvenating the university were, however, short-lived. In the course of reviewing the application for the establishment of the new departments, the Ministry of Education identified a number of inconsistencies in the paperwork submitted—most notably, the misreporting of entries in the curricula vitae of new academic staff. The Ministry considered the transgressions serious enough to warrant a 2-year ban on any further applications. Laureate was not to be deterred, however, and promptly announced a new plan to establish a department of nursing in 2015—for which the application would be lodged when the ministerial ban expired in 2014. By this stage the university's teaching programme had practically come to an end—just one degree-seeking student was left enrolled at the end of 2013.

Eventually, however, it became clear that the plan was not viable, and in late 2014, the management announced that the university would be closed and the Eichi Gakuin corporation dissolved, citing as the reason 'inability to procure the funds necessary for establishment and continued operation of the new department' (*KS*, 3 November 2014). The closure, however, could not take effect immediately: while almost all students had by this time graduated or transferred elsewhere, there remained one 93-year-old non-degree postgraduate student, for whom the university was officially required to remain open throughout the 2014 academic year (Christian Today 2014). This student's term of enrolment finally ended in March 2015, upon which the university was formally closed and Eichi Gakuin dissolved. The Japanese news media gave considerable attention to this bizarre chain of events, portraying the university as something akin to an extremely unfortunate hospital patient: first the doctors abandon all hope of a cure, then botch one final attempt at resuscitation, and ultimately, after declaring the patient clinically dead, nonetheless refuse to allow the body to be transported to the morgue.

'Schools do not close easily. They close hard.' These were the only words of consolation offered by one potential investor who turned down an eleventh-hour request for an injection of capital to save Eichi Gakuin. The fate of the university's academic and administrative staff became a major topic of discussion as the Eichi Gakuin management team prepared for the closure. In a sector where tenure was almost universal, the prospect of having to look for alternative employment was both new and unattractive. Collective bargaining sessions between management and the university's staff union—set up shortly after the initial closure announcement in 2009—were highly acrimonious, with the union continuing, both before and after the Laureate takeover, to argue that all staff should be retained right until the point of dissolution. Ultimately the union was unsuccessful in advancing its demands, and the university's staff was reduced to an absolute minimum, based on a close reading of the rules regarding how many instructors and administrators were required to service a student enrolment of just one individual. The university closed, but its alumni association continues to operate to this day and regularly holds gatherings on the former university campus, which now houses a number of education, sporting, and public welfare facilities (Sapientia Alumni Association 2018).

The painful death of St Thomas' University cannot be put down merely to poor management, but there are a number of managerial features in this example which were not apparent at MGU: namely reliance on external expertise of variable quality; preparedness to forego traditional academic identity and embark on major transformations at short notice; preparedness to dispose of assets and even cede control over the organization; ineffectual engagement with government regulators; inability to mobilize strengths such as staff loyalty and community support until the institution's fate was sealed. What St Thomas' lacked, in summary, was the kind of inbuilt resilience which institutions such as MGU possessed: resilience deriving from a preference for dealing with problems in-house and with the absolute minimum of disruption to the existing *modus operandi*; resilience built on a network of educational operations extending beyond a single university and allowing for significant cross-subsidies; robust connections with local business interests and strong recognition of academic identity; and above all, an overriding concern with maintaining the integrity of the *gakkō hōjin* corporation. All of these features are most clearly manifested in family-run universities such as MGU.

Patterns of Response

In Chapter 1 we noted the prediction in the early 2000s that 15–40 per cent of private universities would close, which translated roughly to between eighty and 215 institutions based on the 542 which existed in 2004. The case of St Thomas' University, however, has far fewer parallels than that of MGU. In fact, as explained below, only eleven (St Thomas is one) private universities have completely ceased to exist in the post-2000 era. Each of the private universities which ceased to exist has an interesting story of its own, but clearly what is more important is to explain what the remaining 98 per cent did in order to survive. Below, therefore, with the benefit of hindsight, we consider how private universities responded to the crisis of the 2000s and suggest why they seem, on the whole, to have been so successful in doing so.

Disestablishment

Table 5.1 lists the eleven 4-year universities which existed in the early 2000s and no longer do so. In actual fact, in only three of these eleven cases has the university disestablishment led to complete dissolution of the *gakkō hōjin* behind it: St Thomas' University (as outlined at the start of this chapter), Risshikan University, and the University of Creation. The latter two of these were prompted by the discovery of shady accounting practices or other forms of improper activity conducted by the *gakkō hōjin*'s directors.

In the other eight cases, the *gakkō hōjin* has remained viable and continues to operate secondary schools and other affiliated institutions. In some cases *gakkō hōjin* have even used the real estate and facilities of the defunct institution to launch new universities. An example is Junshin Gakuen, the family-run *gakkō hōjin* behind Tohwa University, an engineering college which was forced to close its doors owing to severe under-enrolment in 2011. Junshin Gakuen has continued to operate two junior colleges and a senior high school and, upon the disestablishment of Tohwa University in 2011, promptly opened a new university to train nurses and medical technicians on the same site. Another approach is that of Shukugawa Gakuin, operators of Kobe Shukugawa Gakuin University. In this case, the financial pressures which prompted the university closure appear to have been less connected to under-enrolment and decline in tuition revenue than to losses which Shukugawa Gakuin incurred during the 2008 financial crisis, when a large proportion of its assets were invested in the derivatives market (*SS*, 18 April 2014).[1] The university itself was disestablished in 2015, but Shukugawa

---

[1] Many private universities suffered major investment losses in the financial crisis. For example the Keio Gijuku *gakkō hōjin*, owner of the prestigious Keio University, revealed in 2009 that the market value of its securities investments had dropped 53.5 billion yen (*SD*, 11 July 2009). Keiō recorded 16.9 billion yen of this sum as an appraisal loss in the same fiscal year, leaving the rest as an unrealized (off-the-books) loss in the expectation that the share market would recover (Keio Gijuku 2008). Huge losses were recorded in the same year in other large private universities too, including Komazawa (15.4 billion) and Risshō (14.8 billion) (Okuda 2009). The fact that losses of a scale sufficient to bankrupt many large corporations could be incurred without any major operational impact hints at the very substantial overall fortune amassed by these well-established *gakkō hōjin*.

Table 5.1 Private university disestablishments, 2000–18[2]

Name	Private university established	Private university closed	Current status
1 Risshikan University (*Risshikan Daigaku*)	2000 (conversion from *tandai*; name at time of founding was Hiroshima Aki Women's University)	2003	Disestablished; *gakkō hōjin* dissolved; campus facilities now used by Hiroshima Bunka Gakuen University
2 Fukuoka Social Medical Welfare University (*Fukuoka Iryō Fukushi Daigaku*)	2002 (name was Daiichi University of Welfare until 2004)	2014	Disestablished; *gakkō hōjin* conglomerate (family-run) continues to operate a number of other universities and schools
3 Tohwa University (*Tōwa Daigaku*)	1967	2011	Disestablished; new university (Junshin Gakuen University) opened by same *gakkō hōjin* (family-run) on same campus in 2011
4 University of Creation; Art, Music and Social Work (*Sōzō Gakuen Daigaku*)	2004 (amalgamation of *tandai/senmon gakkō*)	2013	Disestablished; *gakkō hōjin* dissolved by MEXT order
5 Kobe University of Fashion and Design (*Kōbe Fashion Zōkei Daigaku*)	2005 (conversion from *tandai*)	2013	Disestablished; *gakkō hōjin* (Fukutomi Gakuen; family-run) continues to operate Kobe Fashion Institute
6 Mie Chukyo University (*Mie Chūkyō Daigaku*)	1982 (name was Matsuzaka University until 2005)	2013	Disestablished; *gakkō hōjin* group (Umemura Gakuen; family-run) continues to operate another university and secondary school
7 Aichi Shinshiro Otani University (*Aichi Shinshiro Ōtani Daigaku*)	2004 (*kōsetsu min'ei* establishment by Shinshiro City)	2013	Disestablished; *gakkō hōjin* (Owari Gakuen) continues to operate secondary schools

[2] Universities offering full undergraduate degrees. Does not include *tanki daigaku* (2-year junior colleges) or *daigakuin daigaku* (institutions offering graduate school curricula exclusively). Likewise for Tables 5.2 and 5.3.

8	Kobe Shukugawa Gakuin University (*Kōbe Shukugawa Gakuin Daigaku*)	2007	2015	Disestablished; *gakkō hōjin* (Shukugawa Gakuin; family-run) continues to operate *tandai* and several schools
9	St Thomas University (*Sei Tomasu Daigaku*)	1963 (name was Eichi University until 2007)	2015	Disestablished; *gakkō hōjin* dissolved
10	Tokyo Jogakkan College (*Tōkyō Jogakkan Daigaku*)	2002 (conversion from *tandai*)	2017	Disestablished; *gakkō hōjin* (Tokyo Jogakkan) continues to operate primary and secondary schools
11	Fukuoka International University (*Fukuoka Kokusai Daigaku*)	1998 (conversion from *tandai*)	2019	Disestablished; *gakkō hōjin* (Kyushu Gakuen) continues to operate *tandai* and kindergarten

Gakuin entered into an agreement under which the nearby Kobe Yamate University took over the defunct university's students, staff, and curriculum in their entirety to create a new department of tourism studies, leaving Shukugawa Gakuin to continue operating its 2-year junior college, kindergarten, and secondary schools (the latter were then devolved to another *gakkō hōjin*, the family-run Suma Gakuen, in 2019).

It is difficult to draw a clear line between such cases and others where the university has technically avoided disestablishment (and thus does not appear in Table 5.1) but has nonetheless undergone major transformations in order to stay in business: two notable examples of the latter type are Poole Gakuin University (now Momoyama Gakuin University of Education) and Hagi International University (now Shiseikan Hall University; discussed later in this chapter). In cases of both actual disestablishment and near-closure but technical survival, however, the failure of the university has generally not proven fatal to the *gakkō hōjin* as a whole which, as we have seen, like MGU, usually has multiple sources of revenue on which to draw.

Closing a university in Japan is not only extremely unusual but also very difficult, as we saw in the case of St Thomas'. In most cases, MEXT requires universities applying voluntarily for disestablishment (*haishi shinsei*) to remain open until the very last students graduate. This does not always go according to plan: Tokyo Jogakkan College ceased admitting new students in 2012 and was scheduled to close when the final cohort graduated in 2016, but had to stay open for an extra year because a number of students failed to fulfil graduation requirements on schedule (*AS*, 28 February 2016). Occasionally a university has successfully arranged for the remaining students to be taken on by other institutions nearby, as in the previously mentioned case of Kobe Shukugawa Gakuin University. Transfer has also been necessitated where the closure is sudden, such as the fraud scandal which destroyed Risshikan University. In that case, the nearby Kure University (now Hiroshima Bunka Gakuen University) accepted the abandoned students, and now operates on the former Risshikan University campus site.

Only once has the ministry ordered disestablishment of a university while students were still enrolled. This happened in the case of the abovementioned University of Creation: MEXT issued a *gakkō hōjin* dissolution order which came into effect in March 2013, allowing one last cohort of forty-five final year students to graduate, but still leaving 106 students enrolled in more junior years. Authorities worked assiduously to arrange spaces for these students at other institutions, but three of them reportedly still remained unplaced at the time of the dissolution (Okamoto 2016: 55; MEXT 2012).

Merger

A merger may be considered a more attractive alternative to complete closure, allowing some continuity and a degree of certainty for students and staff, even if the distinct institutional identity is lost. It may also, at the same time, allow the new entity to reduce the salaries of staff in the university which has been absorbed. Yet there have been only nine private university mergers in the post-2000 period (Table 5.2). This is an extraordinarily small number given that mergers were widespread among Japan's national universities in the same period, and that waves of mergers had also occurred at other times of major upheaval in Japan's higher education sector both in the pre-war period and upon the establishment of the post-war university system (Hata 2004; see also Chapter 2).[3] Moreover, not all of the mergers in the 2000s took place as an eleventh-hour survival measure: at least three of the institutions that merged (Seibo College, Kyoritsu College of Pharmacy, and Seiwa College) enjoyed healthy enrolments but elected for strategic reasons to join forces with high-profile comprehensive universities. In the case of Seiwa, for example, there were reportedly family links and they also shared a Methodist Christian

---

[3] An interesting parallel can be made here to the United Kingdom, where there were some twenty-seven university mergers between 1997 and 2008 but no closures (Fazackerley and Chant 2009).

Table 5.2 Private university mergers, 2000–18

Name	Private university established	Private university closed	Current status
1 Osaka International University for Women (*Osaka Kokusai Joshi Daigaku*)	1965 (name was Teikoku Women's University until 1992)	2002	Absorbed into Osaka International University (same *gakkō hōjin*; family-run)
2 Kyoritsu College of Pharmacy (*Kyōritsu Yakka Daigaku*)	1949	2008	Absorbed into Keio University; *gakkō hōjin* disestablished
3 Hokkaido Tokai University (*Hokkaidō Tōkai Daigaku*)	1977	2008	Absorbed into Tokai University (same *gakkō hōjin*; family-run)
4 Kyushu Tokai University (*Kyūshū Tōkai Daigaku*)	1973	2008	Absorbed into Tokai University (as above)
5 Seiwa College (*Seiwa Daigaku*)	1964 (name was Seiwa Women's College until 1981)	2013	Absorbed into Kwansei Gakuin University
6 Seibo College (*Seibo Daigaku*)	2004 (conversion from *tandai*)	2014	Absorbed into Sophia University
7 Hamamatsu University (*Hamamatu daigaku*)	1988	2016	Absorbed into Tokoha University (same *gakkō hōjin*; family-run)
8 Fuji Tokoha University (*Fuji Tokoha Daigaku*)	2000 (conversion from *tandai*)	2018	Absorbed into Tokoha University (as above)
9 Hokkaido College of Pharmacy (*Hokkaidō Yakka Daigaku*)	1974	2018	Absorbed into Hokkaido University of Science (same *gakkō hōjin*)

background (*SS*, 20 January 2006). As Ichikawa (2007: 205–6) observes, in the post-1991 deregulated environment, creative restructuring of existing academic offerings is a much more attractive option than the much more complex merger, which also has a number of structural disincentives.[4] Notably, Ichikawa also acknowledges that in many cases founders and operators feel a strong obligation to sustain the independent identity of the university they created rather than risk losing it within a larger entity, even if there is a compelling business case for the latter option. We argue that this drive for preservation is especially strong in family-run universities.

---

[4] The disincentives Ichikawa identifies pertain mostly to the fact that a merger involves at least one of the existing universities being disestablished, requiring the parties to negotiate restrictions on disposal of assets while the university is still operating and requirements to gain the assent of a number of stakeholders (as stipulated by the act of endowment), as well as the approval of the Ministry.

In contrast to the dearth of cases of university mergers, Morozumi (2016) notes the recent trend for strategic 'vertical' mergers of *gakkō hōjin* operating universities with those operating secondary schools, citing examples including the merger of Seiryo Gakuen, the operator of the Sakai Senior High School, into Tanioka Gakuen, a family-run organization incorporating (among other institutions) the Osaka University of Commerce. Those vertical mergers can be a means of increasing revenue for the *gakkō hōjin* which has the university, but they also enable more university enrolments to be sourced through recommendations from the secondary school. This in turn reduces the university's reliance on enrolments through the regular entrance examination system, and thereby averts the need to lower the entrance exam pass marks even if the overall number of applicants drops—a move which would in turn affect the university's *hensachi* ranking.

Conversion to Local Public Status

A further eight private universities were thrown a lifeline by local government and converted into local public universities (see Table 5.3). With much higher subsidies and therefore lower fee levels, they have since found their way out of the crisis of under-enrolment. When the first of these conversions, Kochi University of Technology, was announced in 2008, the news media tended to paint it as setting the mould for what would become a common 'last resort' survival strategy for private universities on the brink of bankruptcy (see, for example, *AS*, 22 February 2008). In fact these conversions were actually something of a natural transition for institutions whose establishment had been funded by local governments under the publicly established, privately run (*kōsetsu min'ei*) model (cf. Chapter 2) in the first place. Local governments often chose this model either because they did not have the resources or know-how to run the universities themselves or because the local public university structure at that time did not provide sufficient scope for independent operation. The rollout of a quasi-corporate public university structure, similar to that of national universities, has to some extent made the 'private' element redundant.

Establishment of New Markets

If so few private universities actually closed, what did the rest of them do? The short answer is that the majority did what MGU did: downsized, adjusted their

Table 5.3 Private university conversions, 2000–18

	Name	Private university established	Private university closed	Current status
1	Kochi University of Technology (*Kōchi Kōka Daigaku*)	1997 (*kōsetsu min'ei* establishment by Kochi Prefecture)	2009	Converted to local public university; continues to operate
2	Shizuoka University of Art and Culture (*Shizuoka Bunka Geijutsu Daigaku*)	2000 (*kōsetsu min'ei* establishment by Shizuoka Prefecture)	2010	Converted to local public university; continues to operate
3	Meio University (*Meiō Daigaku*)	1994 (*kōsetsu min'ei* establishment by Okinawa Prefecture and several municipalities)	2010	Converted to local public university; continues to operate
4	Nagaoka Institute of Design (*Nagaoka Zōkei Daigaku*)	1994 (*kōsetsu min'ei* establishment by Nagaoka City)	2014	Converted to local public university; continues to operate
5	Tottori University of Environmental Studies (*Tottori Kankyō Daigaku*)	2001 (*kōsetsu min'ei* establishment by Tottori Prefecture and Tottori City)	2012	Converted to local public university; continues to operate
6	Seibi University (*Seibi Daigaku*)	2000 (conversion from *tandai*; university named Kyoto Sosei University until 2010)	2016	Converted to local public university; continues to operate (as The University of Fukuchiyama)
7	Tokyo University of Science, Yamaguchi (*Yamaguchi Tōkyō Rika Daigaku*)	1995	2016	Converted to local public university; continues to operate (as Sanyo-Onoda City University)
8	Nagano University (*Nagano Daigaku*)	1966 (*kōsetsu min'ei* establishment by Shioda Town, Nagano; university named Honshū University until 1974)	2017	Converted to local public university; continues to operate

offerings, and dug deeper into the shrinking market of school leavers. We examine these moves in some detail below, but it is important first to remind ourselves that this was not at all what universities were predicted to do in response to the declining number of school leavers.

As discussed in Chapter 1, it was assumed that the private university sector would be forced eventually to shift some of its attention to different demographic sectors and explore more creative business models. Ideas commonly put forward included the exploitation of promising alternative student markets such as working adults, distance learners, and international students, as well as pursuing more partnerships with industry to boost research income. Approaches such as these had, after all, enabled universities in the US and UK to ride out major demographic changes in the 1970s and 1980s. Meanwhile, deregulation in the early 2000s opened up possibilities for developing new profession-specific postgraduate degrees and using the *kabushiki kaisha* (joint-stock company) business structure to pursue a more entrepreneurial approach to university management. It is remarkable how little progress was made towards these expected methods of reinvention.

In 2018, the traditional *gakkō hōjin* (educational corporation) is still the default operating structure for private universities; student fees are still the main source of revenue; classroom-based teaching of secondary school leavers is still the dominant educational model. The breakdown of private university revenue has remained remarkably stable since 2000: between 75 and 80 per cent from student fees, approximately 10 per cent from public subsidies, and the rest a combination of sources including asset management, donations, and business income. The latter, for which such high hopes were held, remains at around 2 per cent—almost unchanged since the 1990s (PMAC 2018c).

Research income is on the rise, but the private university sector still lags far behind national universities in this area, in terms of both industry research contracts (15.3 billion vs 44.1 billion yen in 2016; MEXT 2018e) and the *kakenhi* system of government research grants (12.3 billion vs 40.4 billion yen in new grants awarded in 2017; MEXT 2017d). Moreover, deregulation has failed to attract new players to the sector from the business world. Only eight *kabushiki kaisha* universities were ever established and only four remain in operation today; there have been no new such establishments since 2007.

It is worth looking a little more closely at some areas of the student market which did promise particular hope in the 2000s: postgraduate and continuing education, and international education. The expansion of postgraduate education was one of the major reform themes, with key initiatives including the establishment of law schools (see Chapter 4) and other professional degrees and a re-vamping of doctoral education. Meanwhile, international student intake was promoted strongly through the flagship 100,000 students' plan (1983–) and 300,000 students' plan (2008–) and associated initiatives for campus internationalization. Government support was not the only driver in these areas: there was expected to be growing demand from employers for highly qualified talent and continuing university-based training, while the dramatic rise in student mobility across the globe, and within Asia especially, promised new international demand for Japanese university education (Breaden 2018; Ota 2014).

None of these markets has been expanded to the extent anticipated. The vast majority of Japan's university students are still enrolled in undergraduate programmes—in 2018, 89 per cent overall and more than 95 per cent of those in the private sector (MEXT 2018a)—and the average age of entrants to these programmes is still 18 years old: the lowest of any OECD country (OECD 2018b). There was a rise in postgraduate enrolments (from 205,311 students in 2000 to 272,566 in 2011) following the reforms in the early 2000s, but numbers dropped away again to just over 254,000 in 2018 (MEXT 2018a). By far the largest proportion of postgraduate enrolments are in engineering (41 per cent) at Master's level and medicine/dentistry (29.1 per cent) at doctoral level; the numbers are far lower for the humanities (6.3 per cent at Master's level; 7.3 per cent at doctoral) and social sciences (10.0 per cent and 7.9 per cent) respectively, which is where most offerings in the non-elite private sector are located (MEXT 2018a).

Moreover, the average age of students commencing postgraduate degrees is also the lowest in the OECD (OECD 2018b), suggesting that the increased popularity of postgraduate education does not reflect the exploitation of a significantly new demographic sector. Only 12 per cent of enrolees in Master's degrees are classified as *shakaijin* or working adults (MEXT 2018a), and there has been an almost universal failure to extend undergraduate degrees to different age groups, with only 2.4 per cent of new undergraduate enrolees in 2018 being aged 21 or over and only 0.6 per cent over the age of 24 (MEXT 2018a).

Two other new markets which came to the rescue of US universities when they faced demographic pressures in the 1970s (Kelly 1999), part-time students and mature students, have rarely been mentioned in the context of Japanese universities. It is hard to imagine how Japanese students could study part-time when on average full-time students are already working outside the university for over 14 hours a week (Inaba 2016: 82). The long-term view of employment which still prevails in most Japanese organizations makes taking a career break for those in full-time jobs unattractive and such practices are not encouraged by most companies which prefer to undertake career development in-house. Those in part-time jobs or not in the job market at all, such as housewives, have a range of attractive options, such as Asahi Cultural Centres, foreign language conversation schools, and a bewildering array of institutes offering certifications in everything from financial planning to pet psychology. These options are often much cheaper and more flexible than taking a full university degree, which is, in any case, unlikely to lead to enhanced employment opportunities because employers still prefer to employ graduates straight from university (*shinsotsu ikkatsu saiyō*) who they can train most easily in their own company culture.

Greater, but similarly qualified, success has been achieved in promoting the number of international students. The vast majority of international university students are self-funded rather than government-sponsored, and most (83 per cent of undergraduates) are enrolled in private institutions, suggesting at least a partial opening up of private higher education to the burgeoning global market of internationally mobile, fee-paying students. Some universities, mostly small-scale and low-ranked, have successfully established international student intake as a viable substitute for declining domestic enrolments. Japan University of Economics, for example, has more than 70 per cent international students and does not even apply for private university subsidies from the government.[5] While the overall number of international students in Japan grew from around 64,000 to nearly 300,000 between 2000 and 2018, much of this growth was in the non-university sector, primarily Japanese language institutes and vocational schools (JASSO 2019). At undergraduate level the overall increase was from around 28,000 to 85,000, meaning that international students still constitute only around 5 per cent of all university students in Japan.[6] One-third of private universities still have no international students at all.

In terms of internationalization, government support has been focused over-whelmingly on the elite institutions, supported by flagship funding schemes such as Global 30 and the Top Global University project, which are designed to raise the standing of Japanese higher education internationally and to aid in the cultivation of elite talent (Breaden 2018). The generation of fee revenue, how-ever, has seldom been a primary concern. As Huang and Horiuchi (2019: 14) observe, 'the internationalization of Japan's universities is not primarily moti-vated by the market, but exhibits strong non-commercial characteristics and stresses more its academic and cultural values, and its global public

---

[5] Of the 4,184 students at Japan University of Economics in 2017, 2,983 (71.3 per cent) were international (PMAC 2019c; JASSO 2019). This is significantly higher than the number one university, Ritsumeikan Asia Pacific University (53.4 per cent) in the 2018 *Times Higher Education* ranking of Japanese universities by proportion of international students. Presumably this omission is attributable to Japan University of Economics' failure to supply data to the ranking's publishers. The university is part of the family-run Tsuzuki Gakuen Group.

[6] While they constitute only 3 per cent of undergraduates, they are much more significant in Japan's still small postgraduate sector, where they currently account for around 18 per cent of all students.

goods.' In this climate, private universities which have developed a reliance on international students as an alternative revenue source are inevitably viewed with some suspicion. Such reliance is undoubtedly risky owing to the backlash if there is any hint that the university is providing a gateway for foreign nationals seeking illegitimate entry to Japan's labour market (so-called *dekasegi ryūgakusei*). A particularly sensational case is that of Tokyo University of Social Welfare, which in early 2019 was found to have lost track of more than 1,600 of its international students over the past 3 years (*JT*, 11 June 2019). It became clear that the university had been pursuing a business model based on the enrolment of large numbers of fee-paying, non-degree-seeking international students with minimal admission requirements and scant concern for academic progress (NHK, 2019). The reputational fallout of such highly publicized cases cannot be underestimated. An earlier example was that of Hagi International University which, struggling to attract domestic students to its campus in rural Yamaguchi prefecture, developed a heavy reliance on students from mainland China. When it became clear that many of the students were off working in the cities rather than studying, the immigration authorities took the unprecedented step of denying visas to all of the university's prospective students from China in 2003. The university became synonymous with an unsavoury commercialism in international education, and the fallout quickly became apparent in its enrolments: it managed to attract only twenty-two first-year students in 2004, forty-two in 2005, and reportedly just three in 2006 (*JT*, 21 June 2005; *YS*, 1 February 2007).[7]

In addition to these risks, cultural, linguistic, and regulatory impediments make the intake of international students a labour-intensive enterprise, and—unlike many other major destination countries—one which is not compensated by higher fee revenue. Japanese universities across the board offer fee reductions (*jugyōryō genmen*) to attract international students, and the largest discounts are among universities in rural and regional areas which also have

---

[7] Hagi (which later operated under the name of Yamaguchi University of Human Welfare and Culture) persisted with its focus on international students nonetheless, establishing 'satellite campuses' in Hiroshima and Tokyo to enable students to pursue casual work opportunities alongside their studies. These satellites soon outgrew the university's main campus in Hagi (numbers in May 2012 were 171 at the Hagi campus, 606 in Tokyo, and forty-three in Hiroshima), prompting a renewed tightening of visa screenings as well as admonitions from MEXT over the negative impact on educational quality. The high degree of negative publicity Hagi received was undoubtedly linked to an equally highly publicized case earlier the 2000s in which Sakata Junior College, a small private institution in Yamagata prefecture, was discovered to have been knowingly enrolling international students who had no intention of studying and instead were engaged in full-time employment in Tokyo. Sakata's operators had been forced to suspend the college's operations in 2002, filed for bankruptcy in 2003, and in 2004 were issued a dissolution order by MEXT.

the greatest difficulty attracting domestic enrolments. International students attending private universities in rural/regional areas, for example, on average pay only 73 per cent of the standard fee applied to their domestic counterparts (Sato 2018: 185). For these reasons, it is difficult to see international student intake becoming a widespread solution to the problem of a contracting domestic market.

Downsizing, Relocation, Rebranding

While it is still anathema for many in the higher education sector to consider it a business, it seems disingenuous not to do so, perhaps particularly in the case of private universities. The most widespread and, in general, successful changes made by universities as student applications plummeted in the early 2000s involved relatively minor adjustments to their business models within existing institutional parameters. In some cases, such as St Thomas' University, outside consultants were brought in, not always successfully, to advise on these reforms. Advice seems to have varied hugely, but a number of trends can be identified in the responses of the institutions in practice.

Two of the most consistent responses were the review of fees and the casualization of the academic staff. The former is reflected in changing average fee levels, which have continued to rise overall, but at significantly lower rates. The average annual private university tuition fee rose 46 per cent in the decade from 1986 to 1995, 12 per cent from 1996 to 2005, and under 4 per cent from 2006 to 2015 (MEXT 2017e).The trend towards increasing the number of casual staff is observable in the ratio of non-full-time (*kenmu*) academic staff in private universities, which grew from less than half in the early 1990s to over 57 per cent by 2008 (MEXT 2018a). The practice of hiring senior (and expensive) faculty who had retired from national universities seems to have dried up to such an extent that some national universities were forced to increase their retirement age for academic faculty. This had been coming steadily down in the previous decade as academics took up often more lucrative posts in the private sector. The number of faculty aged 65 and over in national universities in 2016 was almost triple that of 2004 (MEXT 2018f).

While in many ways the private university sector looks very much the same as it did two decades ago, one major change is that the universities themselves have changed size. The 478 private 4-year universities in Japan in 2000 had just over 2 million students and the average student population was just over

4,200; the 597 private universities in 2010 had 2.1 million students in total with an population of just over 3,500. This 15 per cent drop in average size was not spread equally across all the institutions.

A phenomenon which was recognized in the early 2000s was that institutions which had higher *hensachi* entrance scores found their application rates going up every year after 1992 as the number of school leavers went down. The common explanation for this counter-intuitive trend was that applicants who failed, in any year after 1992, to get into as high-ranking a university as they had hoped could tell themselves that there would be fewer school leavers in the following year and it would be worth trying again. Unfortunately for them, many others had exactly the same thought and hence the number of applications to such institutions increased rather than decreased (*AS*, 22 February 2007).[8] The net effect was that the average number of applications that students made went up (from 4.56 in 2000 to 5.1 in 2007) at a time when this might have been expected to fall (*YS*, 19 January 2008). Waseda University, for example, had more applications in 2018 than it did in the year 2000 (Yoyogi Seminar 2018). At the other end of the scale, the supplementary education industry created a new classification of 'border free' (BF) to denote under-enrolled universities to which a meaningful pass/fail borderline *hensachi* could not even be assigned.

A reduction in the total size of an institution was often accompanied, as we saw in the case of MGU, by a reduction in official enrolment quotas (*teiin*) as applications dropped rapidly in the early 2000s. This was partly to do with the fear that the impact of under-enrolment would have on reputation. Under-enrolled universities could not afford to be selective in their entrance examinations for risk of further depleting their enrolments; they would drop even lower in the rankings based on *hensachi*, which in turn would affect their capacity to attract new applications. When the implosion scenario entered public discourse in the late 1990s, under-enrolment became popularly associated not only with financial instability but also with low educational standards, making it very difficult for such universities to present themselves to prospective students as either attractive or secure options.

---

[8] A detailed analysis by the *Sunday Mainichi* (14 December 2003) calculated that the borderline point was a *hensachi* of 55: departments with lower *hensachi* entrance scores in the early 1990s saw a big drop in applications; those around the 55 point saw applications remain steady; those with *hensachi* scores considerably higher saw rises in applications. In 2007, for example, almost half of applications to all 559 private universities (3,020,000) were to one of the twenty-three 'strongest' universities (1,440,000) (*YS*, 20 January 2008).

The scant resources available to severely under-enrolled universities to implement any kind of change were further diminished by the rules which MEXT attached to the disbursement of private university subsidies. Universities with enrolments under 90 per cent of capacity were subject to cuts in their subsidy, which increased in proportion with the degree of under-enrolment to a point where, at 50 per cent of capacity, the subsidies were cancelled entirely (MEXT 2018g).[9] By withholding full support for under-enrolled universities, MEXT institutionalized the notion that such universities were also in more general terms substandard and unworthy of public support, contributing further to the reputational downward spiral. Universities found that the only way out was to apply for a reduction in official enrolment quota. The reduction explains in part the apparent paradox of why the proportion of under-enrolled universities is much lower in 2018 than in 2008 while the overall revenue/expenditure balance is slightly worse (see Table 5.4).

Another important variable has been location. Many Japanese universities were forced to move to the suburbs in the 1960s due to government legislation which prevented them from setting up in the largest urban conurbations around Tokyo, Osaka, and Nagoya because of the rapid growth in population that Japan was then experiencing. This restriction was only lifted in 2002 as population pressure in these areas eased and many of the larger universities invested heavily in relocating back to the urban areas. The government

Table 5.4 Under-enrolment and financial hardship in private universities[10]

Year	1998	2008	2018
Number of universities surveyed	439	565	582
Universities at over 100% of quota	404 (92.0%)	299 (52.9%)	372 (63.9%)
Universities at 80–100% of quota	26 (5.9%)	112 (19.8%)	145 (24.9%)
Universities at 50–79% of quota	8 (1.8%)	125 (22.1%)	54 (9.3%)
Universities at less than 50% of quota	1 (0.2%)	29 (5.1%)	11 (1.9%)
Overall operating revenue/expenditure balance	+19%	+5%	+4%
Percentage of universities with negative balance	11%	32%	30%

Sources: MEXT 2018b and PMAC 2018a (enrolment data); MEXT 2015, MEXT 2018b, PMAC 2018c (revenue/expenditure).

[9] The subsidy reduction rates applied to under-enrolled universities were raised further in 2018 (Shinken Ad 2018).
[10] Revenue/expenditure figures are for 2017 (latest available). When compiling these figures, MEXT excluded universities no longer taking applicants, those established by private companies, and those offering only distance education or postgraduate courses.

allocated quota for university places in Tokyo, for example, increased by 10 per cent between 2000 and 2009.

Relocations in some cases brought together all students on the same campus, where previously they had been divided between an urban and a suburban campus. As we saw in the case of MGU, location in urban areas was particularly important for students because it helped with commuting to their part-time jobs. Since, as we have seen, on average students in Japanese universities work over 14 hours a week in part-time jobs, this was not a trivial issue. A comparison of universities in the Nagoya area, all specializing in economics and business studies, suggests that relocating in the early 2000s led to a significant improvement in the average *hensachi* score: Nagoya Gakuin, Aichi University, and Aichi Gakuin University (which all relocated) increased their average *hensachi* by +8, +4, and +4 between 2004 and 2013 while Nagoya University of Economics, Nagoya University of Commerce and Business, and Meijo University (which did not relocate) increased by +2, +1, and, in the final case, decreased by –1 over the same period (Inaba 2016: 73).[11]

While universities changed size and location in response to the problem of enrolment, so they also changed what they offered in terms of courses to their students. Kinmonth (2005: 112) pointed out the surge in popularity in courses with certain buzzwords in the early 2000s, in particular *jōhōka shakai* (information society), *kokusaika* (internationalization), *kankyō* (environment), *fukushi* (welfare), and *ningen kagaku* (studies of the human condition). While in some cases these were genuinely new courses, in other cases it was simply tweaking of a course which already existed in order to make it look more attractive. In Chapter 2 we explained that the diversification of curricular offerings was prompted by the relaxation of curricular establishment standards in 1991 and the partial replacement of ministerial approval requirements

---

[11] A summary of findings from this survey was published just as this book was going to press as Inaba (2020). This re-urbanization has, however, made it increasingly more difficult for students from rural areas to enter university than their city-dwelling counterparts. In 2016 there was a gap of some 33 percentage points between the highest university entrance rate, for students completing secondary education in the Tokyo metropolis (64 per cent), and the lowest, for those from the rural prefecture of Kagoshima (31 per cent); this gap had widened from 25 points a decade earlier (MEXT 2017f: 8). Tokyo and Kyoto have around twice the number of university places as they have high school graduates, while some rural prefectures such has Wakayama and Nagano have less than 40 per cent (Cabinet Office 2017). Improving access to university education outside the major urban centres is becoming an even more pressing issue as students increasingly prefer close-to-home options owing to the prohibitive cost of living away from the family home (NFUCA 2017). MEXT's response is limited at this stage to containment measures: the imposition of stricter penalties on over-capacity enrolment at larger universities—which are typically located in major urban centres—and, in 2018, the institution of a 'provisional' moratorium on both the establishment of new faculties and any increase of enrolment capacity in existing universities for central Tokyo (23 Wards) area (MEXT 2018g). It is difficult to envisage these measures actually producing a levelling-out of access to university education across the urban–rural divide.

with a simpler system of reporting in the early 2000s. Inaba (2016: 62) cites a Kawaijuku survey which logged the names of departments and faculties of Japanese universities based on the School Basic Survey run by MEXT. The range of names of departments and faculties, which had been very stable before the 1990s, increased rapidly thereafter: ninety-seven in 1990, 145 in 1995, 235 in 2000, 360 in 2005, 435 in 2010, and 464 in 2015.

As we have seen in the case of MGU, private universities also improved their position by becoming more student-centred. They responded to the employment demands of their core market of undergraduate students by introducing more practical training alongside academic study. Much of this was in the form of extra-curricular activities, career support, internships, traineeships, and the orchestration of 'double school' arrangements with vocational training colleges[12]—all of which, like many of the renaming exercises noted above, could be achieved economically and without the need for major changes in staffing. The net effect was that these students, many of whom were first-generation students in their families, could get the university degree which their parents had always dreamed for them (and high school career counsellors unanimously pushed) but also some practical skills which made them more employable as the labour market contracted. Overall, the increased investment in student support in multiple forms has been one of the most conspicuous developments on university campuses over the past decade.

This heightened sensitivity to student needs has also, in combination with new statutory obligations regarding organized educational improvement activities,[13] fostered a stronger concern with what goes on in university classrooms. MEXT surveys present impressive evidence of improvement. As of 2016, 79 per cent of universities operated transition programmes for first-year undergraduate students, 85 per cent had mechanisms for ascertaining

---

[12] The term 'double school' refers to students' concurrent attendance both at university and at least one other type of educational institution, typically for the purpose of preparing for examinations leading to vocation-specific licences and certifications in fields such as accountancy, para-legal occupations, and the public service. Reliable figures on the proportion of students in such arrangements are limited, but one government-commissioned survey in 2005 found that it was more than 20 per cent among students in undergraduate social science programmes (but less than 5 percent for those in medical and agricultural sciences) (BERD 2005: 44–5). Many private universities report significantly higher rates than these and proactively advertise an extensive menu of opportunities to 'obtain extra qualifications' (*shikaku shutoku*) as an enticement for prospective students. A 2016 survey found that 60.1 per cent of graduates of 4-year undergraduate programmes (of a sample size of 4,135) held some form of occupational licence or other third-party certification (Morikawa 2017).

[13] The 1998 University Council report on *Vision for Universities in the 21st Century* recommended the inclusion of 'research and training on educational content and methods' as a mandatory activity for universities, and this was actioned in a 1999 revision of the standards for university establishment and in the evaluation standards applied by university accreditation agencies from 2004.

students' study habits and preferences, virtually all operated 'faculty development' (FD) programmes, and 87 per cent had dedicated FD centres of the type that MGU established in the late 2000s (MEXT n.d.c). The introduction of learning tools such as online learning management systems (53 per cent) and learning portfolios (34 per cent) was also on the rise. At the start of the 2000s, only 50 per cent of universities conducted FD activities of any type; one-third did not survey their students about their learning experiences; some did not even publish a syllabus (MEXT n.d.c). While it may be argued that such standardization of teaching formats and methods compromises teacher autonomy, and while enthusiasm for engaging in reform activities varies greatly at individual level,[14] these changes have surely gone some way toward addressing the conventional lack of emphasis on teaching and the image, discussed in Chapter 1, of university as a mere hiatus between school and adult life. An answer to the question of what exactly constitutes a distinctively 'Japanese' university learning experience, however, remains elusive.

Continuity in the Features of Private University Education

If the millennial predictions of a large-scale implosion of the private university sector were so off the mark, what of the other predictions which stemmed from them?

De-valuing of University Credentials?

One predicted outcome of the era when anyone could find a university place (*zennyū jidai*) was that a university degree would come to mean little in the job market. To date, there is a dearth of solid evidence that this is the case. The growth in participation rates suggests that more students than ever perceive some value in a university education; it is also clear that many are prepared to take out loans to attend university. The question, then, is why this demand persists.

There are several ways of answering the question. One is to consider the comparative economic benefit of a university degree—what sociologists sometimes call the 'college premium'. The latest available OECD data on relative

---

[14] Arimoto (2005) gives a good overview of faculty development programmes in the early 2000s. It was commonly joked that most Japanese academics still recognized the acronym FD only in relation to the floppy disks they used in their computers.

earnings by educational attainment (OECD 2018b) shows that in Japan there is a difference in earnings of around 50 per cent between those who are tertiary educated and those who are not. While slightly below the OECD average, this is still a fairly clear endorsement of the value of university credentials. More finely grained studies produced within Japan have similar findings, while also showing little evidence of change over time in the value of a university-level degree compared to other types of educational credential, or in hierarchy of value *within* the university sector. Average wage levels are still much higher for those holding university degrees than any other type of credentials, as are lifetime earnings (JILPT 2018), and '[t]here is no clear evidence that the college premium substantially reduced due to the increase in college-educated people' (Hannum et al. 2019: 8.9). If anything, the gap between university graduates and others may have grown over time, both in terms of earnings and likelihood of regular (*seiki*) employment (He and Kobayashi 2015), suggesting that a university degree has proven a relatively sound insurance against the growing casualization of the Japanese workforce. The close nexus between type of credential and occupational category remains: in other words, university graduates are engaged in occupations different from those with other educational credentials.[15] Not unexpectedly, there is also evidence of continued differentiated outcomes *within* the university sector, with graduates of the most competitive universities recording the highest employment rates in large companies and therefore the highest average salaries (Araki et al. 2015; Nakamuro and Inui 2013).

The brief treatment above clearly overlooks a great many nuances in the data, but all the observations made are repeatedly confirmed in scholarship on educational credentials and employment in Japan, most recently (at the time of writing) in a study by Yamamoto (2019), which reaffirms the persistence of the traditional credential structure which separates university graduates from others and which in turn drives competition for admission to highly prestigious universities. In broad terms at least, it seems safe to endorse

---

[15] The nexus of credential and occupation is best demonstrated by a somewhat counter-intuitive example. There have been a number of high-profile cases in Japan of employees being dismissed for falsifying their educational credentials. The falsification in these cases, however, is not the customary inflation of credentials: rather, it is the under-statement thereof. In November 2006, thirteen cooks employed in the municipal school lunch programme operated by the city of Kobe were dismissed for having given their educational background as 'high school graduate' when in fact they had completed university degrees (*AE*, 27 November 2006). A similar case occurred with an over-qualified bus driver in 2004, and more famously back in 1976, when a worker was sacked from his job on the production line of the national mint for having an associate degree from a 2-year junior college. He sued his former employer for wrongful dismissal, claiming contravention of the constitutional principle of freedom of occupational choice, but lost when the Tokyo District Court declared that an employer was allowed to specify what type of educational credential was most appropriate for the job.

the conventional wisdom that having a university degree is an advantage, and that having one from a top university is even better. Surveys of high school students also reliably confirm the strong preference for university as opposed to other post-secondary study options. A 2018 survey, for example, found that more than 80 per cent of senior high school students hoped to go on to university studies (DISCO Corporation 2018).

This situation is not necessarily, however, an affirmation of the positive value of university credentials. Indeed, it is possible to conjecture that demand for such credentials rises in inverse proportion to their value in the labour market. Under the conditions of mass participation, seeking a university education may be less about gaining a competitive edge than it is a bare minimum choice to guarantee survival in a market already flooded by university graduates. This is the idea of higher education as a 'defensive necessity' or 'hedge against downward mobility' (Marginson 2016); a 'self-perpetuating dynamic' in which the growing cost of not having a university degree justifies greater expenditure on obtaining one (Wright and Horta 2018: 21). It is especially easy to envisage this dynamic in a society like Japan where the rise in university participation rate has been accompanied by economic stagnation and a marked diminishment of job security.

One outcome, theoretically, is a supply of university-educated workers out of proportion with the actual demand for skills in the workplace. This is borne out by at least one recent study, which found that almost 50 per cent of graduates in Japan—the highest of any of the twenty-one countries surveyed—are 'underemployed' in the sense of having educational qualifications in excess of the requirements of their jobs (Green and Henseke 2016). Another outcome as university entrance becomes more of a hedging strategy than a positive step toward upward mobility is a loss of faith among students and parents. Galan (2018: 41–4) cites surveys showing that up to 97 per cent of parents do not believe that a university degree guarantees a stable future, and refers to growth in dropout and leave of absence rates—especially high at low-ranked private universities—as evidence of increasing loss of faith in the promise of university education.

Collapse of Competitive Admission System and Selectivity-based Hierarchy?

The system of applicants submitting to complex and gruelling entrance examinations to prove their worthiness for a university education, and of universities using such examinations rigorously to sift through the hordes of school leavers clamouring for admission, is manifestly untenable in the *zennyū* era. Predictions were that it would only be those top-end institutions, in which applicants continue to outweigh places available, that the logic of the entrance exam system could remain intact. The bulk of the private university sector, not part of this elite stratum, would instead turn to other means of enticing candidates into its depopulated classrooms.

The demise of the entrance exam has, however, been remarkably drawn-out in both practical and ideological terms. Practically speaking, the use of written entrance exams has certainly declined. Enrolments through non-traditional admission methods such as direct recommendations from secondary schools (*suisen*) and interview- and essay-based 'AO' (Admissions Office) screenings accounted for around 51 per cent of all private university enrolments in 2017 (MEXT 2017c), up from 33 per cent two decades earlier. The percentage is higher in under-enrolled universities: as much as 80 percent for those only enrolling half their capacity or lower (Ogawa 2017: 23).

The link between the proportional decline in traditional exams and falling enrolments is, however, far from clear. The largest decline in traditional exam use in private university admissions actually occurred in the late 1990s—from 67 per cent in 1997 to 53 per cent in 2004 (Obunsha Educational Information Center 2018)—rather than in the period thereafter when under-enrolment became a widespread problem. The fact remains that almost half of all private university entrants still take traditional entrance exams—and such exams are offered even by those universities with effectively no need to select between candidates. Regardless of the number of candidates sitting their exams, universities maintain the same orthodox processes and rituals in the setting and marking of exams as observed in the case of MGU in the early 2000s (Chapter 3). These hallmarks of the traditional system are replicated in the context of non-traditional admissions which, while not requiring candidates to sit a conventional written exam, are nonetheless styled as 'entrance examinations' (*nyūgaku shiken*) and conducted with the same procedural rigour.

As discussed in the case of MGU, the adherence to the entrance exam model says a great deal about the model's importance to the fundamental ideas about education in Japan. It is well known in Japanese society that the university entrance exam is far from a perfect means either of evaluating substantive knowledge and skills or ensuring equitable access, but it is equally widely accepted that the exam is the most feasible method of meritocratic selection and an important rite of passage for young Japanese. Secondary schools continue to invest considerable resources in advising their students on university applications and exam strategy, and to measure their own institutional performance on the basis of their students' entrance exam success. Supplementary education schools and other supplementary education providers do the same, although motivated obviously by commercial gain.

The government too remains committed to the primacy of traditional entrance exams. MEXT's official advice to universities is that enrolments through non-traditional admissions should not exceed 50 per cent of overall enrolment capacity. At the time of writing, changes were being proposed to the National Center Test for University Admissions (*centre shiken*)—the centrally administered written exam used for entrance to national universities and also indirectly by many private universities in addition to their in-house exams—to enable better assessment of skills such as reasoning and expression, as well as requiring universities to employ other forms of assessment such as interviews and project portfolios in combination with the exam results (MEXT n.d.b). These reforms face strong opposition from universities who argue that they will confuse students and, even if they are introduced, while they would mean significant changes to the *format* of the university admission process, they would not affect the *process* of exam-taking itself.

The durability of the entrance exam is connected to the persistence of the *hensachi* as the primary measure of university quality and the basis for decision-making regarding post-secondary education. As noted earlier, the importance of selecting a 'good' university has grown rather than diminished in the *zennyū* era, and *hensachi* rankings are thus as widely used as ever. It is true that publishers and commercial education providers have moved to furnish the increasingly discerning market with a variety of alternative sources of information on university quality. Some of those launched in the late 1990s and early 2000s were mentioned in Chapter 1; there are also more recent additions, such as the *Nikkei Business* magazine's University Brand Ranking, launched in 2009. World university rankings have also become highly visible, and *Times Higher Education* even began publishing a Japan-specific version of its rankings in 2017 (Benesse Corporation n.d.). All of these alternative measures are undoubtedly useful reference points for educational consumers, and for universities when conducting self-assessments and marketing their offerings to prospective students. None however offers the same simplicity, universal coverage, and statistical objectivity as the *hensachi* system. Nor do they have the potential to become institutionalized in the same way: they are at best supplementary material, while *hensachi* has become an intrinsic part of the system of university entrance.

On the whole, we can conclude that the key features of the Japanese university system have remained largely intact throughout the period of contraction in the 1990s and 2000s: features such as a well-defined hierarchy of institutions indexed to selectivity and a high reliance on school leavers are still hallmarks of Japanese higher education. Indeed, in a recent precis of the features of Japan's higher education system in comparative context, Ulrich Teichler (2019) makes note not only of these but also many of the other points which were listed in Chapter 1 of this book as being well-established characteristics of Japanese universities back in 1992, including research-oriented professional identities, academic inbreeding, emphasis on STEM over humanities/social sciences, and low levels of international mobility of students and staff. The same observations are perennial features of the OECD's country reports on education in Japan (OECD n.d.). The anticipated 'big bang' in Japanese higher education has turned out to be more of a subdued thud.

Explaining the Resilience of Japan's Private Universities

How is it possible that the predictions outlined in Chapter 1 could have been so far from the mark with the benefit of hindsight in 2018? These were accounts written by those who knew the higher education field well and clearly understood the pressures the private universities were likely to face and how they might respond to them. To be fair, the data did seem unambiguous. Supply outstripped demand; there were too many institutions of higher education with a capacity which would considerably outnumber students willing to take them up, and all this in a system which demanded a very large amount of private investment and which was not generally perceived as a 'public good' (Huang and Horiuchi 2019). Indeed, the neoliberal ethos—praised by an OECD review—of the Japanese government seemed to encourage a system which would cause university closures.

There appear to be a number of key variables which were not properly considered in the accounts we saw in Chapter 1. The role of government turned out to be more ambiguous than anticipated and interest groups which represented the private universities were more nimble than expected. Changes in other parts of the higher education landscape, notably a migration of students from 2-year junior colleges to universities, contributed to rising demand for university education even as the 18-year-old population fell. The private universities themselves were much more proactive in their response than the doomsday scenarios predicted: universities not only diversified and changed their offerings, but in many cases they changed their shape and size very considerably. Perhaps least understood of all was the fact that many of these institutions were much better prepared for the *zennyū* shock in the early 2010s than commentators realized: they had savings from the golden years, often in the form of land, which they could realize in a crisis. They also enjoyed political capital in the local communities which did not want to see them disappear. One of their greatest sources of resilience, however, came from the *gakkō hōjin* structure which allowed for cross-subsidies (in terms of finance, personnel, and knowledge) from other education-related activities.

One factor which was never discussed in the literature of the early 2000s was the family business aspect of many of the private universities. Our argument is that it was this which in part helped ensure the survival of many of the institutions both because the university was often the flagship in a web of family-owned institutions (*dōzoku keiei gakkō hōjin*) and for it to fail would put in jeopardy all the other linked institutions, but also because the family identity and sense of history was so bound up with the maintenance of these institutions. We will look at all these points in more detail below.

Changing Structure of Demand for University Education

There is a certain extent to which the claim that the number of universities and students in Japan actually increased rather than declined in 15 years between 2003 and 2018 is a semantic one. All the examples given in Tables 5.1, 5.2, and 5.3 exclude 2-year junior colleges (*tanki daigaku*), which have experienced a precipitous decline since the early 1990s. The overall number of students in junior colleges in 1995 was 499,000 (at 596 institutions), 219,000 (at 488 institutions) in 2005, and 133,000 (at 346 institutions) in 2015. The average student population of each junior college shrunk from around 840 to around 449 to around 384 over the same 20-year period. As noted in Chapter 2, this decline mainly reflects the breaking down of the traditional gender divide in tertiary education. Put simply, female school leavers who would previously have enrolled in a junior college have increasingly chosen instead to pursue a 4-year undergraduate degree.[16] If this trend had not continued and the number of junior college entrants had remained constant between the years

---

[16] In the early 2000s a number of women-only junior colleges sought to mitigate this trend by becoming co-educational (*AS*, 28 September 2004), but this resulted in only a minor change to the gender balance as a whole (9 per cent male in 1990, 11 per cent in 2000, 13 per cent in 2010; MEXT 2018a) and did not halt the rapid decline in enrolments.

2000 and 2015, it is possible that the number of students at 4-year universities would have reduced by around 80,000. In that context, the *increase* in the number of 4-year university students by around 125,000 over this period does not look so impressive, but it does not, of course, take into account the dramatic overall drop in the population of school leavers over the same period.

The drop in school leavers should also have had a devastating impact on the other major type of post-secondary institution, *senmon gakkō*, or professional training colleges offering advanced post-secondary courses. These, as noted in Chapter 2, are almost exclusively private and even more heavily dependent on student fees than private universities. *Senmon gakkō*, however, have also shown great resilience. Overall enrolments in post-secondary courses at *senmon gakkō* have declined by around 17 percent—from around 691,343 in 1992 to 588,315 in 2018 (MEXT 2018a)—but the *number* of institutions has actually increased: there were 2,494 private *senmon gakkō* offering post-secondary courses in 1992 and 2,805 in 2018 (MEXT 2018a).[17] This is a remarkable success on its own, but importantly for our current purposes, it has been achieved in ways which seem to have benefited universities. One of the strategies which *senmon gakkō* adopted to survive was to develop courses articulated with undergraduate education. In 1985 only 1 per cent of *senmon gakkō* graduates went on to university; in 2006, 27.4 per cent did (*YS*, 28 February 2007). They also introduced 'highly specialized' 4-year courses from which one could enter graduate schools to earn higher professional qualifications rather than proceeding directly into the workforce (*NKS*, 16 July 2007). They proactively marketed their courses to currently enrolled undergraduate students, encouraging the practice of 'double schooling' mentioned earlier. The decline in *senmon gakkō* enrolments appears to have bottomed-out, with numbers largely stable since 2010.

Both *senmon gakkō* and junior colleges were notably absent from the literature examined in Chapter 1, which was focused almost exclusively on the implosion of the private *university* sector. A number of reasons can be posited for this omission. The vast majority of those making the predictions (the authors of this book included) were working in or associated with universities, and were understandably most concerned and interested in what would happen to the university sector. *Senmon gakkō* were, and still are, seen as a different type of post-secondary institution, a non-academic arm of higher education and catering for a completely different type of school

---

[17] The number of national (*kokuritsu*) *senmon gakkō* fell dramatically in the same period, from 148 in 1992 to only nine in 2018.

leaver (although, as noted above, this is not necessarily the case in practice). The junior college sector, meanwhile, was already small and the effects of its implosion would thus be much more subdued. Moreover, it was more difficult to speak of a *forthcoming* implosion in junior colleges because the decline in enrolments was already well under way by the early 2000s. This last reason underscores the naivety of the university implosion scenario: the shift from junior colleges to universities could easily have been factored in to predictions of university enrolment decline.

This redistribution of the student body between junior colleges and universities, combined with the success of universities in tapping further into the (shrinking) body of school leavers and that of *senmon gakkō* in aligning themselves with university education, has sustained an increase in university entrance rates throughout the 1990s, 2000s, and well into the 2010s. This increase, and indeed the recent history of expansion of Japan's higher education sector as a whole, is captured in the master diagram of student enrolments and population change produced periodically by the Ministry of Education (Figure 5.1).

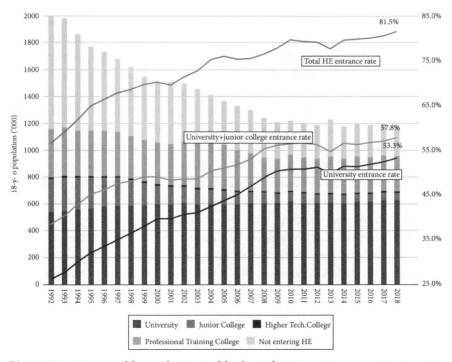

Figure 5.1. 18-year-old population and higher education entrance rates.
Sources: MEXT 2018h and MEXT 2018a.

It is important to highlight the role of government as an agent for this increasing demand. The government enabled the shift from junior college to university through its relaxed standards for university establishment, which allowed many former junior colleges to gain university status or to be reborn as faculties of existing universities within the same *gakkō hōjin*. There is also evidence that the government increased the demand for places at university by making it easier for students to access finance. This was achieved through the government's student loan scheme, administered through the Japan Student Services Organization (JASSO). In Chapter 2 we mentioned the threefold increase in the number of students accessing this scheme in the late 1990s and early 2000s. This number continued to grow, to a peak of over 1.4 million in 2013—compared to around 380,000 in 1998 (JASSO 2017). What this meant was that the amount of financial support provided by families towards students' income declined from 76 per cent in 1996 to 66 per cent in 2008 and 60 per cent in 2016, while the percentage made up by student loans increased in that time period from 6 per cent to 15 per cent to 20 per cent (*JT*, 21 May 2019).

The greatest expansion in the JASSO scheme was in interest-bearing loan recipients (from 110,000 in 1998 to 1.02 million in 2013—an eightfold increase, compared to an increase of 60 per cent for interest-free loans), and especially those enrolled in lower-ranked institutions. The proportion of private university students using JASSO loans overall stands at around 28 per cent in 2018, with a significantly higher proportion (close to 40 per cent) in universities in the lower tiers of the university hierarchy. Loan default rates are very low across the board, but clearly differentiated, with top private institutions recording rates of less than 1 per cent, and low-ranked ones closer to 3 per cent (Sekita 2017). These facts underpin a theory that government 'profligacy' with student loans boosted entrance rates by making university more affordable, and thereby unintentionally forestalled the demise of many private universities struggling with low enrolments. This theory has become so widely accepted that it was adopted almost universally in discussions of the proposal—part of the Liberal Democratic Party's 2017 election manifesto— to expand the JASSO system into a scholarship scheme for students from low-income families.[18] Ministry of Finance officials, for example, admonished that 'providing further [indirect] subsidies in the absence of reform

---

[18] The proposal has been branded by the government rather misleadingly as 'making higher education free' (*kōtō kyōiku no mushōka*), but in fact it entails an expansion of eligibility for loans and the introduction of a new grant-based scheme for student from low-income households meeting certain conditions (MEXT 2018i).

initiatives...extends a lifeline to the management of universities that are unattractive to potential students' (University Journal 2017); the *Nihon Keizai Shimbun* newspaper editors cautioned that the expanded financial aid scheme 'should not extend a further helping hand to under-enrolled universities' (*NKS*, 14 June 2018); even the President of the Japan Association of Private Universities and Colleges acknowledged the existence of 'an argument for avoiding the use of public funds to cover poorly-managed universities' (*MS*, 19 February 2018).[19]

The Role of Government as a 'Protection Fleet'

It is difficult to conclude from the foregoing evidence alone that the government consciously stimulated demand for private university education in a period of population decline. Yet there is also other evidence of the government's active interest in protecting the private sector. Although the government in the 2000s professed a rhetoric of laissez-faire market forces and commentators (Daigaku Mirai Mondai Kenkyūkai 2001: 40) stated that it would no longer act as a 'protection fleet' (*gōsōsendan*) for universities, it actually also put in place a number of systems to pre-empt cases of failure which suggests exactly the opposite. The private sector has always provided a useful buffer and supplement to the state provision of higher education and the representatives of the private sector liked to point this out in their versions of the history of Japanese higher education as we saw in Chapter 2. It seems as if their case may have been heard.

The operators of private universities have benefited from a growing variety of resources and guidance to aid their day-to-day management and financial planning. Some of this is provided by private university associations themselves, but an increasingly crucial role is played by the Promotion and Mutual Aid Corporation for Private Schools of Japan (PMAC), a statutory authority under MEXT jurisdiction which is responsible for distributing government subsidies to private universities as well as offering loans and operating a

---

[19] The theory that the lifespan of struggling universities has been improperly extended by the government through student loans should be handled with care. Clearly the growth in use of loans is also a reflection of the increasingly stretched finances of ordinary Japanese households which, as explained in Chapter 2, have had to contend with the dire combination of declining incomes and rising university fees throughout this same period. Ultimately, it is students and their families, not the government, which must repay the loans, and the reliance on loans does not alter the private-dependent structure of higher education financing in Japan. Nonetheless, the availability of government loans at below-market rates in the 2000s surely contributed in some way to the increasing proportion of high school leavers continuing to university.

number of management support services. A working group on *gakkō hōjin* renewal and revitalization (*gakkō hōjin kasseika/saisei kenkyūkai*) was established within PMAC in 2005. Its final report on management reform and crisis response delivered in 2007 set out in some detail a pathology of financial crisis including 'yellow zone' symptoms demanding immediate action and a 'red zone' where recovery was considered impossible without external support (PMAC 2007). The report's outline of both pre-emptive and remedial strategies were developed in some detail in a range of PMAC handbooks, case studies, and self-diagnosis templates (PMAC n.d.).

Meanwhile, policymakers increasingly articulated the view that it was not enough simply to help *gakkō hōjin* help themselves: a stronger framework of official monitoring and mediation was required. This argument can be seen, for example, in the reports of the University Subdivision of the Central Council of Education (*chūō kyōiku shingikai*), the government's peak advisory body on university policy. A June 2010 report on 'medium- and long-term vision for university education' includes a section on 'the healthy development of private universities', which urges *gakkō hōjin* to pursue more in-depth, realistic business analysis and take steps to prepare for possible crisis situations well in advance, at the same time as recommending stronger assistance from MEXT in terms of supporting these self-directed efforts and providing minimum safeguards for universities in crisis (Central Council for Education 2010). A 2014 amendment of the Private Schools Act responded to some of these recommendations, providing for direct ministerial intervention where a *gakkō hōjin*'s operations were considered 'manifestly inappropriate' or in contravention of statutory provisions. MEXT could demand reports, conduct on-site audits, issue orders for remedial action, and hold executive officers to account if they failed to attend faithfully to their duties.

MEXT has continued to bolster the assistance it offers to struggling *gakkō hōjin*. It declared 2015–20 a 'period of intensive support for the strengthening of private university management' and extended a pre-existing system of detailed investigation of individual *gakkō hōjin* and provision of detailed 'guidance and support' for improvement to cover around half of all *gakkō hōjin* in the country by 2020. *Gakkō hōjin* able to demonstrate to the Ministry that they are proactive in pursuing reforms have had their subsidies boosted. Funds allocated under the Comprehensive Support Program for Private University Reform, introduced in 2013, have grown to account for around 5 per cent of the total private university operating expense subsidies (PMAC 2018b). The Ministry also provided some direct financial support to struggling private universities through a scheme launched in 2015, under which, at its peak in 2017, special subsidies totalling 4 billion yen were extended to some 150 institutions.[20] A ministerial working group in 2017 recommended further mechanisms for early intervention in both day-to-day management and strategic development, as well as the cultivation of stronger mutual support networks among private universities themselves, which could see inter-university transfers of students, and indeed whole programmes, become commonplace in the future (Working Group 2017). A new amendment of the Private Schools Act planned for 2020 imposes stricter obligations of transparency and medium-term planning, as well as a more active role for government in the winding-up of a *gakkō hōjin* to protect the interests of students and other stakeholders. This brief and non-exhaustive summary of recent developments evidences the degree to which MEXT has come to view itself not as a regulator of private institutions in an open market but as a proactive supporter of the healthy development of such institutions. It certainly looks as if private universities are benefiting from the 'protection fleet' provided by the Ministry.

The government's position may also reflect problems with the third-party university evaluation and accreditation system to act as a mechanism for identifying problems in university management. The seven-year accreditation cycle has proven too long to enable an effective response to problems which, as we have seen in the case of MGU, became very acute in a relatively short space of time. Moreover, the evaluation process has not proven to be a sound mechanism for distinguishing truly terminal cases from the much larger pool of universities which were under-performing, but not incurable. For example, Poole Gakuin was successfully accredited by Japan Institution for Higher Education Evaluation (JIHEE) in 2008 and received high praise for its focus on educational experience and student wellbeing (Poole Gakuin 2008), yet by 2015 had announced its intention to close. Another failed university, Tokyo Jogakkan College, also passed its 2010 accreditation, but just 3 years later was planning to close. On the other hand, Aikoku Gakuen University failed its JIHEE accreditation evaluations on multiple occasions (decision deferred pending improvements in 2010; not suitable for accreditation 2014; decision deferred pending improvements 2017), yet has survived and managed to recuperate from a disastrous enrolment of just seventeen new students (out of a quota of one hundred) in 2014 to a more healthy 117 in 2017 (Aikoku Gakuen 2017).

---

[20] Only when the scheme came under direct fire in 2018 for gratuitously propping up operations otherwise destined to fail was it cut by more than half to 1.8 billion yen and forty to fifty universities (MEXT 2018i).

What is clear from the above account is that there has often been a great deal of negotiation between *gakkō hōjin* operators and MEXT officials when it has looked as if a private university was in serious danger of closing. This is where much of the uncertainty has resided in relation to the final outcome for individual institutions. Officials generally have couched their position not in terms of a positive desire to leave private universities to their own fate, but rather as a constraint on their own options. Before the closure of Tohwa University, for example, when petitioned by students and other supporters seeking to keep the university afloat, a MEXT official explained patiently that 'the principle of "private university autonomy" precludes the Ministry from intervening' (*YS*, 6 February 2007). A similar attitude was expressed in the case of St Thomas' University, where a MEXT official asked to comment on how the Ministry would deal with the university's eleventh-hour proposal to establish a new faculty, commented dispassionately that it 'would make a decision about whether or not to approve [the faculty] after hearing what the university management thinks about its own prospects for continued existence' (*KS*, 21 January 2014). Throughout the past 20 years, there appears to have been confusion as to whether the emphasis is to be placed on the process of helping universities out of trouble or, in the spirit of respect for autonomy and market forces, allowing them to die a natural death.

The situation was further complicated by the personal connections between private university management and MEXT officialdom. University officials have liaised routinely with the Ministry, even when not subject to the monitoring processes outlined earlier, and especially when planning new initiatives. Numerous rounds of consultation with MEXT advisors have been mandatory in the lead-up to any application to alter curricular structures or student quotas, and there were many other day-to-day operational circumstances where such consultation was considered highly advisable. It is unsurprising therefore that *amakudari*, the practice of retired public officials finding work in the sectors they used to oversee, was widespread in the private higher education sector during this period. A 2009 survey by the Democratic Party of Japan found that eighty-one *gakkō hōjin* had a total of 123 former MEXT officials among their executive officers, and a further 576 former officials were working as non-executive administrative staff members in 152 *gakkō hōjin* (DPJ 2009).[21] Whether or not these connections fostered ministerial sympathy

---

[21] A more recent internal probe by MEXT itself identified sixty-two cases of officials engaging in active procurement of jobs for retired colleagues, the direct form of *amakudari* facilitation which has been outlawed since 2007 (*JT*, 30 March 2017).

for private universities—let alone influenced decisions about funding or approval of applications—is entirely a matter of speculation, but clearly many *gakkō hōjin* considered their cultivation important in an era of competition and uncertainty.

If the role of central government in stepping in to support struggling private universities was somewhat inconsistent with its apparent agenda of laissez-faire economics, the role of *local* governments in supporting such institutions was much more consistent. As explained in Chapter 2, local governments frequently invited private universities to set up in their areas with large subsidies or gifts of land in the belief that they would help to drive the regeneration of the local economy. Some of these have proven successful, such as Ritsumeikan Asia Pacific University, which was established by the Ritsumeikan *gakkō hōjin* with major grants of land and other infrastructure from the governments of Oita Prefecture and Beppu City, where it is located. Another interesting case is Akita International University (AIU), a local public university established by the Akita Prefectural authorities in 2004, but inheriting its campus and many staff from a branch campus of Minnesota State University which had previously operated in Akita. AIU has gone on to become one of the very top public universities in the whole of Japan with a *hensachi* in some of its departments rivalling that of the University of Tokyo.

There are other cases, however, where the support of the local authorities has yielded less positive outcomes. Hagi Gakuen, the *gakkō hōjin* behind Hagi International University—mentioned earlier in relation to international students—obtained 2 billion of the 6.4 billion yen it required for university establishment from the City of Hagi, and a further 2 billion from Yamaguchi Prefecture (*YS*, 28 June 2005). From its inauguration in 1999, Hagi International University struggled to meet its enrolment quota and eventually became so deeply in debt that in June 2005 the *gakkō hōjin* had to file for civil rehabilitation.[22] The rehabilitation plan proved unsuccessful, however, and a second civil rehabilitation process was initiated in 2012 and concluded in 2016. The university continues to operate today (under the name Shiseikan Hall University; its second name change since 1999) but can hardly be judged

---

[22] The Civil Rehabilitation Act allows for an organization facing bankruptcy to continue operating under a rehabilitation plan approved by a certain majority of its creditors. The plan generally entails drastic restructuring and disposal of many of the organization's assets, with creditors entitled to receive no less than what they would in the event of actual bankruptcy, but it has the great benefit of affording the organization a pathway to autonomous recovery. The civil rehabilitation process was originally designed for companies, and Hagi Gakuen claimed the dubious honour of being the first *gakkō hōjin* to invoke it owing to an inability to attract students to its university.

a local success: in 2017 it welcomed 285 new students to its Tokyo satellite campus, all of whom were international students, while just twenty-three new students enrolled at the 'main' campus in Hagi.

The struggles of Hagi International University are especially notable in light of the fact that, on paper, in many ways it embodied the state's vision for higher education reform. As Akabayashi (2015) notes, Hagi International University assiduously followed the recommendations laid out by government advisory councils in the 1990s and early 2000s: it developed curricula based on buzzwords such as international studies and information science; it pro-actively recruited students from overseas; it collaborated with local public authorities; it developed creative approaches to course delivery such as satellite campuses; it even functioned as a test case in the application of the civil rehabilitation process to private university management. Despite all these efforts to be a truly twenty-first-century university, it has been on the brink of failure for much of its existence.

The Role of Family Business

MGU is a family-run university and, as we have seen, this appeared at some points to be a weakness when it came to responding to the pressures of the early 2000s. In the long term, however, it was the source of remarkable resilience. The same can be said of family-run universities as a whole, which are conspicuously absent from the ranks of universities which have closed since 2000, summarized in Tables 5.1, 5.2, and 5.3 earlier in this chapter. No family-run university has converted to local public status. Several of the cases of merger involved family-run institutions, but none of these led to closure of the *gakkō hōjin* itself (merely merger with another university within the same family-run *gakkō hōjin* group). A number of the outright university closures were of family-run universities, but in only one of these cases did the family-run *gakkō hōjin* itself actually close, and that (Horikoshi Gakuen, the operators of the University of Creation) was a forced closure as a result of serious fraud. In the remaining cases the *gakkō hōjin* has survived and even thrived. The conclusion that family-run institutions have been especially adaptable is not a watertight account, owing both to the difficulties of defining and identifying 'family-run' in the first place (about which more will be said in the next chapter) and to the invisibility of cases in which the university has survived, but the *gakkō hōjin* itself may have fallen out of family hands. Overall, however, it is clear that family-run universities have proven unexpectedly adaptable to the dramatic changes of the past two decades. This success deserves more attention.

There are several features of family-run institutions which can be extrapolated from the MGU case. Perhaps most conspicuous is the pattern of vertical institutional integration. The university is often the 'flagship' institution in the *gakkō hōjin* conglomeration of institutions which goes all the way down to attached nurseries and kindergartens. Non-family *gakkō hōjin* too can have such conglomerations, but the family approach to management enables a degree of integration and coordination which may be difficult to achieve when management of the constituent institutions is more diffused. Conglomerations allow for cross-subsidies, which we believe was an important factor in the survival of successive institutions as the wave of demographic decline passed through the educational stages from elementary school up to university. Family-run universities can also generally rely on the commitment and support of extended family who have grown up with and understand the values of the institution. Leadership can be direct and unambiguous because it coincides with ownership. It can generate a family-type atmosphere which fosters relations based on trust and loyalty and which some sociologists of Japan has defined as 'kintractual' as opposed to 'contractual' (Murakami 1984: 351; Goodman 1999: 128).

All of these features suggest that when accounting for the unexpected resilience of family-run universities, we need not only to examine the strategies formulated and actions taken by their leaders in response to specific situations, but also to look more closely at patterns of *inbuilt* resilience deriving from the basic fact that they are family-run. There is a rich literature on kinship structures in traditional and modern Japanese society, and the unusual prevalence of family business in Japan has been examined in the wider international and comparative context of family business studies. Yet insights from these fields have almost never been applied to the analysis of higher education institutions. In the next chapter, we attempt just such an analysis.

6

Private Universities as Family Business

This chapter looks more closely at one very common, but almost completely unresearched, sector of Japanese private higher education: the family-run university. We develop the argument, outlined in the previous chapter, that the resilience of private universities in the face of the many challenges of the past two decades can be explained partly by the fact that so many of them are family businesses. This type of business has developed a particularly important role in Japan in a variety of areas, including the educational, medical, and welfare fields.

Situating Family-run Universities in Japanese Private Higher Education

No official data is published on family-run universities in Japan, but they are widely known to be numerous. Citing a survey by one of Japan's private university associations (APUJ 2018), Obara (2019) suggests that approximately 40 per cent of all private universities in Japan are family-run.[1] This suggestion appears to conflate institutions still run by their original founder (and which have the potential to become a family business if close relatives of the founder become involved and/or if control is passed to a second generation) with those which have already made this leap in succession.[2] That said, there are many *gakkō hōjin* which are well known to be controlled by a single founding family and the existence of such organizations is entirely predictable in light of the prevalence of family business overall in Japan.

---

[1] This figure is very similar to the figure gleaned from a survey on private university management conducted by the Promotion and Mutual Aid Corporation for Private Schools of Japan (PMAC 2019b) which shows that in 37.1 per cent of *gakkō hōjin* which operate universities (and 46.8 per cent of those with junior colleges [but not universities]), the chair of the board of trustees (*rijichō*) is either the original founder of the *gakkō hōjin* or a relative thereof. The PMAC and APUJ figures are based on surveys of 608 and 274 *gakkō hōjin* respectively.

[2] An amendment to the Private Schools Act, which comes into force in 2020, will oblige *gakkō hōjin* to publish the names of their executive officers as well as more transparent financial reports, which may make it easier to calculate the actual number of family-run or managed institutions in Japan.

Family-Run Universities in Japan: Sources of Inbuilt Resilience in the Face of Demographic Pressure, 1992–2030. Jeremy Breaden and Roger Goodman, Oxford University Press (2020). © Jeremy Breaden and Roger Goodman. DOI: 10.1093/oso/9780198863496.001.0001

Family-run organizations are generically referred to as *dōzoku keiei*, meaning literally 'same-family management' (sometimes *ichizoku keiei* or 'single-family management'). The expression *dōzoku keiei* can be combined with any form of conglomeration, to describe a group of institutions in a particular field all run or controlled by members of the same family, as in *dōzoku keiei gakkō hōjin* (family-run educational corporations) or *dōzoku keiei shakai fukushi hōjin* (family-run welfare corporations, discussed later in this chapter). The term *dōzoku keiei* does not, however, appear within the conventional typologies of Japanese higher education. As explained in Chapter 2, these typologies hinge on formal (legal) institutional type, the public/private distinction, and criteria such as size and era of establishment. We need to develop a more qualitative picture of the private university sector in order to understand where *dōzoku keiei* universities sit within this highly heterogeneous collection of institutions.

A useful starting point here is Kaneko's (2007) Japanese private university 'typology by birth', comprising *voluntary association*, *sponsored*, and *entrepreneurial* universities. In the *voluntary association* type are universities which trace their origins back to the private schools established in feudal times, and those which began life in the late 1800s as academies founded by prominent intellectuals, often with ideas about education different from those of the Meiji government. Understandably, such academies tended to emphasize values such as innovation, free-thinking, and self-reliance.[3] In the contemporary era, many of the universities which emerged from these academies still associate themselves proactively with prominent historical figures—mainly progressive Meiji-period thinkers—although as Kaneko (2004: 48) notes, these figures rarely had any direct involvement in the running of the institutions themselves. Nonetheless, they represent the 'spirit' of private education in Japan which, as seen in Chapter 2, the private university associations are currently so keen to promote and with which other private universities are happy to associate themselves.

The *sponsored* category covers universities established, both pre-war and post-war, by various entities beyond the education sector to advance specific educational or social causes, including universities sponsored by religious

---

[3] Many of these were schools of western learning which exposed students not only to new technological and administrative knowledge but also to the social values espoused in western scholarship, which were considered progressive in the context of post-feudal Japanese society. Leading examples include Keio University (founded as a school of Dutch language and later western studies by Fukuzawa Yukichi, one of the leading figures in Meiji modernization) and Doshisha University (founded as an English language school by Japanese missionary Joseph Hardy Neesima).

organizations. There are over eighty so-called 'mission' (*mission-kei*) universities in Japan with contemporary or historical ties with the Christian Church and almost fifty with Buddhist affiliations. The degree to which religious doctrine informs the university's activities varies greatly: for some, the religious connection is a matter of pedigree and prestige rather than practice, but for others the connection is much more overt, including an explicitly religious mission and a prominent place for religious studies in the curriculum.[4] To this category we could also add the small number of universities whose establishment was sponsored by business corporations, generally to contribute to technological advancement and industry-specific human resource development. A good example of a university originally founded by a company is present-day Seikei University (alma mater of the current Prime Minister, Abe Shinzō), the predecessor of which was founded in 1906 with the support of Iwasaki Koyata, the fourth head of the Mitsubishi *zaibatsu*. Until it received its own charter in the post-war period, Seikei was largely run on donations from the Mitsubishi Group, and the university still has close connections with the company. More recent examples include Toyota Technological Institute (*Toyota Kōgyō Daigaku*, sponsored by the automobile manufacturer) and the University of Marketing and Distribution Sciences (*Ryūtsū Kagaku Daigaku*, sponsored by Daiei—a major supermarket chain).[5]

Finally there are the *entrepreneurial* universities, established by individuals and groups already active in the business of education. Most are relatively small operations, sometimes founded by a single wealthy individual or family which is influential in local educational, political, and/or business circles, and whose operation has expanded across generations or attracted a wider consortium of supporters. The university is often the final addition to a suite of interests which may include primary and secondary schools, junior colleges, and/or advanced vocational schools.[6] As Kaneko (2007) acknowledges, the category of 'entrepreneurial' universities is so large and diverse that it is extremely difficult to achieve a meaningful breakdown of institutions within it. Generalizations about their founders' motivations or educational outlooks

---

[4] The Basic Act on Education (Article 15) prohibits national and local public educational institutions from engaging in education or other activities specific to any single religion, but this prohibition does not extend to private institutions.

[5] These are distinct from the handful of universities which are directly established and operated by commercial enterprises (*kabushiki kaisha-ritsu daigaku*) rather than *gakkō hōjin*.

[6] An article in the Nihon Keizai Shimbun (*NKS*, 21 September 2004) suggests that the large growth in entrepreneurial universities in the 1990s and early 2000s introduced a new culture among *gakkō hōjin* which meant that the earlier view that these institutions were naturally virtuous (*seizensetsu*) could no longer be maintained and that they required much closer scrutiny. It may have been in part this change of view which led to the revision of the Private Schools Act to be introduced in 2020.

are especially difficult. Some institutions clearly serve specific academic interests and vocational training needs, while others address broader social themes such as internationalization (the word *kokusai*—international— appears in the names of thirty universities and *fukushi*—welfare—in seventeen). Sixty-three private universities enrol women only. Others are deeply community-oriented—to the extent, as we have seen in Chapter 2, that their establishment may have been underwritten by local government. The usefulness of the 'entrepreneurial' categorization is also compromised by the fact that the circumstances of a university's birth are not necessarily the decisive factors in shaping its present-day character. Nonetheless, it is within this problematic category that the vast majority of *dōzoku keiei* (famly-run) universities are located.

There are many organizations and groups which undertake research on private education in Japan in general and on *gakkō hōjin* in particular.[7] It is the fact that there is so much research in this general area that it makes the complete absence of formal research on *dōzoku keiei gakkō hōjin* so conspicuous.

An important part of the explanation for the lack of this research lies, we propose, in the negative image of family-run institutions in Japan in general and the reluctance of such institutions to draw attention to this facet of their organization. There are indeed some very negative images of family-run private universities in Japan. Any internet search quickly reveals a host of aspersions concerning everything from fraud and embezzlement to association with organized crime groups and right-wing organizations. The more extreme of these allegations tend to be unconfirmed and are often vigorously denied by those accused, but, at the very least, they do point to a general suspicion of the credentials of family businesses as operators of educational institutions.

The sheer scale and success of some family-run organizations is enough to raise eyebrows in some quarters. Kindai University, which has been run across three generations by members of the Seko family, attracts more undergraduate applications (154,000-plus in 2019) than any other university in Japan (*SA*, 8 March 2019). The Teikyo University Group, founded by the Okinaga family,

---

[7] The largest organization undertaking research in this area is probably the Nihon Shigaku Kyōiku Kenkyūjo (Japan Private Education Research Centre) (http://www.shigaku.or.jp/) established in 1962. More practitioner-oriented research groups which look at the management of private education and *gakkō hōjin* include the Shigaku Keiei Kenkyūkai (http://sikeiken.or.jp/) and the Gakkō Keiri Kenkyūkai (http://www.keiriken.net/), which includes almost all private universities in Japan in its network. Both of the private university associations also have their own in-house research platforms: https://www.shidaikyo.or.jp/riihe/about/ and https://www.shidairen.or.jp/activities/forum/

encompasses no less than thirty-nine different universities, colleges, schools, and kindergartens, generating revenue in the order of 100 billion yen annually (*STK*, 15 May 2017). The Tsuzuki Gakuen Group (Tsuzuki family) has an even more extensive portfolio of schools, including six universities across the country. Some universities are run by families with business interests spreading far and wide beyond education. The Miyata family, whose members head both Asahi University and Meikai University, were responsible for major condominium developments in Tokyo in the 1960s and also operate the successful Nangoku Shuka chain of eateries.

Family-run universities rarely feature in the mainstream Japanese news media, but when they do, it is almost always in cases of financial misconduct. In 2011 for instance, the former head of Asai Gakuen (Asai family) was sentenced to four years and six months imprisonment for fraudulently obtaining 57 million yen in government subsidies (*NKS*, 10 March 2011). In 2001 the National Tax Agency presented the above-mentioned Tsuzuki Gakuen Group with a bill for more than 160 million yen in extra taxes for under-reported income across two of its *gakkō hōjin* (*NKS*, 6 September 2001). In some cases there is a long-running pattern of misbehaviour. Horikoshi Gakuen (University of Creation; Horikoshi family) was the subject of a number of police investigations into fraudulent activity and suspected breaches of labour laws throughout the 2000s, had its government subsidies cancelled in 2010, failed its third-party accreditation review in 2011, and was expelled from both prefectural and national associations of private universities in the same year, before being dis-established by government order in 2013.

In some cases the misbehaviour is not only financial. The head of Tokyo University of Social Welfare, Nakajima Tsuneo, received a 34-month prison sentence in 2008 for a series of indecent assaults perpetrated on the university campus (*JT*, 28 June 2008). After release, he regained an influential positon in the organization, by that time headed by his mother, and proceeded to implement a new commercial model for the university which involved the mass recruitment of poorly qualified, international students. Nakajima returned to the headlines in 2019 after it was found that over 1,600 of these international students had disappeared from the university in the previous 3 years (Sawada 2019).

Other family-run operations have close connections with centres of political power in Japan. In some cases these are openly declared as part of the organization's history: an example is Josai Gakuen (operator of Josai University, among others), which was founded by Mizuta Mikio, a minister in several Liberal Democratic Party governments of the 1950s to 1970s and presided over by his daughter Noriko until 2016. A problematic scandal involved the current Abe government and Kake Gakuen, the operators of Okayama University of Science, which gained unusually swift and trouble-free approval from the government to establish a new veterinary faculty. This family-run organization, which runs two other universities and a number of schools and professional training colleges, is headed by Kake Kotaro, a close acquaintance of Prime Minister Abe.

There is no evidence that cases such as these are more prevalent in family-run universities than in other private higher education institutions, or indeed more common in private higher education than in any other sector of private enterprise. Nonetheless, the existence of such cases and the negative images they foster do help explain, as Obara (2019: 144) in his generally positive account of such institutions acknowledges, the dearth of serious attention to family-run universities as a category. Operators and supporters of private higher education institutions in Japan prefer not to draw attention to such cases lest they be implicated by association; scholars writing about private higher education may wish to avoid mixing tabloid fodder with serious analysis, and be conscious of the risks of skewing readers' impressions by giving such cases unwarranted exposure. The suggestion by some informants that the topic of family-run universities is 'taboo' in Japan may well stem from concerns such as these. At any rate, it is not difficult to understand why family-run universities rarely take proactive steps to identify themselves as such, let alone suggest that such universities might actually be better in certain aspects than institutions not run by families.

Despite the absence of research on *dōzoku keiei gakkō hōjin* by researchers inside Japan, there is some work undertaken on these institutions by researchers working outside the country. One of these is in a rarely-cited book from the late 1980s in which an economist, Estelle James, and an anthropologist, Gail Benjamin, explain why there may be so many 'entrepreneurial' universities in Japan, and why so many of these are family-run.[8] The starting point for their analysis is the demand-absorbing role of the private higher education sector which we outlined in Chapter 2. James and Benjamin (1988: xvi–xviii) suggest that whereas elsewhere the rise of the private sector has been a response to cultural heterogeneity, generally linguistic and religious,

---

[8] One of the very few other explicit references we can find to the role of families in running private educational institutions in Japan at this time is in Holmes (1989: 210) who writes that 'Private education in Japan is a family...affair. Members of the family (often grandchildren) of the men and women who founded them still own many private schools'.

in Japan it has been a response to excess demand which the government has been unwilling to meet. They write (1988: 56, 58):

> The private sector serves as a shock absorber, responding rapidly to the ups and downs in the relevant population, while the public sector gradually adjusts... [This] pattern of service delivery chosen by Japan was consistent with the interests of the supporters of the Liberal Democratic Party (LDP), which has consistently governed Japan since the 1950s... Ultimately, the public/private division of responsibility for education (and other quasi-public social services) may be designed to maximise the welfare of those in power and provide necessary pay-offs to allied groups.

James and Benjamin (1988: 62–4) discuss how this profit can be generated through measures such as the vertical integration of institutions which provides a guaranteed supply of students who can be charged fees along the whole track of their educational experience (what they call 'sales maximization'); by the senior members of the organization receiving substantial funds through legal means of 'disguised profit distribution' such as receiving an income for each of the different positions they hold in the organization;[9] or by non-taxable perks (from expense accounts, free accommodation, cars—to the occasional examples of illegal 'kickbacks' for offering contracts to external parties).[10] Indeed, it was the combination of 'disguised profit maximization' with assured demand as a result of limited government supply, plus the easy availability of borrowed capital which made the establishment of private universities not only easy but also attractive to many families in the 1960s, 1970s, and 1980s.[11] At the same time, the government—which needed such

---

[9] A widely reported example of this practice was the retirement package received by the demitting head of the Tanioka Gakuen Gakkō Hōjin in 2007 who received three payments—as head of the university, junior college, and school board (see NKS, 14 September 2007).

[10] Kempner and Makino (1993: 190) make a similar point when they write: 'Many private universities merely increase the status, prestige, power or profit of a particular family.... The motives for private ownership are often simply for the accrual of personal benefits to a small family or group of owners and not for the production of knowledge or cultural enrichment.' While families cannot take out 'dividends' from non-profit organizations, one way in which they can invest profits is through expansion which creates job opportunities and salaries for members of the family.

[11] An explanation that one sometimes hears for the establishment of so many private educational institutions in the period immediately after the war was that they benefited from the financial policies which were put in place by the American occupation authorities to protect religious, especially Christian, organizations from government interference. These policies made it more difficult for the tax authorities, and even the Ministry of Education, to directly investigate their affairs. The tax breaks which accrued from running a private university meant that they not only received exemptions in terms of income but also that the owners of educational institutions could pass on property to the next generation while avoiding inheritance tax. There was also very little auditing of the salaries paid by gakkō hōjin to those running the organization. It is interesting that, while this topic has been fairly

institutions to prevent the requirement to invest more taxpayers' money in the higher education system—provided a large amount of latitude to private institutions in how they ran themselves. The product of this mixture of conscious blindness, student demand, and family profiteering was that the whole issue of family-run universities become something of a sensitive topic for researchers in Japan from the 1960s and to a large extent remains so today.[12]

A rather more positive account of family-run universities is provided in a doctoral thesis from UCLA by Obara Kazuhito (2005) that is complemented by his case study contribution to the volume by Altbach, de Wit, and Choi (Obara 2019). Obara's thesis is ostensibly on leadership in private universities, but in contextualizing his survey material he provides an excellent summary of the contemporary debates and fears which were swilling around private universities in the early 2000s. He (2005: 1) describes a situation where 'due to the convergence of several socio-environmental factors, the private sector in Japan is currently facing a crisis which may possibly threaten the entire Japanese private higher education system and its continuance.' Obara (2005: 9) lists seven socio-environmental issues—the decline in the number of 18-year-olds; the growing number of private universities, the establishment of for-profit universities, the incorporation or privatization of the national sector, economic recession and job shortages for graduates, international pressure for Japan to liberalise its educational services, and tension over whether universities should focus on character building or academic skills— and suggests (2005: 175), in line with common assumptions of the period, that 'perhaps more than 150 private universities in Japan face bankruptcy within the next ten years.'

Obara sets out to collect data from university leaders on how they are going to respond to what he (2005: 103) calls 'the upcoming reality of the "law of the jungle"'. The focus for Obara's data collection is on what he describes as 'second-tier private universities'. He (2005: 102–3) estimates that roughly one hundred of Japan's private universities in the mid-2000s fit into the category of 'second-tier' based on their *hensachi* scores which, as explained in Chapter 1,

---

widely discussed in the case of the religious organizations which were established in the post-war period, we have found no references in the literature to educational institutions.

[12] In general, there seems to be a reluctance among Japanese researchers to examine any area which is considered 'private', but a further reason sometimes given for the lack of research on family-run universities is that the owners of many of these institutions are academically trained and considered to be colleagues by the researchers in the field who might undertake such projects in Japan. If this is true, then it is a good example of what Wisniewski (2008) calls 'the averted gaze'.

denote the competitiveness of their entrance examinations.[13] Obara sent his survey to forty-two board chairs and university presidents of these one hundred second-tier universities, selected to cover as many of Japan's prefectures as possible. Thirty-four (81 per cent) agreed to participate in his project. Obara describes twenty-one of these thirty-four institutions as 'family owned'. They share a number of key characteristics. All the universities in the survey have attached institutions: more than half of them have a graduate school, a junior college, a senior high school, a junior high school, and a kindergarten; one quarter have attached professional training colleges and elementary schools.[14] Two-thirds of the presidents interviewed were also the heads of at least one other institution in the *gakko hōjin* (which generally meant that they received more than one salary). Presidents talked about: creating a university which was a 'big-family system' (Obara 2005: 155); having set up their own staff agency so that they could hire their administrative support staff on temporary contracts (Obara 2005: 156); running other businesses to support the university financially (Obara 2005: 157); a sense that academic staff at the university showed little understanding of their current predicament and were reluctant to sign up to any reforms which would make the university more market-oriented (Obara 2005: 158).

Obara expands on these points in a case study of Tamagawa Gakuen in the Altbach et al. (2019) volume on family-run higher education institutions examined later in this chapter. His great grandfather was the founder of the university, which is famous for being family-run over four generations, and indeed he (2005: 2) freely admits that one of the reasons that he undertook his PhD at UCLA on Japanese private higher education was because he was training to 'run a private university in Tokyo'. He (2019: 144) is equally candid about the sensitivities which surround such inherited positions in Japan when he says that 'The concept of hereditary occupations is often criticized for its exclusive, feudalistic and anti-democratic characteristic. This type of criticism is levied in the education industry'. Or, as editors of the volume in which his

---

[13] Obara (2005: 102) clearly distinguishes this group from what he calls 'first-tier private universities', of which he lists just forty-four, and 'lower tier', which presumably includes all of the remaining 350 or so. First-tier private universities, according to Obara, range from Keio, Waseda, the MARCH (Meiji, Aoyama Gakuin, Rikkyo, Chuo, and Hosei), and Kan-Kan-Do-Ritsu (Kansai, Kansai Gakuin, Doshisha, and Ritsumeikan) at the top to other highly rated and hard to enter if less well-known institutions such as, in the Kansai region, Konan, Kyoto Bunkyo, Kyoto Joshi, Kyoto Sangyo, and Ryukoku.

[14] The physical proximity of different educational institutions within the same *gakko hōjin* is one indication of how closely they operate. The Kansai University *hōjin*, for example, has a kindergarten, junior high school, senior high school and graduate school all on the same campus as ten of its undergraduate faculties.

case study appears (Altbach et al. 2019: 300) put it: 'In Japan, family succession, understood as a form of wealth transfer, has become the subject of societal criticism and perceived as perpetuating class divisions.'

Obara (2019) picks out a number of features which make Tamagawa Gakuen distinctive. It is 'traditional' for the same person to hold the roles of chair of the board of trustees (*rijichō*), university president (*gakuchō*), and school principal (*kōchō*). The current incumbent has been in post for 24 years. There has been a clear and long plan for training his successor who 'must win the trust of his or her subordinates'. This long apprenticeship assures continuity, consistency, and stability in the organization: 'Family ownership handed down from parents to children reflects *isshisōden* (passing on knowledge). The vision of parents is inherited by their children who grew up within "the family business" and appreciate its contributions and challenges intimately.'

One theme which is muted in Obara's accounts is intra-family conflict, particularly when it comes to the point of succession. He (2005: 156) does, however, cite one example of an institution which he says 'prohibits inheriting by one family member, assigning multiple family members for the board of trustees, appointing any relatives at the same workplace, and allowing both husband and wife to work at the same workplace'. This is apparently due to a series of internal disputes during the institution's 120-year-history. To understand this fully, we need to look at how family-run universities fit within the private university governance structure introduced in Chapter 2.

In theory, the Private Schools Act of 1949 prevents a single family from controlling a *gakkō hōjin*. Article 38 (7) provides that the 'officers [that is, trustees and auditors] must not include the spouse of any officer or more than one relative within the third degree of kinship of any officer.' In other words, the owning family can never occupy more than two positions on the board of trustees. Importantly, however, this restriction only applies to a single *gakkō hōjin*. It is possible therefore for one family to form groups of *gakkō hōjin*, each of which can be headed by a family member without infringing the law. An example is the aforementioned Kake Gakuen Group where at least five members of the Kake family hold key executive positions within the group, but no more than two in any one *gakkō hōjin*—an arrangement which is perfectly legal (*GB*, 31 July 2017). Moreover, there is no statutory restriction on family membership of the board of councillors (which is supposed to function as a check on the power of the trustees), nor on the number of family members occupying other key executive positions such as university president, dean, or administrative director-general.

The education ministry does use administrative guidance to express some disapproval of family-dominated institutions, advising that *gakkō hōjin* should take care not to select large numbers of councillors from the same family (MEXT 2004), and occasionally naming and shaming institutions which do not comply with this (see, for example, APUJ 2010; MEXT 2007). In the absence of a legal foundation, however, these admonishments are usually expressed in a rather mild tone[15] and not followed up with any concrete intervention. As James and Benjamin (1988) argued back in the 1980s, it is always important to remember that the existence of private family-run institutions reduces the need for government investment in the higher education sector.

It is again conspicuous how little attention has been focused on questions of governance in family-run *gakkō hōjin*, given the detailed legislation that exists. At times, it is almost possible to see researchers shying away from the topic. Egnor (2001), for example, has written an ethnography of a *dōzoku keiei* university which he anonymized as Toshi (literally 'metropolitan') Gakuen. Toshi Gakuen is part of a *gakkō hōjin* which includes a junior college, senior and middle high school, an elementary school, and kindergarten which was run by the founder until 1973 when it was passed on to his son who served as president until 1994 (Egnor 2001: 51–2). The current president is the grandson of the founder who has served as both president of the university and chair of the board of trustees since 1994. Even though Egnor's thesis is entitled *Governance of a Private Japanese University*, there is no mention or analysis at all of the family-run aspect of Toshi Gakuen—apart from an oblique reference (Egnor 2001: 195–6) to the challenges that the grandson had because of his relative youth when he took over as president and chair.

Family-Owned/Managed Higher Education Institutions (FOMHEIs): The Global Picture

Family-run universities are thus both very common and significantly understudied in Japan. This combination of features is not uniquely Japanese. In a short, but seminal, article published in 2005, Altbach (2005: 10) described family-run universities as a phenomenon that is 'largely ignored ... growing rapidly and not well understood'. He highlights the importance of family-run

---

[15] The stock advice is to 'consider adjusting the composition of the board of councillors, as it is heavily weighted toward family members' (MEXT 2007).

universities, particularly in Central and South America (Mexico and Argentina) and in Asia (India, China, Japan, Taiwan, Korea, Philippines, and Thailand). While he was unable to give exact figures on the number of such institutions either globally or nationally, he suggested that in Thailand, for example, half of all the private universities were family-owned.[16]

Altbach (2005: 29) defines a family-run university as 'an institution established by an individual or a family group in which family members remain directly involved and generally dominant in the administration, governance, financial control, and/or direct ownership of the institution'. He (2005: 30) points out the positive aspects of universities set up by families: 'they allow new and innovative educational and management ideas to be developed and tested. They give rein to charismatic educational leaders with a zeal for reform.' The reasons for their establishment, he suggests, are extraordinarily varied: some are set up from a purely philanthropic or social sense of mission; some may have been established to bring honour and status to the founding individuals and their families; some may have been started in order to make money or employment for extended members of the family; some may have been developed for political reasons, for example by contributing to the local economy in order to develop a political base. In general, he concludes, 'family ownership is seen as a way to ensure stability and control, the ability to keep financial aspects of the institution as confidential as possible, and to maintain the original mission or purpose of the institution's characteristics.' He delineates these characteristics as follows:

- Structures that permit centralized overall control of the institution with family members generally occupying senior positions, especially in relation to financial management; this often means—within the regulations of individual countries—having boards of trustees dominated by family

---

[16] Interestingly, while Altbach suggests that this might be a growing phenomenon in countries which were just developing their higher education systems, an article hosted by a US organization called University Business (UB) suggests that in the United States 'family-owned and operated schools, colleges, and universities numbered several hundred just two generations past' (Martin and Samuels 2010). Martin and Samuels' article picks out three examples of such institutions in the US: Herzing University, Sullivan University, and Rasmussen College. An organization called America's Focus representing America's Family Owned Colleges, Universities and Schools wrote on its website that 'America's FOCUS members feel that our varied histories, our student driven philosophies and entrepreneurial foundations have guided us for generations with a unique family-style, hands-on approach to modern career education.' The organization appears to have been lobbying primarily against government regulation linking student loan repayments to starting salaries, and by 2018 it no longer seemed to have a web presence. According to Levy (2019: 20), in the US in the 1980s, there was a rapid growth in corporate for-profit higher education institutions, which meant that many family for-profit institutions had to close or merge.

members with final decision-making authority over both financial and academic issues;

- Academic staff with very little decision-making authority; and administrative offices, in particular the role of president, generally occupied by members of the owning family;
- Strategic direction of the institution very much in the hands of the owning family, which can be positive (in responding to market pressure) but potentially negative if there is a conflict of interest between financial gain and academic integrity;
- Top-down nature of the institution meaning potential constraints on the academic freedom of members of staff, both in relation to teaching and research.
- Maintenance of sustained leadership and effective long-term management can be a particularly serious issue for family-owned universities as control inevitably passes from one generation to another.

Following his seminal article in 2005, Altbach spent over a decade trying to raise funds in order to undertake a rigorous and systematic investigation into the phenomenon of family-owned universities. Unable to secure funding, he teamed up with some colleagues to pull together what information was already available on the topic and to commission case studies of family-run universities from around the world. These latter were largely written by family members who had undertaken research on their own institutions in order to help qualify them to take over. Altbach and colleagues coined the acronym FOMHEI (family-owned or managed higher education institutions) to cover the range of case studies they collected and published the book under the title *The Global Phenomenon of Family-owned/Managed Universities* (Altbach, de Wit, and Choi 2019).[17] They set these universities in the context of the growth of private universities worldwide (Levy 2019) and the literature on comparative family business studies (Allen and Choi 2019). They conclude (Altbach, de

---

[17] The case studies are from Armenia, Bangladesh, Brazil, China, Colombia, Ethiopia, India, Japan, Korea, Mexico, the Philippines, and the United Arab Emirates. Most of these case studies do not give accurate figures about the number and proportion of FOMHEIs in each country, but a few of the chapters do give an indication of their prevalence. In Brazil, family-owned HEIs represent 26 per cent of all HEIs (Reis and Capaleto 2019). In China, around 22 per cent of students are currently studying in private HEIs, most of which are established and managed by private individuals; the number is expected to rise as the government has been encouraging the establishment of private HEIs since 2000 in order to meet unmet demand for higher education (Yu 2019). In Colombia, 25 per cent of HEIs are controlled by families enrolling 14 per cent of all students (Mantilla 2019). In Korea, more than 70 per cent of students attend one of the country's 320 private HEIs of which, according to Choi (2019) over 200 (60+ per cent) are FOMHEIs meaning that nearly half of all students attend such institutions.

Wit, and Choi 2019) that while there are no official statistics on FOMHEIs, they 'number in their thousands worldwide and exist in most countries. They are, without question, a key dimension of the private higher education environment.'[18] As Levy (2019) points out,

> Just as entering students often do not know whether a HEI is owned by a private, public, for-profit, non-profit, or religious entity . . . , so they often do not know whether or how much their institution is family-owned or managed . . . . The non-elite nature of most FOMHEIs makes them especially vulnerable to the vagaries of the marketplace, including demographically induced stagnation or even declines in demand.

He picks out the cases of Japan and Korea as exemplars of this phenomenon.

The chapter in Altbach et al.'s volume by Choi (2019), subtitled 'A future of dark speculation?', demonstrates the significant parallels between the Japanese and Korean situations. Many of the Korean institutions are, as in Japan, part of large educational conglomerations under the direction of a single family with a single, centralized board. Despite their scale, Choi (2019: 162) describes them as having 'a typically rural base of operations, local focus, profit-driven owners who may engage in unethical practices, negative public perception, short history, financial instability or government administrations critical of private enterprises'. He (170–5) recounts a number of the scandals and negative perceptions surrounding FOMHEIs in Korea and lists the names of those which have been forced to close or merge as a result of the introduction of stricter controls and regulations in recent years.

Allen and Choi (2019: 3) draw two specific conclusions from their review of the family business literature, in particular about socio-economic wealth, which can aid an understanding of FOMHEIs. The first is the potential link between 'non-financial social benefits and the respect and prestige often afforded institutions of higher learning . . . . For example . . . reputational wealth . . . is perhaps higher than it might be in owning another kind of a business'. The second is what they describe as 'the potential fit between a family's long-term approach, effort to avoid significant risks and the slow rate of change often found in higher education'. Both of these points are relevant, we believe, to our case study of Meikei Gakuin University (MGU): as to why it was established and why it initially responded so slowly to the demographic threats it faced. Allen and

---

[18] Tamrat (2018), in a short survey of FOMHEIs in Africa, lists twenty countries where they can be found.

Choi (2019: 35–6) also point towards the comparative advantages which 'familiness' can bestow on a business, in particular a focus on future generations and a 'participatory family culture'.

Whilst acknowledging that each FOMHEI has its own history and trajectory, Altbach et al. (2019) are able, from twelve case studies from different countries, to draw up a list of the key characteristics of FOMHEIs which add important depth to Altbach's original exploratory article in 2005. The key features of FOMHEIs which they identify are that:

- They focus on teaching, in particular courses with market relevance;
- They rely heavily on tuition revenue to sustain their operations;
- They have little research culture;
- They are often part of larger, family-owned educational conglomerations where revenue can be shared among different organizations and where the schools, for example, can subsidize the university if needed;
- They are subject to government oversight and guidelines but, even when these are in place, families can exercise control through occupying key leadership and board positions; where they occupy both, this can lead to fewer 'agency problems', i.e. disagreements between owners (principals) and managers (agents). This is especially the case when the same individual can occupy multiple roles;
- Families look to recruit from within the family and there is an expectation that family members will work for the organization;
- Potential successors are integrated into the culture of the organization early; they are expected to obtain appropriate credentials (such as a PhD) and experience of leadership;
- The reputation of the family is closely linked with the success of the institution; institutional failure portends financial and social risk to the whole family;
- They often suffer from a poor public image; their governance structure is criticized as anti-meritocratic and offering more opportunities for corruption than non-family institutions and their motives, however genuine, can be interpreted in that context;
- They can be nimbler in times of crisis; can be better at preserving the values, beliefs and practices of the organizational culture; can demonstrate long-term stability (family presidents can stay in post for several decades); can demonstrate high levels of family and personal financial investment to ensure continuity.

Altbach et al. (2019: 304) summarize this last point well when they write:

> The prospect of personal financial stability and social prestige drives the family's continued commitment to organizational success... Faculty, staff, students and the local community stand to benefit from the high engagement of the family when the institution climbs rankings, attracts top talent or attracts resources.

As we have seen, all of these points are applicable to the case of MGU. Several of them, we suggest, are indeed the sources of 'inbuilt resilience' which allowed MGU to recover to become the institution it is today. The involvement of family members in so many key positions in the *gakkō hōjin*, combined with the expectation that such involvement would continue into the future, may have fostered a degree of tunnel vision, but also provided coherence in management and enabled decisions to be implemented efficiently. The focus on undergraduate education and the relegation of research to the status of an esoteric pastime ensured that reforms, when they finally came, were focused on catering to the university's primary market of fee-paying students. MGU was also a typical family-run institution in that it was part of a larger conglomeration of institutions. In purely business terms, the prospect of closing the 'flagship' university within the conglomeration was likely to have reputational damage for the whole *gakkō hōjin* such that the status—not to mention the jobs and income—of all the institutions as well as family which ran them were likely to suffer. It was imperative, therefore that the university survive even if it meant reducing its size and income; possibly even if it meant running it at a loss.

Many of these attributes of inbuilt resilience in family-run universities are specific manifestations of features which exist in family-run organizations in other sectors of society. At the same time, the conception of an institution as 'family-run' invites further consideration of the nature of family and kinship more generally. Below therefore we situate our account of family-run universities within the wider literature on family business internationally and Japan specifically, together with anthropological insights into kinship and family relations in Japan.

The Study of Family Businesses

In his book, *Dynasties*, the Harvard economic historian David Landes (2006: xi–xii) explains how he became converted to the importance of family businesses for the modern world:

In the European Union, family firms make up 60–90 percent of businesses, depending on the country, and they account for two thirds of GNP and jobs. In the United States in the mid-1990s, more than 90 percent of firms were family units, accounting for more than half of the country's goods and services; further, one third of the Fortune 500 (the country's five hundred largest firms) were said to be family controlled or to have founding families involved in management. What's more, these family firms tended to be the best performers, far outpacing on average their managerial (non-family) competitors.

According to Colli and Rose (2008: 201), actually as many as 95 per cent of registered companies in the US might be defined as family businesses, collectively responsible for 40 per cent of the country's GDP; in Brazil the figures are respectively 90 per cent and 65 per cent; in Spain 70–80 per cent and 65 per cent; and in Germany 60 per cent and 55 per cent. According to an article in the *Harvard Business Review* (Kachaner, Stalk, and Bloch 2012), family-owned businesses account for over 30 per cent of companies which have sales over $1 billion. Many of the world's best-known companies such as Walmart (United States), Michelin (France), IKEA (Sweden), Benetton (Italy), Heineken (Netherlands), Lego (Denmark), Samsung (Korea), Kikkoman (Japan) and Tata (India) are still regularly described as family businesses.[19]

Family businesses are the oldest and still by far the most common form of economic organization, so why are they not the object of more study? The reasons, according to Landes (2006: 290–1) is that 'Contemporary students of business history...largely ignore the struggles and successes of family firms because they assume family enterprise is merely a transitional stage model, if not obsolete altogether...Business dynasties..are seen as intrinsically inadequate, a thing of the past...[G]rowth in both production and distribution creates problems and tasks that impose functional specialization...and thus compels recourse to appropriately trained personnel'. Landes adds the success of the business itself to the list of challenges to family firms, as heirs find other things to do with the wealth that previous generations have accrued.

Family businesses, therefore, have not enjoyed the same level of academic scrutiny as new advanced forms of company management and ownership which enjoy purportedly better leadership by being run as professional organizations on purely economically rational grounds for the interest of

---

[19] As a counter-example, the premise of *The Lehman Trilogy*, a play documenting the rise and fall of Lehman Brothers, is it was the decisive shift in the late 1960s with the creation of a trading division run by non-family members which led eventually to the firm's demise.

external partners such as shareholders and consumers. In much of the literature on management organizations, indeed, family businesses are seen as an anachronism or as a historical relic which, over time, will become proper companies.

A major issue for research on family businesses has been the question of definition. Landes (2006: xiv), for example, defines a dynasty as 'three successive generations of family control' and gives an account of some of the best known 'business family names' from the past two centuries: Barings, Rothschilds, Morgans, Fords, Agnellis, Peugeots, Rockefellers, Guggenheims. From Japan, he takes the case study of the Toyoda family which established and continue to play a leading role in the Toyota Motor Corporation. While interesting in their own right, these case studies actually demonstrate very different trajectories: from continuing family control in the case of the Rothschilds stretching back more than 250 years, to the Peugeots and Morgans who moved from successful family enterprises to a managerial arrangement, to the Rockefellers who long ago gave up their control over Standard Oil to concentrate on philanthropy and politics.

The figures cited by Colli and Rose above are reliant on a very broad definition of what constitutes a family business. Such a definition, for example, might require only that the family had some degree of control over the strategic direction of the company and an intention for the company to remain in the family. A very narrow definition would be one that required multiple generations to be actively involved in the daily operations of the company and at least one member to have significant management responsibility (see Sharma, Melin and Nordqvist, 2014: 16–7). Using a narrow definition in the US, for example, would reduce the number of companies to a quarter of the figure quoted by Colli and Rose (see Shanker and Astrachan, 1996).

Colli and Rose (2008: 195) themselves admit that, 'There is no general consensus among scholars as to what constitutes a family business in quantitative, qualitative...or historical terms'. As they (2008: 196) point out, 'The notion of family is as variable as that of the family business, shifting through time and having very specific and distinctive meanings in particular countries and even different regions'. In order to allow some level of comparative analysis, however, they break down the core components of family business into three elements: kin (however culturally defined), property (as in the ownership of a crucial element of capital) and succession (as in the ownership of, and succession to, the control of the strategic management of the firm). This allows them to propose a broad, working definition of the family firm as 'one where a family owns enough of the equity to be able to exert control over strategy *and* is involved in top management positions' (Colli and Rose, 2008: 194; italics in original). This fits well with another definition sometimes used by business management scholars where family businesses are described as 'organizations where two or more extended family members influence the direction of the business through the exercise of kinship ties, management roles, or ownership rights' (Tagiuri and Davis, 1996: 199).

As all those who have tried to find a definition for family businesses point out, such attempts raise as many questions as they answer about institutional, cultural and governance arrangements.[20] Sharma (2004: 4), for example, points out, firms are rarely 'an either-or scenario', that is either a family business or not a family business, but frequently a mixture of the two. Instead, it can make more sense to talk about the *extent* to which a family has influence over a business. Families can have different levels of financial and emotional investment in their companies which can and do change over time. Astrachan, Klein and Smyrnios (2002), therefore, have tried to establish a scale to measure this influence through three key variables: power, experience and commitment or culture. Sharma (2004: 4–7) describes mapping 72 distinct non-overlapping categories of family firm according to the extent of family involvement in terms of ownership and management. Astrachan and Zellweger (2008) suggest a priority is to distinguish between founding ownership (i.e. first-generation family influence) and descendant ownership (i.e. influence of the family via second or later generations).

Much of the research on family businesses in the past two decades has been focused on the examination of the actual individuals or groups of family members involved. There has been considerable research on the characteristics of founders, successors and non-family employees as the key stakeholders in the business. There has been research on the nature and types of contracts which exists in such organizations; on sources of conflict and their resolution; and on intergenerational transition and how each of these differ from those in 'professional firms' (where ownership and management are separated). According to Sharma (2004: 21–2) there has been much less research at the organizational level, trying to identify, for example, what 'familiness' as a form of capital brings to the firm or why indeed family firms have endured and shown so much resilience in the face of the 'rationalization' of business.

One of the scholars who has attempted to examine the element of 'familiness' of family business is W. Gibb Dyer, initially in his article 'Culture and

---

[20] For a recent summary of research approaches to family business, see *The Sage Handbook of Family Business* edited by Melin, Nordqvist, and Sharma, 2014.

continuity in family firms' (1988) which was published in the inagurual issue of the journal *Family Business Review* (itself the first scholarly journal in the field).[21] He started by outlining a number of key variables—the concept of the person as good or bad; the nature of relationships (hierarchical, egalitarian, individualistic); the nature of truth (to be found in authority figures such as founder or developed through personal testing); the view of morality (universal or situational)—and used them to map four 'cultural patterns' of family business which he named 'paternalistic', 'laissez-faire', 'participative' and 'professional'.

In the 'paternalistic pattern', which Dyer believed to be by far the most common, leaders who are family members retain all power and make all the key decisions; the family distrusts outsiders and closely watches over employees; family members enjoy preferential treatment; employees are expected to carry out instructions from above without question. In the 'laissez-faire' model, the only substantive difference is that employees are seen as trustworthy and given autonomy to make decisions. The family may still determine the ends, but the employees may determine some of the means. The author could find few examples of the 'participative culture' where the status and power of the ruling family was de-emphasised and relationships are more group-centred and egalitarian than the first two models. Finally, the 'professional culture' pertained generally to where the owning family has turned over the running of the business to non-family members. In Dyer's study, 80 per cent of firms were paternalistic in the first generation; and two-thirds of these changed in the next generation, mostly to become 'professional'.

In a more recent study (Dyer 2018: 244) draws on the idea of 'socio-economic wealth' as a new dependent variable to measure how well family firms perform. This idea has been developed in the work of Berrone, Cruz and Gomez-Meija (2012: 266-7) who use the acronym FIBER to capture the elements of this concept:

1. *F*amily control and influence
2. *I*dentificiation of family members with the firm.
3. *B*inding social ties
4. *E*motional attachment of family members
5. *R*enewal of family bonds through dynastic succession

---

[21] In another article (Dyer 2018: 241), Dyer says that when he published his first article (with Beckhard) on family business in 1983, they could only find six citations, one of which was another of their articles in press.

Dyer constructs a 2×2 matrix with socio-economic wealth on one axis and firm financial performance on the other. Those which score high on both he dubs 'clan' family firms; those which score low on both he dubs 'self-interested' family firms. Those with high financial performance and low socio-economic wealth and low financial performance and high socio-economic wealth, he dubs 'professional' and 'mom and pop' firms respectively.

As we have seen, the examples of Japanese family universities do not fit exactly into any of the typologies which Dyer has developed. Nor would he necessarily expect them to do so. These are Weberian ideal types and are useful as heuristic devices for comparing family businesses both across time (as they change) and across space (as there are many variants at any one time). Meikei Gakuin University, as we have seen, has elements of 'paternalistic' and 'laissez-faire', 'clan' and 'mom and pop' firms. While some authors have looked at how each of these may introduce problems for family businesses, they can also confer considerable comparative advantages.

Kuper (see Norton, *I*, 24 July 2000; Taylor, *G*, 19 July 2000) is among the scholars whose research has focused on emphasising the strengths of family businesses which can provide them with resilience that other forms of management might lack. Family businesses are particularly willing to make long-term investments. They also score heavily on flexibility of labour and reduce the problems of having to train new workers by the simple expedient of ensuring that children acquire an inside knowledge of the business at an early age. But the most significant advantage may lie in the special element of trust between family members. This not only reduces the need for formal contracts but also ensures that capital can be readily raised from members of the wider family.

The net effect of these positive features, as Kachaner, Stalk and Bloch (2012) point out, is that family-owned businesses across all continents outstrip their competitors when economies go into a downturn. They pinpoint seven differences in approach which they suggest might account for this resilience. Family businesses, in general, are more frugal in good times and bad; they keep the bar high for capital expenditures; they carry little debt; they acquire fewer (and smaller) companies; they often show surprising levels of diversification; they are more international; they retain talent better. All of these features, apart from the international dimension, are observable in family-run universities in Japan.

While students of company organization like Kuper can see the benefit of the loyalty and dedication which can arise within family businesses, they also worry about the potential conflicts of interest, irrationalities, and inefficiencies which can also occur in such types of organizations. As Pounder (2015: 121) says, 'the main historical cause of the challenges and problems with family businesses has been the management of the interrelationship between family concerns and business concerns.' The personal interests of family members and the needs of the business might not be aligned, for example, when it comes to assigning senior roles or deciding how much to take out of the company for personal expenses as opposed to how much to reinvest. Individual family members may have inherited equal rights in the company but have different views on its direction. There are multiple examples of family businesses being torn apart by such conflicts—often expressed as 'emotional capital' versus 'business demands'—and they are used to interrogate the advantages and disadvantages of a professional organization which avoids this possibility (see Shafieyoon and Mansouri 2014).

Much of the literature on family businesses (see, for example, Carlock, de Vries, and Florent-Treacy 2007), therefore, explores key questions such as: How are the resources allocated? How are decisions made? How are individuals selected for senior leadership positions? How are the family and business values sustained and transmitted to owners, employees, and younger family members? By far the biggest issue covered in the literature, however, is the question of succession: what happens when the founder of the company needs to hand over the reins to the next generation? It is in this context that the case of Japanese family businesses is particularly interesting.

Family Business in Japan

Goto (2013: 555–6) quotes a widely cited report that globally only 30 per cent of family businesses reach the second generation, that less than 16 per cent reach the third generation, and that, in the US, the average life span of a family business is a mere 24 years. In the case of those family firms which survive more than 60 years, two-thirds of them stop growing, but, as he and others point out, there is one very clear exception to this pattern: Japan.

In Japan, the average life span of a family business is 52 years, and eight of the world's twelve longest surviving family businesses are Japanese, including the Hoshi Guest House, founded in 717, and the construction company Kongo Gumi which reportedly was operated for a record-breaking 1,400 years by a succession of heirs until it was taken over in 2006 (McNeill, I, 29 December 2013). There are 517 still extant businesses founded in Japan before 1700 AD including eighty-five sake breweries, seventy confectioners, and sixty-four inns or hotels (Campden FB n.d.). The nearly 4,000 Japanese companies which have been in business for more than 200 years represent almost 45 per cent of all businesses worldwide with histories of this length (Takei 2016). Some of the biggest companies in Japan are widely known as family firms: Toyota Motor Company (Toyoda family), Suntory (Torii and Saiji families), Kikkoman (Mogi family), Canon (Mitarai family), Panasonic (Matsushita family), and the Mitsui family.[22]

Family businesses became particularly important in Japan in the post-war period in helping society rebuild and develop its medical, welfare, and educational provision. Very similar to the legislation that allowed families to establish educational and welfare organizations in the post-war period, the 1948 Medical Service Act allowed physicians to own medical facilities as sole proprietors, and amendments in 1950 allowed physician-directed-and-owned medical corporations (known as *iryō hōjin*) to own medical facilities. As Rodwin (2011: 171) says: 'Often misleadingly referred to as not-for-profit, medical corporations are for-profit firms that do not pay dividends. They distribute profits to physician owners through salaries, expense accounts, and fringe benefits.' These medical corporations grew rapidly in the post-war period and some of them become huge: one chain included fifty hospitals and 170 clinics with 12,000 employees (Rodwin 2011: 177). As hospitals consolidated, they developed a web of affiliated facilities; medical corporations owned hospitals, clinics, health or social service institutions for the elderly, and home care agencies. Powell and Anesaki (1990: 152) have described some of the tax and other financial advantages that the families who ran such facilities managed to accrue for themselves, particularly following revisions to the Medical Service Act in the early 1980s, which led to the diminishing of government control over private hospitals. This also led to huge growth in the number of such facilities.

Rodwin (2011) gives a very detailed account of some of the conflicts of interest which can occur for the owners of private medical facilities in Japan—in which Japanese patients stay longer in hospitals than in other nations and also receive more drugs for medical treatment—and the efforts by the Japanese government to rein these in over the past three decades. In 1983, a special

---

[22] For examples of detailed histories of current Japanese family-run companies, see Fruin (1983) on Kikkoman, Roberts (1973) on Mitsui, and Landes (2006) on Toyota. For ethnographic accounts of family businesses, see Hamabata (1990) and Kondo (1990), who both provide excellent ethnographies of the complex ties and relations among the members of family-owned manufacturing businesses in Tokyo although, as Stewart (2014: 68) points out, they offer few insights into business as such and focus almost completely on the family element and how that effects domestic transactions.

'medifraud inspectorate' was established after a number of spectacular cases of fraud forced the Ministry of Health and Welfare to intervene again.

Today, around 80 per cent of all hospitals and around 90 per cent of all clinics in Japan are private, mainly family, businesses. As Rodwin says (2011: 161), 'Most private practitioners have entrepreneurial conflicts of interest from owning facilities and from selling medication and ancillary services.' This may explain the current discussion regarding the government converting physician-owned hospitals into institutions that resemble not-for-profit charitable hospitals in the United States.

While accounts of Japanese medical institutions point out that they are largely physician-owned, they do not obviously link this with being a family business. There is virtually no discussion in the literature, for example, of the issue of succession though this is widely known to be a major concern for families who own clinics and hospitals where there can be intense pressure on children, especially oldest sons, to become medically trained. The only English language reference we have found to this issue is in a volume examining the Japanese health system for lessons for the US system (Goldsmith 1984: 29) where a background chapter, co-authored with the leading expert on Japanese health policy and management, Ikegami Naoki, states: 'Nearly 70 per cent of the hospitals are privately owned by physicians. It is imperative for the physician owner of the hospital or clinic to ensure that it stays within the family. It is for this reason that some of the private medical schools can afford to charge high entrance fees.' Indeed, it is likely that it was pressure to secure places for oldest sons to become qualified to take over the family business which was, in part at least, responsible for the series of scandals which hit Japanese medical schools in 2018, where they were found to be illegally discriminating against female applicants by arbitrarily lowering their entrance examination scores (*JT*, 14 December 2018).

In relation to the development of post-war welfare systems, Goodman (2000; 2003) describes the establishment of private welfare corporations (*shakai fukushi hōjin*) set up under the 1951 Social Welfare Services Act. This allowed private welfare institutions to receive public funds in a very similar way to that in which *gakkō hōjin* and *iryo hōjin* were operated for educational and medical institutions. Once corporations had received this accreditation, they found it much easier to get licences to open other institutions. When those were set up, they were often, as was the case with the medical and educational establishment, staffed by members of the extended family, although the law limited the number of family members on any board of trustees (*rijikai*).

The idea that families could continue to hold the major positions in the different organizations of the same corporation or *hōjin* was, however, accepted and is a practice that continues today. In a study of a large *shakai fukushi hōjin* in West Tokyo in the 1990s (Goodman 2000: 70), only two of the 14 institutions (those most recently opened) were not being headed by the direct or adopted direct descendants of the original founder of the *hōjin* in 1949. Putting this the other way around, the current head of the main institution in 1991 estimated that around 90 per cent of the descendants of the original founder and their families either had worked, were working or would be working in some form of social welfare institution, most, though not all, linked with the *hōjin* he had set up.

As with the medical and educational sectors, family-run *shakai fukushi hōjin* quickly came to dominate the field in the immediate post-war period. It would otherwise not have been possible for the state to support all the children who came into its care as Japan was still suffering from extreme poverty and deprivation. By the early 1980s, around 90 per cent of all children's homes (*yōgoshisetsu*) were private organizations and part of *shakai fukushi hōjin*. In many cases, the *yōgoshisetsu* was the flagship institution within the *shakai fukushi hōjin*, especially if it could trace its origins back to the pre-war period as over one-third could (Goodman 2000: 52). If the *yōgoshisetsu* was not able to continue for any reason, it was likely to have a profound impact on the reputation and future survival of the whole *shakai fukushi hōjin*. In a story which has considerable resonance for the problems of family-run universities in Japan today, this was exactly the situation that *yōgoshisetsu* found themselves in in the early 1990s. Put simply, the 30 per cent drop in the number of children in the Japanese population between 1975 to 1990 was a serious threat to the future of these child welfare institutions.[23] In order to survive, they would need to find new markets and sources of income. This they did very successfully, in particular by raising consciousness of the problem of child abuse in Japan (which had long been ignored) and the role they could play in helping children who had been victims. Remarkably, through such measures, the number of such institutions in 1995 was the same as in 1980 at around 480 (Goodman 2000: 51). Even more remarkably, the official number of children's homes in Japan today has grown to over 600, despite concerted attempts from external agencies such as the UN and Human Rights Watch and internal agencies such as the Ministry of Health and Welfare to deinstitutionalize child welfare in

---

[23] The birth rate per 1,000 live births dropped from 1.9 million in 1975 to 1.22 million in 1990; in 1998 there were fewer children in Japan than at the time of the first census in 1920.

Japan in favour of adoption and fostering. This example of the survival of the family-run welfare institutions provides a good comparator for the 'inbuilt resilience' which we ascribe to family-run universities.

The Concept of the *Ie*, Adoption, and the Ideology of Continuity in the Japanese Family

Why do Japanese family businesses survive so long and show such resilience in the face of external challenges? At the same time, why are they, as the leading scholar of Japanese family business, Goto Toshio, is quoted (*SD*, 14 April 2018), not just 'less appreciated' (*dōzoku kigyō ga hyōka sarete inai*) than they are in other parts of the world, but actually viewed so negatively that they often do not even admit to being family businesses? This is despite the fact that, according to the same article in *Shūkan Diamond* (*SD*, 14 April 2018), more than 50 per cent of all Japanese listed companies today can still be described (although it is not made clear by what criteria) as family businesses and, on average, family businesses outperform non-family businesses in Japan.

Goto (2013) and Takei (2016) both see the reason for the longevity of Japanese companies as lying in Japan's historical past and in particular in the *ie* (household) model of kinship. Few subjects have engaged anthropologists of Japan more than the *ie* household system which has widely been seen as the clue to understanding multiple forms of social organization which extending beyond the family. The key elements of the *ie* system can be summarized as follows:

- The *ie* is a corporate body which has its own status, assets, career, and goals;
- Certain roles and positions, for example head or successor, are only defined in the context of the *ie*. Hence, an *ie* is distinct from 'family' where genealogy rather than position is paramount;
- There is clear distinction between those who are inside and outside the *ie*;
- The head (*katoku*) of the *ie* (who is appointed by the previous head) is expected to take responsibility for the actions of all members of the household and the latter are expected to show loyalty to the head in return for this benevolence;
- The *ie* incorporates all those who have gone before as well as all those who are yet to be born; it is imbued with a strong sense of its own history and sees its primary responsibility as ensuring household continuity

(known in Japanese as *iesuji*) in the strongest possible form for the sake of future generations such that it can override the primacy of the blood line (*chisuji*).

In purely anthropological terms, therefore, while the preferred form of succession as the head of the *ie* remains male primogeniture, i.e. the oldest son, if the oldest son is not considered competent, then a younger son or even daughter might replace him. If there is no appropriate successor within the family, then an 'outsider' should be recruited. Whatever happens, continuity must be ensured. As Colli and Rose (2008: 205) put it, 'In Japan, social values and attitude to the family...are not defined in biological terms. Instead...[the] family is defined as those who contribute to the economic welfare of the group or "*ie*".' The primary objective of the *ie* is to protect and expand the wealth of the family even if this is achieved as a result of an adoption rather than by a blood relative.

The rules around adoption are well understood and well-established in Japan. According to Bachnik (1988: 14) 'adoption has been practised in Japan for at least 1300 years' but became the dominant mode of family organization among the samurai class in the Tokugawa feudal period between the middle of the seventeenth and nineteenth centuries. It was then disseminated through the wider population as part of the so-called samuraization process (Befu 1981) in the years after the Meiji Restoration of 1868. The defining characteristics of adoption in Japan historically (Bachnik 1988: 14–15) have been that the primary focus is on the welfare of the *ie* not the adoptee; adoptees are not foundlings but usually close relatives; adoptees are relatively old; no legal distinction exists between adoptive and natural children (unlike with illegitimate children). This system of adoption is remarkably flexible. At its simplest, anyone in Japan can legally adopt anyone else, as long as they are not of a previous generation, such as an uncle or aunt in the case of kin, or, in the case of non-kin, older than the adopter. Adoption in Japan does not require any form of actual co-residence and even, according to Lebra (1995), it was historically possible for someone to adopt retrospectively after they had died. Adoption ties can also be revoked (*rien*) in the same way that marriages can change with divorce (*rikon*).

Over the years, multiple forms of adoptive relationships have developed in Japan. A younger brother can be adopted as a son. A daughter from a lower status family can gain 'suitability' for marriage to a higher status spouse by being adopted by another household even if she never actually lives with her adoptive parents. *Kaiyōshi* (buyer-adoptive son) relates to a person on the verge of bankruptcy selling his property to a stranger who is willing to take over the family occupation and continue the family name. Lebra (1995) points out that these adoptions quickly become 'normalized' in the family record because of a Japanese tendency towards 'genealogical amnesia'. This explains, in part, the frequent claim that the Japanese Imperial family has continued for 125 generations unbroken; often the continuity was as a result of adoptions which have now been forgotten.

By far the most common form of adoption in Japan has been the adoption of sons-in-law (*muko yōshi engumi*), generally between the ages of 25 and 30, and generally at the moment when they marry the daughters of the family which needs a new head. In Japan, sexual relations with social kin, such as adopted brothers or sisters, as opposed to biological kin, are not considered incestuous. Ninety-five per cent of all the roughly 90,000 adoptions—a number which has remained remarkably steady for the past 50 years—which occur in Japan each year are of adults by adults and the great majority of those are of sons-in-law (Mehrotra et al. 2013).

In the immediate post-war period, Japan was democratized by the SCAP administration. Some of the very large family conglomerations, known as *zaibatsu*, seen as a key part of Japan's military build-up, were abolished. A new civil law technically abolished the *ie* system and all biological children were given equal rights in terms of inheritance. The *ie* system was considered a feudal relic which vested too much power in hierarchical relations and in particular in the power of the head of the family. Adult adoption, however, continued at a very high rate, but it began to develop a negative image and a view developed that there was something suspicious about people decided to adopt. Adoption became associated, for example, with avoiding paying inheritance tax (every year several thousand people over the age of 50 are adopted); as a means for homosexual partners to pass on their inheritance in a country which does not formally recognize homosexual partnerships; as a means of keeping otherwise illegal foreign workers in the country; even as a means of avoiding debt collectors since it is one of the few ways to legally change one's family name in Japan (Goodman 2000: 147). Despite the persistence of adoption in contemporary Japan, therefore, these days it is often seen as old-fashioned and dating from a pre-war or even feudal system of kinship.

As with the increasingly negative view of adoption in the post-war period, so with the introduction of western thinking of professional management practices, family businesses began to be looked down upon as old-fashioned. Takei (2016), indeed, goes as far as to say, 'family business became taboo.' This may explain why family-run businesses in Japan and the existence of corporations (*hōjin*) of family-run organizations, while they are highly dominant in many spheres—not just business, but also medical, welfare, and educational—have been so little researched. In the case of universities, the absence of research on the role of families in their management and ownership is not just limited to Japan. As we have seen, the category of family-owned and managed higher education institutions remains poorly understood and in many societies—Japan included—viewed with a good deal of misapprehension and suspicion. The very family-oriented features which give rise to such negative views are also those which predispose FOMHEIs to cope especially well with crisis.

Conclusions, Reflections, Predictions

The book started out with a social science puzzle: why were so many people in Japan in the early 2000s convinced that there was going to be a major implosion in the private higher education sector during the next decade? Toivonen and Imoto (2012: 6–7) asserts that social science can be broken down into approaches that either look at structure or agency. The former, 'focusses on how people are constrained by the rules, norms and categories of a society'; the latter 'place the human agent, rather than the social structure, at the centre of sociological inquiry'. The approaches which look at structure can be further broken down into what they call 'the consensus model' and the 'conflict model'. In the 'consensus model', often associated with the functionalist theories deriving from the work of Emile Durkheim in the late nineteenth century, 'social phenomena are explored in terms of what functions they serve for the integration and cohesion of society.' By contrast, in the 'conflict model', deeply influenced by Marxist thinking, 'society is seen as inherently unstable. The state of harmony and consensus assumed in the functionalist model is instead regarded as an ideology...imposed on society...by the dominant class.'

The struggle between consensus-based functionalist approaches versus conflict-based social action and Marxist theories for understanding Japan has been a hot topic of debate in the field of Japanese studies. This has been the case particularly since the 1980s when scholars began to interrogate the dominance of the so-called Nihonjinron (theories of Japaneseness) literature which tended to present Japan in functionalist, consensus-based terms. Two Australian sociologists, Ross Mouer and Yoshio Sugimoto (1986), characterized these theories of uniformity and consensus as 'The Great Tradition' in the study of Japanese society which they counterpoised with 'The Little Traditions' of conflict and variation. While the 'Little Traditions' could be found in Japanese studies in the 1980s, they argued, they were muted by the collective interests of the state, academia, and the publishing industry.

We suggest that the dominant paradigmatic view of higher education institutions in the early 2000s was coloured by functionalist assumptions of the way that Japanese society would 'naturally' allow such institutions to disappear because the supply of private university education would exceed the demands of a declining population. This perspective did not foresee the actions of several important stakeholders in the higher education system. It did not take into account the actions of parents, especially those who had not been to university themselves, in encouraging and supporting their children to do so, which led to the rapid growth in the proportion going into higher education after school. It did not take into account the growing demand for four-year university education among women who in previous generations would have settled for junior college instead. It did not take into account the conservativeness of companies which still wished to recruit university graduates rather than school leavers, or of school careers advisors in recommending their pupils to attend even low-level universities, rather than no university. It did not take into account the inconsistency of government policy, under pressure from powerful lobby groups, which put in various safety nets and incentivized students to attend university when they could have allowed many more institutions to fail. Most importantly, it treated universities as passive in the face of these crises when in fact they were complex actors able to draw on multiple resources as well as multiple narratives with their staff and students which allowed them to find new ways of existing. In particular, as we have seen, it did not recognize that many of the universities which were most under threat were part of family-run conglomerations which had both the resources and the motivation to ensure their survival. The story of private universities in Japan in the period 1992–2018 has been one of resilience in the face of demographic decline.

To complete the span of time promised by the subtitle of the book, we must also look ahead to the next decade of demographic change and its possible consequences for private universities. The first point to note is that the decline over the two decades from 2018 will actually happen at a much slower pace than in the 1990s and 2000s. The forecast decrease in 18-year-olds over 13 years from 1.18 million in 2018 to 1.04 million in 2031 makes for a rate of decline which is 80 per cent smaller *per year* compared to when the population plummeted over 17 years from 2.05 million in 1992 to 1.19 million in 2009.

A question that policymakers fix on in Japan is not whether private universities are capable of negotiating population decline itself but when and where the rate of decline will finally outstrip the ongoing rise in entrance rates. Adopting a similar modelling approach to that used by the OECD (Vincent-Lancrin 2008), the education ministry (MEXT) has formulated a number of scenarios based on different entrance rates for universities specifically (MEXT 2017f). The most pessimistic of these assumes that the entrance rate will not rise any further, in which case the number of university entrants in 2033 will be around 15 per cent less than in 2015. In order to realize the most optimistic scenario, in which there is no decline at all in the absolute number of university entrants, the entrance rate would have to rise significantly, to 60.3 per cent (from 50.2 per cent in 2015).

In early 2018, MEXT submitted to the Central Council of Education committee drafting the latest 'grand design' for higher education in Japan, a more sophisticated projection based on observations of the changes in entrance rates in the period from 2014 to 2017, by gender and geographical region (MEXT 2018k).[24] This projection—which applies a higher rate of increase in women's entrance rates across the board but acknowledges that entrance rates among men are unlikely to increase further in many regions—produces the results shown in Table 6.1 below. This shows a continued increase in entrance rates, but still not enough to counterbalance the population decline, resulting in a drop in the absolute number of university entrants of close to 20 per cent by 2040. The potential impact on fee-reliant private universities is obvious.[25]

---

[24] Population will not decline at an even rate throughout Japan. Ogawa (2016, see also Ogawa 2017) compares the number of final-year high school students and first-year primary students in each prefecture to establish the extent of the decline over the period it takes for the latter cohort to reach the age of university entrance. The national average drop in the number of 18-year-olds between 2015 and 2033 is 10.7 per cent. Metropolitan Tokyo and neighbouring Kanagawa are under 5 per cent. Far higher proportions are predicted in rural prefectures generally, and especially in northern Japan (over 20 percent in Aomori, Fukushima, Akita, and Iwate) and, less predictably, in the Kansai area (the home to MGU and many of the other universities profiled in this book), with Osaka and Kyoto both around 15 per cent.

[25] Predictions of declining student populations apply to post-secondary education as a whole, not universities specifically. As we have seen, population decline has hit 2-year junior colleges (*tandai*) particularly hard and, in all likelihood, will continue to do so. In junior colleges, the fulfilment rate (enrolments as a percentage of capacity) is 90 per cent overall, and approximately one-third of colleges fail to fill even 80 per cent of their enrolment capacity which, in many cases, has itself been reduced over time. Perhaps more significantly, therefore, 57 per cent of junior colleges in 2018 had a negative balance sheet (MEXT 2018b).

Table 6.1 Government projection of change in entrance rates and number of university entrants

Year	University entrance rate			No. of university entrants	
	Overall	Male	Female		Decrease
2017	52.6%	55.9%	49.1%	629,733	
2033	56.7%	57.8%	55.5%	569,789	59,944
2040	57.4%	58.4%	56.3%	506,005	123,728

Source: MEXT 2018k.

The key difference between the situation in the early 2000s and the late 2010s is that many universities have already been struggling for more than two decades of downturn and are, in the words of Ogawa Yō quoted in the introduction to this book, already 'on the brink' (*genkai*): so severely under-enrolled and financially stretched that they are at constant risk of closure.[26] Ogawa (2017) says that universities in this position tend to have several things in common: (a) they are small-scale, undergraduate institutions; (b) they were established in the boom period, often as upgraded junior colleges or public–private partnerships; and, (c) they are located either in rural areas (which have a declining local population of university-goers and little capacity to attract students from other areas) or on the fringes of major urban centres (which are home to the vast majority of universities and therefore the fiercest competition). These features can be contrasted with the universities that have remained stable in the past two decades of a supposed oversupply (*zennyū jidai*) of higher education: large metropolitan institutions with long histories.

This analysis is borne out by a portrait of the private university sector published by Promotion and Mutual Aid Corporation for Private Schools of Japan (PMAC) (Table 6.2). The finding that smaller, and especially rural, universities are the most precarious is hardly novel or surprising, but PMAC's figures also underline the fact that such universities constitute the majority

---

[26] Ogawa's *genkai daigaku* (universities on the brink) epithet is inspired by the term *genkai shūraku* (communities on the brink), which is used to refer to rural villages that have been so severely depopulated that they are no longer viable and in danger of dropping off the map completely (Ohno 2008). Use of the *genkai* label has been extended recently into a discourse of *genkai kokka* (nation on the brink): see, for example Menju (2017). In a study (Manzenreiter, Lützeler, and Polak-Rottmann 2020) of rural Japan, the editors conclude that the number of cases of rural communities in Japan which have disappeared completely is actually very rare indeed despite the predictions that many hundreds were on the point of extinction. In an analysis that has interesting parallels with our study of Japanese private universities, they set out to explore the sources of resilience of such communities and why predictions of their extinction have so consistently proven wrong.

Table 6.2 Size, location, and financial status of Japanese private universities, 2017[27]

	Universities		Students		Universities in operating deficit	
	No.	%	No.	%	No.	%
Rural/medium-small	304	51.4	505,939	24.8	138	45.4%
Urban/medium-small	227	38.3	506,348	24.8	78	34.4%
Rural/large	16	2.7	229,792	11.3	1	6.3%
Urban/large	45	7.6	800,173	39.1	2	4.4%
TOTAL	592		2,042,252		219	

Source: MEXT 2017f.

in the private university sector. They have known for a long time how to diversify and survive and in all probability will continue to do so.

The prevalence of family-run universities in Japan is related to the system of *gakkō hōjin* governance which, as we have seen, allows a small number of individuals to maintain hands-on control and resist outside scrutiny and intervention. This structure in combination with the overwhelming reliance on private funding sources constitutes the essentially 'private' character of private universities in Japan. It is a combination which has long excused a low level of government investment (both financial and regulatory) in the university system, and it is unlikely to change in the near future. The 2017 report of the ministerial working group on private universities, mentioned in Chapter 5 in relation to the construction of a safety net for struggling institutions, affirms a bare-minimum role for government, stating that 'while MEXT is responsible for approving acts of endowment, issuing dissolution orders and performing other statutory functions, the basic principle is to afford the utmost respect for the independence and autonomy of *gakkō hōjin*' (Working Group 2017: 5).

The question, however, is how the ministry will balance this respect for autonomy with the pressure to furnish a credible safety net and take more tangible action to promote the sound governance and management of *gakkō*

---

[27] PMAC employs the categories of 'urban' (Tokyo and the twenty major cities with special administrative designation [*seirei shitei toshi*] nationwide) and 'provincial' (the rest), and correlates these geographical categories with the factor of size—dividing universities into 'large' (enrolment of 8,000 and over) and 'medium-small' (under 8,000) (PMAC 2018c). The correlation which the PMAC data reveals between size, location, and financial stability is also observable in a 2013 survey of private university leaders' own assessments of their operating position (Yamada 2018). The proportion of leaders expecting their circumstances to become more challenging was predictably high among provincial universities (46 per cent) and those enrolling 1,000 or fewer students (43 per cent), while optimism was highest among those located in Tokyo (32.6 per cent) and those enrolling over 2,000 students (62.5 per cent).

hōjin. We are likely to see a continued tension between arm's-length and hands-on treatment which, as shown in Chapter 2, has been a primary feature of private higher education administration in Japan for the last hundred years. A classic example of this contradictory approach can be seen in allowing new universities to open while imposing harsher financial penalties on existing universities which exceed their enrolment quotas.[28] Plans for expansion of the student financial aid system, mentioned in Chapter 5, are likely to generate further demand for university education and exacerbate the contradiction between policy controls and free market forces. The result may be a prolongation of the current situation in which many universities are on the brink, but not at all certain when they might topple over it.

The government's current position could even be seen as affirming the approach to management which has long prevailed in family-run institutions. At first glance, the 2017 report mentioned above does seem to challenge that approach, calling for *gakkō hōjin* to be more transparent and accountable to a wide range of stakeholders, including alumni, employers, and local communities, and suggesting that private universities 'will need to maintain an even stronger public character (*kōkyōsei*) than they have thus far' (Working Group 2017: 5). It even proposes universities adopt something like a 'code of corporate governance' (Working Group 2017: 8). The emphasis on *corporate* governance, however, is mirrored by a further dilution of *academic* governance mechanisms. The report's emphasis on 'alignment of authority and responsibility' in essence signals an even stronger role for the *gakkō hōjin* board and university president and a further weakening of faculty councils (*kyōjukai*). In such a climate, it is almost impossible to imagine a waning of the model of 'board of trustees' rule' or 'one-man management' which is the norm in family-run universities.

All this leads us to suggest that private education as a family business in Japan will continue for some time to come. Moreover, the support of a structure of family businesses—which has been extant in Japan for over 1,000 years and which exists primarily in order to ensure their own continuity—may

---

[28] In 2016, for example, MEXT granted permission for five new universities to open in 2018 while at the same time reducing the amount by which it allowed large and medium universities to over-recruit without losing their subsidies. The response of some of these universities has been to apply to open new departments or to increase the quotas of their current departments in order to protect their financial position. At the time of writing, large universities were allowed to enrol up to 110 per cent of quota, medium universities 120 per cent, and small universities 130 per cent before losing their subsidies. MEXT also applies incremental subsidy cuts to universities enrolling under 90 per cent of quota. From 2019, universities which manage to stay between 90 and 100 per cent of quota will be *rewarded* with an increase in subsidy of up to 4 per cent (MEXT 2018g).

well prove to be a boon in a period of increasing diversity. We therefore predict that most of the universities which exist in Japan today will also be operating, in some form or other, in 2030 which bodes well for the continued development of family-run universities as part of private education systems elsewhere. If we are wrong, of course, we look forward to analysing why that might be.

Glossary

akahon: literally 'red book', compilations of universities' past entrance examinations which can be used as practice papers by students thinking of applying.

amakudari: literally 'descent from heaven', refers to the appointment of a former government official to a position of responsibility in a private organization.

arubaito: part-time work (from German *arbeit*).

bunkasai: student-led festival on campus.

centre shiken (daigaku nyūshi centre shiken): a nationwide standardized examination for university entrance conducted by the National Center for University Entrance Examinations, an administrative agency under the education ministry. Examination results are used for admission to national, local public, and some private universities. A new format being introduced from 2020 is designed to test a wide range of skills and will eventually include an English language proficiency test conducted by private testing service providers.

chūō kyōiku shingikai: Central Council for Education. The main policy advisory body to the national ministry of education; publishes reports and recommendations which inform educational policymaking. University matters are dealt with by the Council's University Subdivision (*daigaku bunkakai*), whose members include representatives appointed by the ministry from both academia and business circles. The subdivision operated as a separate council, the University Council (*daigaku shingikai*), from 1987 to 2000.

COE/COL: Centres of Excellence/Centres of Learning. Part of Japanese government policy in early 2000s to both foster competition among universities and align university activity more closely with wider economic objectives was the development of mechanisms for allocating public funding on a competitive rather than historical basis. The flagship competitive funding schemes were those for research-based Centres of Excellence (COE) from 2002 and teaching-based Centres of Learning (COL, which eventually became more widely known as GP—Good Practice) from 2003.

daigaku: 'university', covering an extremely broad range of four-year (*yonen-sei*) institutions, from world-class establishments with several thousand students to local colleges with less than fifty.

daigaku kaikaku: blanket term for university reform.

Daigaku Rei: University Ordinance of 1918 which provided formal recognition of private academies as *daigaku* as well as providing for the establishment of public universities at prefectural level.

daigaku hyōka: university evaluation. Part of the goal of making universities more entrepreneurial and results-driven in the early 2000s was a shift from ex ante to ex post evaluation and quality assurance. In association with the 2004 move to corporatization, a new regime of 'accreditation evaluation' (*ninshō hyōka*) was introduced, under which all universities—not only national university corporations—submit to a seven-yearly cycle of evaluation by a government-approved independent accreditation agency.

daigakuin: graduate school(s).

daigakuin daigaku: a university which offers graduate school programmes only.

dokuritsu gyōsei hōjin: literally 'independent administrative corporations', the status given to all national and most local universities in 2004 which afforded them more scope to determine their own institutional identities and directions, as well as requiring them gradually to become more financially autonomous.

dōzoku: group of related households.

dōzoku keiei: literally 'same-family management', management by a group of related households.

fuku-gakuchō: Vice president of a university.

gakkai: learned society.

gakkō hōjin: see shiritsu gakkō hōjin below.

gakubu: undergraduate academic unit; usually termed 'faculty' or 'college' in English. May incorporate a number of individual *gakka* (departments).

gakuchō: president: Directs the business of the university and oversees its staff (School Education Act, Art. 92(3)). In private universities, the president is selected by the board of trustees, selection committee and/or direct ballot. The president may also serve as the chair of the board of trustees. Usually assisted by vice presidents (*fuku-gakuchō*) who may also be trustees.

gakusha: scholar.

haken shain: despatch company employee.

hensachi: a standard deviation score which indicates a prospective university applicant's position relative to her/his peers, as determined through mock entrance exams conducted by major supplementary education providers.

hōjinka: corporatization; usually refers to the corporatization of national universities in 2004.

hōka daigakuin: graduate law schools, first opened in 2004.

hyōgiinkai: board of councillors in a private school corporation (*gakkō hōjin*). The chair of the board of trustees (*rijichō*) is obliged to hear the opinion of the Board of Councillors in advance on certain matters (budgets, borrowing, disposition of assets, business plans, amendments to the articles of endowment, mergers, dissolution, important particulars concerning for-profit business, other important particulars: Private Schools Act Art. 42); it must be provided with reports on previous year's activities (PSA Art. 46) and Auditors' reports (PSA Art. 37), and approve appointment of auditors (PSA Art. 38). Membership varies ('as provided for in the articles of endowment'), but must be more than double the number of trustees (PSA Art. 41(2)) and should include employees of the *gakkō hōjin*'s schools, and alumni 'aged 25 and over' (PSA Art. 44). Trustees (*riji*) can serve concurrently as councillors.

ie: house or household.

iryō hōjin: not-for-profit private medical corporations established under the Medical Service Act of 1948.

Japan Student Services Organization (JASSO; nihon gakusei shien kikō): An independent administrative institution under the umbrella of the education ministry. Provides support services for domestic and international students and administers the national system of higher education loans (*shōgakukin*).

jimu (short for jimu-soshiki, jimu-kyoku, jimu-bu): University administration. No provision in School Education Act other than requirement for universities to have 'administrative staff' (*jimu shokuin*).

juku: supplementary education schools offering programmes to students still in primary or secondary schools.

junkyōju: assistant professor.

kabushiki kaisha ritsu daigaku: corporate universities, category of private university created in 2003 which were not *shiritsu gakkō hōjin*.

kakenhi (short for kagaku kenkyūhi): Grants-in-Aid for Scientific Research. The principal government research grant scheme in Japan.

kanji: auditors. Audit the business and property of the *gakkō hōjin* (Private Schools Act Art. 37(3)(i)(ii)), report to boards of trustees and councillors (Art. 37(3)(iii)), or to the competent governmental authority in cases of misconduct or legal infringement (Art. 37(3)(iv)). Must be at least two auditors (Art. 35(1)); trustees (*riji*) cannot serve as auditors.

kenkyūkai: academic study group.

kenkyūsha: researcher.

kisei kanwa: relaxation of regulations or deregulation, a political philosophy applied to many areas of Japanese life, including higher education, since the 1980s.

kiyō: academic proceedings, transactions, bulletin; often published by universities in-house.

kokuritsu daigaku: national universities.

koma: unit of teaching, normally ninety minutes in length.

kōshi: lecturer.

kōritsu daigaku: local public universities: established and operated by a prefectural or municipal government.

kōsetsu min'ei daigaku: publicly founded, privately operated universities.

kōtō senmon gakkō (kōsen for short): higher technical colleges, which provide qualifications leading mainly to occupations in engineering, science, and technology and enrol just under 2 per cent of students in higher education.

kyōikusha: educationalist.

kyōju: professor.

kyōjukai: Academic Council: Composed of professors and may include associate professors and other members of academic staff. Discusses education and research activities undertaken within in its faculty or organizational unit; gives opinions on student admissions, graduations, curricula and conferral of degrees, and other important matters concerning education and research (School Education Act, Art. 93).

kyōjukai-shihai: literally 'academic council rule'; universities where power resides largely with the academic body.

kyōmuka: administrative office for educational affairs.

kyūsei daigaku: universities established in the pre-war period.

kyū-teidai: former imperial universities.

Meiji period: Period between 1868 and 1912 when Japan was formally ruled by the Emperor Meiji.

MEXT: Japanese Ministry of Education, Science, Sports and Culture. *Monbukagakushō* (or *monkashō* for short) in Japanese.

Monbushō: Former Japanese Ministry of Education, Science and Culture. Now MEXT (above).

nyūgakukin: entrance or enrolment fee, payable when enrolling in university on top of the regular tuition fees charged per year or academic semester. Similar once-off fees are required when starting a new project in many areas of Japanese society.

nyūgakushiki: entrance ceremony.

nyūshi iinkai: entrance examination committee.

nyūshi nittei: schedule of entrance examinations.

nyūshi sōdan kai: 'entrance examination advice meetings', events to attract potential applicants to a university.

rijichō: chair of the board of trustees in a private school corporation (*gakkō hōjin*). Represents the *gakkō hōjin* and presides over its business (Private Schools Act, Art. 37 (1)). Convenes and chairs board of trustees. Convenes (but not necessarily chairs) board of councillors. Appoints auditors with consent of board of councillors.

riji: trustees in a private school corporation (*gakkō hōjin*). Represent the *gakkō hōjin*, administer the business of the *gakkō hōjin* by assisting the *rijichō*, and perform the duties of the *rijichō* when s/he is unable to do so (Private Schools Act, Art. 37(2)). Must number at least five (PSA Art. 35(1)). Must include at least one head of any university/school in the *gakkō hōjin*, persons appointed from board of councillors, any other persons appointed as provided in the articles of endowment (PSA Art. 38(1)). Must include at least one external party (not employee or executive of any the schools established by the *gakkō hōjin*) (PSA Art. 38 (5)). *Gakkō hōjin* which operate universities have an average of 11.58 *riji*. Of these, an average of 6.57 are engaged full-time and 4.82 are part-time external appointments (PMAC 2015).

rijikai: board of trustees in a private school corporation (*gakkō hōjin*). Composed of all *riji*; decides on the business of the *gakkō hōjin* and supervises the *riji* in the execution of their duties. Decisions effected by majority of trustees present at meeting (quorum = majority of trustees) unless otherwise provided for in the articles of endowment (Private Schools Act Art. 36(6)).

rijikai-shihai: literally 'board of trustees rule'; universities where power resides largely with the board of trustees or the president.

rinji kyōiku shingikai (or rinkyōshin for short): Special Advisory Council on Education established in 1984 by Prime Minister Nakasone Yasuhiro to chart a course for Japanese education in the post-high-economic-growth era.

ryūnen: an extra year of university which students do because they do not have enough credits to graduate or if they elect to stay on at university beyond the normal four years rather than graduate, for example when the job market is depressed.

senmon gakkō: professional training colleges; a subcategory of specialized training schools (*senshū gakkō*) which offer specialized post-secondary courses (*senmon katei*) across a very wide range of occupational fields generally over a three-year programme. These colleges enrol around 16 per cent of all students in higher education but are defined by the OECD as offering 'non-university qualifications' and hence are generally omitted in comparative statistics of the proportion of students going to university.

senmonshoku daigaku / senmonshoku tanki daigaku: new category of vocational universities and vocational junior colleges offering undergraduate courses with an emphasis on practical training with direct connection to specific vocational fields, placing them somewhere between the conventional university system and the professional training college system. The first three opened in 2019.

senmonshoku daigakuin: 'professional graduate school', a category of institution introduced in 2003, extending postgraduate education beyond its traditionally heavy focus on pure research.

setchi kijun: standards for establishment of a university; administered since 1956 by the Ministry of Education.

shakai fukushi hōjin: literally 'social welfare juridical person': corporate status provided for under Article 22 of the 1951 Social Welfare Services Act, whereby a private welfare administrative organization can be accredited to provide specified publicly recognized welfare services and receive public funding for these programmes.

shakaijin gakusei: literally 'students who belong to adult society'. In practical terms, a student who has spent significant time not being a student—for example while working or raising a family full time. Sometimes, but not always, defined as those over twenty-one when entering undergraduate courses and over twenty-five on postgraduate programmes.

Shidaikyō: Association of Private Universities of Japan (APUJ), established in 1948 and counts around two-thirds of all private universities as its members.

Shidairen: Japan Association of Private Universities and Colleges (JAPUC), established in 1951, by a group of *kyūsei* institutions which felt that their influence within *Shidaikyō* was diluted by the growing number of *shinsei* universities. Formerly known in English as the Japan Association of Private Colleges and Universities.

Shidai Rengōkai: Federation of Japanese Private Colleges and Universities Associations, a joint body for both APUJ and JAPUC, founded in 1986.

shinsei daigaku: universities established after the post-war reforms to the structure of the education system.

shiteikō: literally 'designated schools'; schools with a quota of places which they can directly allocate to students to study at a particular university.

shiritsu daigaku: private university.

Shiritsu Gakkō Hō: Private Schools Act of 1949 which provided for the establishment of *shiritsu gakkō hōjin*.

Shiritsu Gakkō Rei: Private Schools Ordinance of 1899 which placed private educational institutions under the control of regional government heads.

shiritsu gakkō hōjin: private school corporations (referred to simply as '*gakkō hōjin*' throughout this book) established under the Private Schools Act (*shiritsu gakko hō*) of 1949.

Shiritsu Gakkō Shinkō Josei Hō: Act on Subsidies for Private Schools of 1975 which formalized the ad hoc system subsidizing private universities with public money, which had been instituted in 1970.

shuei-san: security staff.

sōchō: president or chancellor. Often refers to cases where the same individual serves as president (*gakuchō*) of multiple institutions within the same *gakkō hōjin*, or as both university president and chair of the board of trustees (*rijichō*).

sotsugyō ronbun: graduation thesis.

sotsugyōshiki: graduation ceremony.

suberidome: backstop, as in a university to which a student applies in case they are unable to get into a higher level institution.

suisen seido: literally 'recommendation system', system whereby universities allow students to enter directly through recommendations from their schools or other agencies, including individuals themselves (*jiko suisen*).

taigaku: dropping out of university.

tanki daigaku: two-year higher education colleges, established in the post-war period and mainly attended by women.

teiin: quota for number of students an institution is allowed to accept and qualify for the full subsidy available. Determined and monitored by the Ministry of Education.

teiin-ware: 'enrolment below the government-approved quota'—an obvious sign of danger for fee-reliant private universities.

yobikō: supplementary education institutions offering programmes to students who have left school and have, typically, taken a year out to apply or re-apply to university.

yutori kyōiku: 'relaxed' educational curriculum introduced in 2003 in the light of the widespread belief in the 1980s that the education system was overheating and applying too much pressure on children but which paradoxically quickly led to a widespread panic over declining scholastic standards.

zemi: seminar class for students in the final (and sometimes penultimate) year of an undergraduate degree programme. Typically involves small class sizes and self-directed study.

zennyū jidai: 'the era of university admission for all', referring to the point in time when university places outnumber students seeking admission.

References

Abe, Shigeyuki, Shoji Nishijima, Shyam Sunder and Karen Lapardus. (1998). 'Why do students take it easy at the university', in Japan: *Why it Works, Why it Doesn't: Economics in Everyday Life*, eds. James Mak, Shyam Sunder, Shigeyuki Abe and Kazuhiro Igawa, pp. 73-81. Hawaii: University of Hawaii Press.

AFCSPU (The Association of Faculty Councils on Subsidies for Private Universities). (2004). *Shiritsu daigaku no mirai: kaikaku to tenbō* [The future of private universities: reform and prospects]. Tokyo: Ōtsuki Shoten.

Aichinger, Theresa, Peter Fankhauser, and Roger Goodman. (2017). 'The Happiness of Japanese Academics: Findings From Job Satisfaction Surveys in 1992 and 2007', in *Life Course, Happiness and Well-being in Japan*, eds. Barbara Holthus and Wolfram Manzenreiter, pp. 158-74. Abingdon: Routledge.

Aikoku Gakuen. (2017). *Nyūgakusha ni kansuru ukeire hōshintō* [Admission policies, etc.]. Online: https://www.aikoku-u.ac.jp/jp/outline/disc/fre (accessed 3 June 2018).

Akabayashi, Hideo. (2015). 'Private Universities and Government Policy in Japan'. *International Higher Education* 42: 117-19.

Allen, Matthew and Edward Choi. (2019). 'Family involvement in university management', in *The Global Phenomenon of Family-Owned/Managed Universities*, eds. Philip G. Altbach, Edward Choi, Matthew R. Allen, and Hans de Wit, pp. 29-41. Leiden: Brill.

Altbach, Philip G and Lionel S. Lewis. (1995). 'Professional attitudes: An international survey', *Change* 27: 51-7.

Altbach, Philip G. (2004). 'The Past and Future of Asian Universities: Twenty-first Century Challenges', in *Asian Universities: Historical Perspectives and Contemporary Challenges*, eds. Philip Altbach and Toru Umakoshi, pp. 13-31. Baltimore and London: The Johns Hopkins University Press.

Altbach, Philip G. (2005). 'Universities: Family Style', in *Private Higher Education: A Global Revolution*, eds. Philip G. Altbach and Daniel C. Levy, Rotterdam, pp. 29-32. Rotterdam: Sense Publishers.

Altbach, Philip G., Edward Choi, Matthew R. Allen, and Hans de Wit. (eds.). (2019). *The Global Phenomenon of Family-Owned/Managed Universities*. Brill: Leiden.

Amano, Ikuo. (1986). *Kōtō kyōiku no nihon teki kōzō* [Structure of higher education in Japan]. Tokyo: Tamagawa Daigaku Shuppanbu.

Amano, Ikuo. (1988). *Daigaku: shiren no jidai* [Universities in trying times]. Tokyo: University of Tokyo Press.

Amano, Ikuo. (1990). *Education and Examination in Modern Japan*. Tokyo: University of Tokyo Press.

Amano, Ikuo. (1997). 'Structural Changes in Japan's Higher Education System: From a Planning to a Market Model'. *Higher Education* 34: 125-39.

Amano, Ikuo. (2000). *Gakuchō: daigaku kaikaku eno chosen* [University presidents: the challenge of university reform]. Machida: Tamagawa University Press.

Amano, Ikuo. (2004). *Daigaku kaikaku: chitsujo no hōkai to saihen* [University reform: collapse and restructuring of the existing order]. Tokyo: University of Tokyo Press.

Amano, Ikuo. (2006). *Daigaku kaikaku no shakaigaku* [Sociology of university reform]. Tokyo: Tamagawa University Press.

Amano, Ikuo. (2011). *The Origins of Japanese Credentialism*. Melbourne: Trans Pacific Press.
Amano, Ikuo and Gregory Poole. (2005). 'The Japanese university in crisis'. *Higher Education* 50(4): 685–711.
Anderson, Kent and Trevor Ryan. (2010). 'Gatekeepers: A Comparative Critique of Admission to the Legal Profession and Japan's New Law Schools', in *Legal Education in Japan: Globalization, Change and Contexts*, eds. Stacey Steele and Kathryn Taylor, pp. 45–67. London: Routledge.
Anderson, Ronald S. (1975). *Education in Japan: A Century of Modern Development*. Washington DC: US Government Printing Office.
Aoki, Masahiko, Akihiro Sawa, Michio Daitō, and Tsūsan Kenkyū Rebyū Henshū Iinkai. eds. (2001). *Daigaku kaikaku: kadai to sōten* [University reform: Challenges and debates]. Tokyo: Toyo Keizai Shimposha.
APUJ—Association of Private Universities of Japan. (2010). 'Setchishin gakkōhōjin bunka-kai' [Schools establishment council, educational corporations subcommittee]. *Kyōiku gakujutsu onrain* no. 2391 (17 February 2010). Online: https://www.shidaikyo.or.jp/newspaper/online/2391/1_1.html (accessed 18 August 2018).
APUJ—Association of Private Universities of Japan. (2018). 'Shidai governance/management no genjō to sono kaizen.tsūyoka ni mukete'[The present state of governance and management of private universities and directions for their improvement and strengthening]. Online: https://www.shidaikyo.or.jp/riihe/book/pdf/2018_p01.pdf (accessed 6 August 2019).
Arakaki, Daryl Masao. (2004). '"Please Teach the 3 Hs", A Personal Request to Japan's New American-Style Law Schools'. *Osaka Gakuin University Faculty of Law Kiyō* 30(1): 107–46.
Araki, Shota, Daiji Kawaguchi, and Yuki Onozuka. (2015). *University Prestige, Performance Evaluation, and Promotion: Estimating the Employer Learning Model Using Personnel Datasets*. PRIETI Discussion Paper Series 15-E-027. Online: https://www.rieti.go.jp/jp/publications/dp/15e027.pdf (accessed 5 July 2018).
Arimoto Akira. (2005). *Daigaku kyōjushoku to FD* [The university professoriate and faculty development]. Tokyo: Toshindo.
Arimoto, Akira and Shinichi Yamamoto. eds. (2003). *Daigaku kaikaku no genzai* [University reform today]. Tokyo: Toshindo.
Asahi Shimbun Kyōiku Shuzaihan. (2003). *Daigaku gekidō: tenki no kōtō kyōiku* [University upheaval: Higher education at a turning point]. Tokyo: Asahi Shimbunsha.
Asahi Shimbunsha. (2002). *Daigaku ranking* [University ranking]. Tokyo: Author.
Aspinall, Robert. (2013). *International Education Policy in Japan in an Age of Globalisation and Risk*. Leiden: Brill.
Association of Private Universities of Japan. (2004). *Shigaku shinkōshi: hanseiki no chōsen* [History of private education development: the 50-year challenge]. Tokyo: Author.
Astrachan, Joseph H, Sabine B. Klein, and Kosmas X. Smyrnios. (2002). 'The F-PEC Scale of Family Influence: A Proposal for Solving the Family Business Definition Problem'. *Family Business Review* 15(1): 45–58.
Astrachan, Joseph H. and Thomas Zellweger. (2008). 'Die Performance von Familienunternehmen: Literaturübersicht und Orientierungshilfe für künftige Forschungsarbeiten' (Performance of family firms: A Literature review and guidance for future research). *ZfKE—Zeitschrift für KMU und Entrepreneurship* 56(1–2): 83–108.
Baba, Masateru and Yukimasa Hayata. (1997). 'The Changing Role of JUAA in Japanese University Evaluation'. *Assessment and Evaluation in Higher Education* 22(3): 329–35.
Baba, Masateru. (2002). 'The Rationale Behind Public Funding of Private Universities in Japan'. *Higher Education Management and Policy* 14(1): 75–86.
Bachnik, Jane. (1988). 'Adoption'. *Kodansha Encyclopedia of Japan*. Vol. 1. Tokyo: Kodansha.

Bachnik, Jane. ed. (2003). *Roadblocks on the Information Highway: The IT Revolution in Japanese Education*. Lanham, Boulder, New York, and Oxford: Lexington Books.

Bailey, F. G. (1977). *Morality and Expediency: The Folklore of Academic Politics*. Oxford: Blackwell.

Barretta, Mary Jane. (1987). *Rikkyo University, Tokyo, Japan: A case study of governance at a private university*. PhD thesis, University of Pittsburgh.

Bartholomew, James R. (1989). *The Formation of Science in Japan: Building a Research Tradition*. New Haven: Yale University Press.

Befu, Harumi. (1981). *Japan: An Anthropological Introduction*. Tokyo: C. E. Tuttle.

Benesse Corporation. (n.d.). 'THE sekai daigaku ranking nihonban' [THE World University Rankings, Japan edition]. Online: https://japanuniversityrankings.jp/ (accessed 18 August 2018).

BERD—Benesse Educational Research and Development Institute. (2005). 'Shinro sentaku ni kansuru furikaeri chosa' [Survey of reflections on graduate pathway choice]. Online: https://berd.benesse.jp/berd/center/open/report/shinrosentaku/2005/houkoku/furikaeri2_6_9.html (accessed 20 June 2017).

Berrone, Pascual, Christina Cruz, and Luis R. Gomez-Meija. (2012). 'Socioemotional wealth in family firms: Theoretical dimensions, assessment approaches, and agenda for future research'. *Family Business Review* 25(3): 258–79.

Birnbaum, Alfred. ed. (1991). *Monkey, Brain, Sushi: New Tastes in Japanese Fiction*. Tokyo, London, New York: Kodansha International.

Birnbaum, Robert. (2005). 'Professor and Sensei: The Construction of Faculty Roles in the United States and Japan'. *Higher Education Forum* 2: 71–91.

Breaden, Jeremy. (2013). *The Organisational Dynamics of University Reform in Japan: International Inside Out*. Abingdon: Routledge.

Breaden, Jeremy. (2018). *Articulating Asia in Japanese Higher Education: Policy, Partnership and Mobility*. Abingdon: Routledge.

Breaden, Jeremy and Roger Goodman. (2014). 'The Dog that Didn't Bark: 3/11 and International Students in Japan', in *Internationalising Japan: Discourse and Practice*, eds. Jeremy Breaden, Stacey Steele, and Carolyn S. Stevens, pp. 13–31. Abingdon and New York: Routledge.

Cabinet Office. (2017). *Kihon shiryō nyūgaku teiintō no jōkyō* [Basic reference materials (enrolment capacity, etc.)]. Online: https://www.kantei.go.jp/jp/singi/sousei/meeting/daigaku_yuushikishakaigi/h29-04-18-siryou5.pdf (accessed 20 June 2017).

Campden FB. (n.d.). 'Japanese Family Businesses'. Online: http://www.campdenfb.com/sites/campdendrupal.modezero.net/files/Japan_infographic_large.jpg (accessed 11 July 2018).

Carlock, Randel S., Manfred Kets de Vries, and Elizabeth Florent-Treacy. (2007). 'Family Business', in *International Encyclopedia of Organizational Studies*, eds. Stewart R. Clegg and James R. Bailey, pp. 499–502. London: Sage.

Central Council for Education University Subdivision. (2008). *Gakushi katei kyōiku no kōchiku ni mukete* [Toward the development of undergraduate education]. Online: http://www.mext.go.jp/b_menu/shingi/chukyo/chukyo4/houkoku/080410.htm (accessed 10 June 2017).

Central Council for Education University Subdivision. (2010). *Shitsu hoshō o sasaeru tame no kokkōshiritsu daigaku no kenzen na hatten* [Sound development of national, public and private universities to support quality assurance]. Online: http://www.mext.go.jp/b_menu/shingi/chukyo/chukyo4/houkoku/attach/1297042.htm (accessed 11 May 2018).

Central Council for Education. (2003). *Kore made no kōtō kyōiku keikakutō ni tsuite* [Higher education plans, etc. to date]. Online: http://www.mext.go.jp/b_menu/shingi/chukyo/chukyo4/gijiroku/030201fb.htm (accessed 19 July 2017).

Central Council for Education. (2005). *Wagakuni no kōtō kyōiku no shōraizō* [A vision for the future of higher education in Japan]. Online: http://www.mext.go.jp/b_menu/shingi/chukyo/chukyo0/toushin/05013101.htm (accessed 19 July 2017).

Chen, Xi. (2003). 'Daigaku settchi botai toshite no senshūgakkō no kenkyū' [Research on specialised training colleges as founders of universities]. Paper delivered at Nihon Kyōiku Shakai Gakkai, Meiji Gakuin University, 21 September.

Choi, Edward. (2019). 'Korea: Family-owned universities and colleges—A future of dark speculation?', in *The Global Phenomenon of Family-Owned/Managed Universities*, eds. Philip G. Altbach, Edward Choi, Matthew R. Allen, and Hans de Wit, pp. 182–197. Leiden: Brill.

Choi, Edward, Matthew Allen, Hans de Wit, and Philip G. Altbach. (2019). 'A model of family-based higher education management: Challenges and opportunities', in *The Global Phenomenon of Family-Owned/Managed Universities*, eds. Philip G. Altbach, Edward Choi, Matthew R. Allen, and Hans de Wit, pp. 257–280. Leiden: Brill.

Christian Today. (2014). 'Kōbe no seitomasu dai: rainen 3gatsu haishi e' [St Thomas University, Kobe to close in March next year]. *Christian Today*, 5 November 2014. Online: https://www.christiantoday.co.jp/articles/14491/20141105/thomas-university.htm (accessed 10 March 2018).

Clark, Burton R. (1983). *The Higher Education System: Academic Organisation in Cross-National Perspective*. Berkeley: University of California Press.

Clark, Burton R. (1995). *Places of Inquiry: Research and Advanced Education in Modern Universities*. Berkeley, London, and Los Angeles: University of California Press.

Clark, Gregory. (2003). *Naze nihon no kyōiku wa kawaranai no desu ka?* [Why doesn't Japanese education change?]. Tokyo: Tōyō Keizai.

Coleman, Samuel. (1999). *Japanese Science: From the Inside*. London: Routledge.

Colli, Andrea and Mary Rose. (2008). 'Family business', in *The Oxford Handbook of Business History*, eds. Geoffrey G. Jones and Jonathan Zeitlin, pp. 194–218. Oxford: Oxford University Press.

Cummings, William K. (1994). 'From Knowledge Seeking to Knowledge Creation: The Japanese University's Challenge'. *Higher Education* 27(4): 399–415.

Cummings, William K. (1997a). 'Human Resource Development: The J-model', in *The Challenge of East Asian Education: Implications for America*, eds. William K. Cummings and Philip G. Altbach, pp. 275–91. New York: State University of New York Press.

Cummings, William K. (1997b). 'Private Education in Eastern Asia', in *The Challenge of East Asian Education: Implications for America*, eds. William K. Cummings and Philip G. Altbach, pp. 135–54. New York: State University of New York Press.

Daigaku Mirai Mondai Kenkyūkai. (2001). *Daiyosō: 10nen go no daigaku* [Forecast for universities 10 years from now]. Tokyo: Tōyō Keizai Shimbunsha.

Dima, Alina M. (2004). 'Organizational Typologies in Private Higher Education'. Paper presented at 17th Annual CHER Conference 2004, Enschede, Netherlands.

DISCO Corporation. (2018). 'Kōkōsei ni kiita shinro kibō jōkyō ankēto' [Survey of senior high school students' post-graduation preferences] (Press release, 22 May). Online: https://prtimes.jp/main/html/rd/p/000000404.000003965.html (accessed 5 July 2018).

Dore, Ronald P. (1965). *Education in Tokugawa Japan*. Berkeley and Los Angeles: University of California Press.

Dore, Ronald P. (1976). *The Diploma Disease: Education, Qualification, and Development.* Berkeley: University of California Press.

Dore, Ronald P. and Mari Sako. (1998). *How the Japanese Learn to Work.* London and New York: Routledge.

DPJ—Democratic Party of Japan. (2009). *Amakudari ni kansuru yobiteki chōsa* [Preliminary survey into *amakudari*]. Online: http://www1.dpj.or.jp/special/yobicyousa/02.html (accessed 16 July 2017).

Dyer, W. Gibb. (1988). 'Culture and continuity in family firms'. *Family Business Review* 1(1): 37–50.

Dyer, W. Gibb. (2018). 'Are family firms really better? Reexamining "examining the 'family firm effect' on firm performance"'. *Family Business Review* 31(2): 240–8.

Eades, Jeremy S. (2000). '"Why don't they write in English?" Academic Modes of Production and Academic Discourses in Japan and the West'. *Ritsumeikan Journal of Asia Pacific Studies* 6: 58–77.

Eades, Jeremy S. (2005). 'The Japanese 21st Center of Excellence Program: Internationalisation in action?', in *The "Big Bang" in Japanese Higher Education: The 2004 Reforms and the Dynamics of Change*, eds. J. Eades, R. Goodman, and Y. Hada, pp. 295–323. Melbourne: Trans Pacific Press.

Egnor, Clark Marshall. (2001). *Governance of a private Japanese university before and after the 1998 university council reforms.* Doctor of Education in Higher Education Administration dissertation, West Virginia University, Morgantown.

Ehara, Takekazu. (1998). 'Faculty Perceptions of University Governance in Japan and the United States.' *Comparative Education Review* 42(1): 61–72.

Ehara, Takekazu and Hitoshi Sugimoto. (2005). *Daigaku no kanri un'ei kaikaku: nihon no yukue to shogaikoku no dōkō* [University governance in transition: world trends and implications for Japan (publisher's translation)]. Tokyo: Toshindo.

Ellington, Lucien. (1992). *Education in the Japanese Life Cycle: Implications for the United States.* Lewiston, NY: Edwin Mellen Press.

Fazackerley, Anna and Julian Chant. (2009). 'Sink or swim? Facing up to failing universities'. Policy Exchange Research Note, April 2009. Online: https://www.policyexchange.org.uk/wp-content/uploads/2016/09/sink-or-swim-apr-09.pdf (accessed 1 August 2018).

Federation of Japanese Private Colleges and Universities Association. (2017). *Asu o hiraku: shiritsu daigaku no tayō de tokushoku aru torikumi (zōhoban)* [Pathways to tomorrow: the diverse and distinctive activities of private universities (augmented edition)]. Tokyo: Author.

Flaherty, Darryl E. (2013). *Public Law, Private Practice: Politics, Profit and the Legal Profession in Nineteenth-Century Japan.* Cambridge, Mass.: Harvard University Asia Centre.

Foote, Daniel H. (2006). 'Forces driving and shaping legal training reform in Japan'. *Australian Journal of Asian Law* 7(3): 215–40.

Foote, Daniel H. (2013). 'The trials and tribulations of Japan's legal education reforms'. *Hastings International and Comparative Law Review* 36(2): 369–442.

Fruin, W. Mark. (1983). *Kikkoman Company: Clan and Community.* Cambridge: Harvard University Press.

Fu, Huiyan. (2012). *An Emerging Non-Regular Labour Force in Japan: The Dignity of Dispatched Workers.* London and New York: Routledge.

Fujii Kayo. (1997). *Daigaku "zōge no tō" no kyozō to jitsuzō* [The truth and fallacies of the university's ivory tower]. Tokyo: Maruzen.

Fujimura-Faneslow, Kumiko (1995). 'College women today: Opinions and dilemmas', in *Japanese women: New feminist perspectives on the past, present and future*, eds. Kumiko Fujimura-Faneslow and Atsuko Kameda, pp. 125–54. New York: The Feminist Press.

Fukudome, Hideto. (2019). 'Higher Education in Japan: Its Uniqueness and Historical Development', in *Education in Japan: A Comprehensive Analysis of Education Reforms and Practices*, eds. Yuto Kitamura, Toshiyuki Omomo, and Masaaki Katsuno, pp. 41–51. Singapore: Springer.

Fukudome, Ruriko. (2004). 'Daigaku shokuin no yakuwari to nōryoku keisei: shiritsu daigaku shokuin chōsa wo tegakari toshite [The role and development of university staff: A survey of private universities]. *Kōtō Kyōiku Kenkyū* [Japanese Journal of Higher Education Research] 7: 157–76.

Fukui, Yū. (2004). 'Hyōka ni taeuru daigaku zukuri; shiritsu daigaku no survival senryaku' [Making universities which can stand up to evaluation: a survival strategy for private universities]. *Shigaku Keiei* 348: 1–10.

Funabiki, Takeo. (2005). *Daigaku no ethno-graffiti* [University ethno-graffiti]. Tokyo: Yuhikaku.

Furusawa, Yukiko. (2001). *Daigaku survival: saisei eno sentaku* [University survival: choices for survival]. Tokyo: Shueisha.

Galan, Christian. (2018). 'From Youth to Non-adulthood in Japan: The Role of Education', in *Being Young in Super-Aging Japan: Formative Events and Cultural Reactions*, eds. Patrick Heinrich and Christian Galan, pp. 32–50. London: Routledge.

Geiger, Roger L. (1986). *Private Sectors in Higher Education: Structure, Function and Change in Eight Countries*. Ann Arbor: University of Michigan Press.

Goldfinch, Shaun. (2006). 'Rituals of Reform, Policy Transfer, and the National University Corporation Reforms of Japan'. *Governance* 19(4): 585–604.

Goldsmith, Seth B. (1984). *Theory Z. Hospital Management: Lessons from Japan*. Maryland and Tunbridge Wells: An Aspen Publication.

Goodman, Roger. (1999). 'Culture as Ideology: Explanations for the Development of the Japanese Economic Miracle', in *Culture and Global Change*, eds. Tracey Skelton and Tim Allen, pp. 127–36. London and New York: Routledge.

Goodman, Roger. (2000). *Children of the Japanese State: The Changing Role of Child Protection Institutions in Contemporary Japan*. Oxford: Oxford University Press.

Goodman, Roger. (2003). 'Can Welfare Systems be Evaluated Outside their Cultural and Historical Context? A Case Study of Children's Homes in Contemporary Japan', in *Asian Politics in Development: Essays in Honour of Gordon White*, eds. Robert Benewick, Marc Blecher, and Sarah Cook, pp. 214–29. London: Frank Cass.

Goodman, Roger. (2009). 'The Japanese Professoriate', in *Higher Education in East Asia: Neoliberalism and the Professoriate*, eds. Gregory Poole and Ya-chen Chen, pp. 15–32. Rotterdam, Netherlands: Sense Publishers.

Goodman, Roger. (2010). 'The rapid Redrawing of Boundaries in Japanese Higher Education'. *Japan Forum* 22(1–2): 65–87.

Goodman, Roger, Sachi Hatakenaka, and Terri Kim. (2009). *The Changing Status of Vocational Higher Education in Contemporary Japan and the Republic of South Korea*, UNESCO-UNEVOC Discussion Paper Series, No. 4. Bonn: UNESCO-UNEVOC International Centre for Technical and Vocational Education and Training.

Goodman, Roger and Chinami Oka. (2018). 'The Invention, Gaming and Persistence of the *hensachi* ('standardised rank score') in Japanese Education'. *Oxford Review of Education* 44(5): 581–98.

Goto, Toshio. (2013). 'Secrets of family business longevity in Japan from the social capital perspective', in *Handbook on Research on Family Business (Second Edition)*, eds. Kosmas X. Smyrnios, Panikkos Zata Poutziouris, and Sanjay Goel, pp. 554–85. Cheltenham UK and Northampton, MA: Edward Elgar.

Green, Francis and Golo Henseke. (2016). 'Should Governments of OECD Countries Worry about Graduate Underemployment?' *Oxford Review of Economic Policy* 32(4): 514–37.

Gunderman, Richard and Mark Mutz. (2014). 'The collapse of big law: A cautionary tale for big med', *The Atlantic*, 11 February.

Hall, Ivan P. (1975). 'Organizational paralysis: The case of Todai', in *Modern Japanese Organization and Decision-Making*, ed. Ezra G. Vogel, pp. 304–30. Berkeley, Los Angeles, and London: University of California Press.

Hall, Ivan P. (1998). *Cartels of the Mind: Japan's Intellectual Closed Shop*. New York: W.W. Norton.

Hamabata, Matthews Masayuki. (1990). *Crested Kimono: Power and Love in the Japanese Business Family*. Ithaca and London: Cornell University Press.

Han, Min Cho. (1996). *Gendai nihon no senmon gakkō* [Professional training colleges in contemporary Japan]. Tokyo: Tamagawa University Press.

Hannum, Emily, Hiroshi Ishida, Hyunjoon Park and Tony Tam. (2019). 'Education in East Asian Societies: Postwar Expansion and the Evolution of Inequality'. *Annual Review of Sociology* 45: 8.1–23.

Hata, Takeshi. (2004). 'Mergers and Cooperation of Higher Education Institutions in Japan', in *Mergers and Cooperation among Higher Education Institutions: Australia, Japan, Europe*, ed. Research Institute of Higher Education, pp. 33–52. Hiroshima University, Hiroshima: Author.

Hatakenaka, Sachi. (2010). 'What's the Point of Universities? The Economic Role of Universities in Japan'. *Japan Forum* 22(1–2): 89–119.

He, Fang and Tōru Kobayashi. (2015). *Gakurekikan no chingin kakusa wa kakudai shite iru noka* [Is the educational credential-based wage differential increasing?]. *Panel Data Research Center at Keio University Discussion Paper Series*, September 2015. Online: https://www.pdrc.keio.ac.jp/publications/dp/1195/ (accessed 19 July 2017).

Henderson, Dan Fenno. (1997). 'The Role of Lawyers in Japan', in *Japan: Economic Success and Legal System*, ed. Harald Baum, pp. 27–67. Berlin: de Gruyter.

Holmes, Brian. (1989). 'Japan: Private education', in *Private Schools in Ten Countries: Policy and Practice*, ed. Geoffrey Walford, pp. 200–17. London and New York: Routledge.

Honda, Yuki. (2004). 'The Formation and Transformation of the Japanese System of Transition from School to Work'. *Social Science Journal Japan* 7(1): 103–15.

Hood, Christopher P. (2001). *Japanese Education Reform: Nakasone's Legacy*. London: Routledge.

Horta, Hugo, Machi Sato, and Akiyoshi Yonezawa. (2011). 'Academic Inbreeding: Exploring Its Characteristics and Rationale in Japanese Universities Using A Qualitative Perspective'. *Asia Pacific Educational Review* 12(1): 35–44.

Hōzawa Yasuo and Yūji Shirakawa. (2006). 'Shiritsu daigaku ni okeru shōgakukin jukyūritsu no kitei yōin' [Factors governing the rate of financial aid receipt among private institutions of higher education in Japan]. *Kyōiku Shakaigaku Kenkyū* 78: 321–40.

Huang, Futao. (2019). 'Field of Higher Education Research, Asia', in *Encyclopedia of International Higher Education Systems and Institutions*, eds. Pedro Teixeira et al. Netherlands: Springer.

Huang, Futao and Kiyomi Horiuchi. (2019). 'The public good and accepting inbound international students in Japan'. *Higher Education* 79: 459–75.

Hunt, Stephen and Vikki Boliver. (2019). *Private Providers of Higher Education in the UK: Mapping the Terrain.* Centre for Global Higher Education (working paper no. 47). London: UCL.

Ichikawa, Shōgo. (2000). *Kōtō kyōiku no henbō to zaisei* [The transformation of higher education and finances]. Tokyo: Tamagawa Daigaku Shuppanbu.

Ichikawa, Shōgo. (2004). 'Shigaku no tokusei to josei seisaku' [Private education characteristics and subsidy policies]. *Daigaku Zaisei Keiei Kenkyū* 1: 169–85.

Ichikawa, Taichi. (2007). *30nengo o tenbō suru chūkibo daigaku: management, gakushū shien, renkei* [Prospects for medium-sized universities in 30 years' time: management, learning support, partnership]. Tokyo: Toshindo.

Iida, Yoriko. (2013). *Women's Higher Education and Social Position before and after World War II in Japan.* Hyogo: Kwansei Gakuin University Press.

Imai, Takeshi and Imai, Mitsuaki. (2001). *Daigaku marketing no riron to senryaku* [The theory and strategies of marketing universities]. Nagoya: Chūbu Nihon Kyōiku Bunkakai.

Inaba, Yushi. (2016). *Higher education in a depopulating society: survival strategies of Japanese universities.* MSc dissertation, the Department of Education, University of Oxford.

Inaba, Yushi. (2020). 'Higher education in a depopulating society: Survival strategies of Japanese universities'. *Research in Comparative & International Education.* DOI: 10.1177/1745499920910581

Inagaki, Kyoko. (2007). *Jogakkō to jogakusei: kyōyō, tashinami, modan bunka* [Women's schools and female students: cultivation, accomplishment, and modern culture]. Tokyo: Chuo Koronsha.

Ishida, Hiroshi. (2007). 'Japan: Education expansion and inequality in access to higher education', in *Stratification in Higher Education: A Comparative Study,* eds. Yossi Shavit, Richard Arum, and Adam Gamoran, pp. 63–86. Stanford: Stanford University Press.

Itoh, Akihiro. (1999). *Senkanki nihon no kōtō kyōiku* [Higher education in Japan in the interwar period]. Tokyo: Tamagawa University Press.

Itō Ayumi. (2013). 'Shigoto Hōkai' (The Collapse of Work), *Shūkan Tōyō Keizai,* 31 August: 100–7.

James, Estelle and Gail Benjamin. (1988). *Public Policy and Private Education in Japan.* Basingstoke: Palgrave Macmillan.

Jannuzi, Charles. (2008). 'Demographic Disaster for Higher Ed in Japan? Parts II–III', *Japan Higher Education Outlook (JHEO),* 27 October 2008. Online: http://japanheo.blogspot. com/2008/10/demographic-disaster-for-higher-ed-in.html (accessed 11 August 2017).

Japan Association of Public Universities. (2017). *Heisei 29nendo kōritsu daigaku binran* [2017 handbook of public universities]. Online: http://www.kodaikyo.org/?page_id=937 (accessed 12 June 2018).

JAPCU—Japan Association of Private Colleges and Universities. (1984). *Shiritsu daigaku: kinō, kyō, ashita* [Japan's private colleges and universities: yesterday, today and tomorrow]. Tokyo: Author.

JAPCU—Japan Association of Private Colleges and Universities. (1987). *Japan's Private Colleges and Universities: Yesterday, Today and Tomorrow.* Trans. Simul International. Tokyo: Author.

JASSO—Japan Student Services Organization. (2017). *Shōgakukin jigyō kanren shiryō* [Materials on scholarships programme]. Online: http://www.mext.go.jp/b_menu/

shingi/chousa/koutou/069/gijiroku/__icsFiles/afieldfile/2016/02/23/1367261_7.pdf (accessed 6 March 2018).

JASSO—Japan Student Services Organization. (2019). *Heisei 30 nendo gaikokujin ryūgakusei zaiseki jōkyō chōsa kekka* [Survey results on enrollment status of international students in FY2018]. Online: https://www.jasso.go.jp/about/statistics/intl_student_e/2018/index.html (accessed 1 June 2019).

J-CAST. (2009). 'Hajimatta "daigaku tōta": St. Thomas dai "haisen no ben"' [University shakeout begins: 'words of the defeated' from St Thomas University], *J-Cast News*, 21 June 2019. Online: https://www.j-cast.com/2009/06/21043456.html (accessed 8 March 2018).

JFBA (Japan Federation of Bar Associations). (2017). *White Paper on Attorneys, 2017*. Online: https://www.nichibenren.or.jp/library/en/about/data/WhitePaper (accessed 30 March 2018).

JILPT—Japan Institute for Labour Policy and Training. (2018). Useful *rōdō tōkei* [Useful labour statistics 2018]. Online: https://www.jil.go.jp/kokunai/statistics/kako/2018/index.html (accessed 8 July 2018).

Kachaner, Nicolas, George Stalk Jr., and Alain Bloch. (2012). 'What You Can Learn from Family Business'. *Harvard Business Review* 90(11): 1–5.

Kaneko, Motohisa. (2004). 'Japanese Higher Education: Contemporary Reform and the Influence of Tradition', in *Asian Universities: Historical Perspectives and Contemporary Challenges*, eds. Philip Altbach and Toru Umakoshi, pp. 115–44. Baltimore: Johns Hopkins University Press.

Kaneko, Motohisa. (2007). 'Japanese Private Universities in Transition: Characteristics, Crisis and Future Directions', in *Frontier of Private Higher Education Research in East Asia*, ed. Akiyoshi Yonezawa, pp. 47–62. Tokyo: Research Institute for Independent Higher Education.

Kano, Yoshimasa. (2015). 'Higher Education Policy and the Academic Profession', in *The Changing Academic Profession in Japan*, eds. Akira Arimoto, William K. Cummings, Futao Huang and Jung Cheol Shin, pp. 27–40. Switzerland: Springer.

Kariya, Takehiko. (2011). 'Credential Inflation And Employment in "Universal" Higher Education: Enrolment, Expansion and (In)Equality Via Privatisation in Japan'. *Journal of Education and Work* 24(1–2): 69–94.

Kariya, Takehiko and Ronald Dore. (2006). 'Japan at the Meritocracy Frontier: From Here, Where?' *The Political Quarterly* 77: 134–56.

Kawahara, Junji. (2004). *Daigaku keieisenryaku* [Management strategy for universities]. Tokyo: Toyo Keizai Shimposha.

Kawaijuku. (2016). *Hiraku nihon no daigaku: 2016nendo chōsa kekka hōkoku* [Japan's universities: report on 2016 survey results]. Online: https://www.keinet.ne.jp/gl/16/11/01toku.pdf (accessed 25 June 2018).

Kawanari, Yo. (2000). *Daigaku hōkai!* [University collapse!]. Tokyo: Takarajimasha.

Keio Gijuku. (2008). 'Heisei 20nendo shūshi kessan ni tsuite' [2008 fiscal year budget settlement]. Online: https://www.keio.ac.jp/ja/news/2009/kr7a43000000wz5g.html (accessed 5 March 2018).

Kelly, Curtis. (1999). 'The Coming Educational Boom in Japan: Demographic and Other Indicators That Suggest an Increase in the Number of Adults Seeking Education'. *Japanese Society* 3: 38–57.

Kempner, Ken and Misao Makino. (1993). 'Cultural Influences on the Construction of Knowledge in Japanese Higher Education'. *Comparative Education* 29(2): 185–99.

Kida, Ryūtarō. (2012). 'Kōtō keizoku kyōiku no nihonteki tenkai ni kansuru ichikōsatsu' [A study of Japanese-style development of higher and continuing education]. *Waseda Review of Education* 26(1): 159–72.

Kimura, Makoto. (2012). *Abunai shiritsu daigaku nokoru shiritsu daigaku* [Private universities at risk and those which will survive]. Tokyo: Asahi Shimbun Publishing.

Kimura, Makoto. (2014). *Shūshokuryoku de minuku! Shizumu daigaku nobiru daigaku* [Universities which will sink and those which will flourish: insights from their performance in graduate job placement]. Tokyo: Asahi Shimbun Publishing.

Kimura, Makoto. (2017). *Daigaku daitōsan jidai* [The era of mass university bankruptcy]. Tokyo: Asahi Shimbun Publishing.

Kimura, Makoto. (2018). *Daigaku daihōkai* [The great university collapse]. Tokyo: Asahi Shimbun Publishing.

Kinmonth, Earl H. (2005). 'From Selection to Seduction: The Impact of Demographic Change on Private Higher Education in Japan', in *The 'Big Bang' in Japanese Higher Education: The 2004 Reforms and the Dynamics of Change*, eds. Jerry S. Eades, Roger Goodman, and Yumiko Hada, pp. 106–35. Melbourne: Trans Pacific Press.

Kinmonth, Earl H. (2008). 'Review of Brian McVeigh's The State Bearing Gifts: Deception and Disaffection in Japanese Higher Education'. *Journal of Japanese Studies* 34(2): 419–23.

Kinukawa, Masakichi. (2002). 'Shiritsu daigaku no sōshiki: keiei saikō' [Reconsidering organisation and management strategies of private universities]. *Kōtō Kyōiku Kenkyū* [Japanese Journal of Higher Education Research] 5: 27–52.

Kinukawa, Masakichi and Akira Tachi. eds. (2004). *Gakushi katei kyōiku no kaikaku* [Reform of baccalaureate education in Japan]. Tokyo: Tōshindō.

Kitamura, Kazuyuki. ed. (1989). *Gakkō tōta no kenkyū: daigaku 'fushi' mōsō no shūen* [Research on school shakeout: the end of the illusion of university 'immortality']. Tokyo: Tōshindō.

Kitamura, Kazuyuki. (1997). *Daigaku tōta no jidai: shōhi shakai no kōtō kyōiku* [The university shakeout era: consumer society and higher education]. Tokyo: Chūkō Shinsho.

Kitamura, Kazuyuki. (2002). *Daigaku wa umarekawareru ka* [Can universities be reborn?]. Tokyo: Chūkō Shinsho.

Kitamura, Kazuyuki and William K. Cummings. (1972). 'The "Big Bang" theory and Japanese university reform'. *Comparative Education Review* 16(2): 303–24.

Kiyonari, Tadao. (2001). *21seiki shiritsu daigaku no chōsen* [The challenge for private universities in the 21st century]. Tokyo: Toyo Keizai Shimposha.

Kiyonari, Tadao. (2003). *Daigaku tōta jidai no daigaku jiritsu kasseika sen'ryaku* [Strategies for university autonomy and revitalization in the shakeout era]. Tokyo: Tōyō Keizai Shimposha.

Kiyonari, Tadao and Yukimasa Hayata. eds. (2005). *Kokuritsu daigaku hōjinka no shōgeki to shidai no chosen* [The impact of national university corporatisation and the challenge to private universities]. Tokyo: Eidell Institute.

Kobayashi, Tetsuya. (2008). 'Henbō suru gakuchō wa kiki wo sukuu ka? [Can reforming university presidents deal with the crisis?], *Chūō Kōron*, February: 64–73.

Kondo, Dorinne. (1990). *Crafting Selves: Power, Gender, and Discourses of Identity in a Japanese Workplace*. Chicago: Chicago University Press.

Kuroki, Hiroshi. (1999). *Meisō suru daigaku* [Universities gone astray]. Tokyo: Ronsōsha.

Kuroki, Toshio. (2009). *Rakkasan gakuchō funtōki: daigaku hōjinka no genba kara* [The struggles of a president in freefall: from the front lines of university corporatisation]. Tokyo: Chūō Kōronsha.

Kusaka, Kimindo, Kazuo Noda, Yasunori Nishijima, Mineo Nakajima, Kazuaki Tanaka, and Teiichi Sato. (2003). *Ima, nihon no daigaku o dō suru ka?* [What is to be done with Japan's universities today?]. Tokyo: Jiyū Kokuminsha.

Landes, David S. (2006). *Dynasties: Fortunes and Misfortunes of the World's Great Family Businesses*. New York: Viking.

Lawley, Peter. (2005). 'The Post-"Law School" Future of Japanese Undergraduate Legal Education: A Personal Perspective Comparison with Australia'. *Journal of Japanese Law* 20: 81–100.

Lebra, Takie. (1995). *Above the Clouds: Status Culture of the Modern Japanese Nobility*. Berkeley, CA: University of California Press.

Lee-Cunin, Marina. (2004). *Student Views in Japan: A Study of Japanese Students' Perceptions of their First Years at University*. Lancashire: Fieldwork Publications.

Levin, Mark A. and Adam Mackie. (2013). 'Truth or Consequences of the Justice System Reform Council: An English Language Bibliography from Japan's Millennial Legal Reforms'. *Asia-Pacific Law and Policy Journal* 14(3): 1–16.

Levy, Daniel C. (1986). *Private Education: Studies in Choice and Public Policy, Yale Studies on Nonprofit Organisations*. New York: Oxford University Press.

Levy, Daniel. (2008). 'Global Trends in Private Higher Education Research and East Asia'. Pp. 11–21 in *Frontier of Private Higher Education Research in East Asia*, Research Institute for Independent Higher Education (RIIHE), RIIHE Research Series, No. 3.

Levy, Daniel. (2018a). 'Too Big to Marginalize: Higher Education's Private Sector', *Inside Higher Ed.*, 15 April.

Levy, Daniel C. (2018b). 'Global Private Higher Education: An Empirical Profile of Its Size and Geographical Shape'. *Higher Education* 76(4): 701–15.

Levy, Daniel C. (2019). 'The Family Album—Inside the World's Private Higher Education Landscape', in *The Global Phenomenon of Family-Owned/Managed Universities*, eds. Philip G. Altbach, Edward Choi, Matthew R. Allen, and Hans de Wit, pp. 9–28. Leiden: Brill.

Mak, James, Shyam Sunder, Shigeyuki Abe, and Kazuhiro Igawa (1998). 'Why do students take it easy at university', in *Japan: Why it Works, Why it Doesn't. Economics in Everyday Life*, pp. 73–81. Hawaii: University of Hawaii Press.

Mantilla, Gabriel Burgos. (2019). 'Columbia: The complex reality of family universities', in *The Global Phenomenon of Family-Owned/Managed Universities*, eds. Philip G. Altbach, Edward Choi, Matthew R. Allen, and Hans de Wit, pp. 116–129. Leiden: Brill.

Manzenreiter, Wolfram, Ralph Lützeler, and Sebastian Polak-Rottmann (eds.). (2020). *Japan's New Ruralities: Coping with Decline in the Periphery*. London: Nissan Institute of Japanese Studies/Routledge.

Marginson, Simon. (2016). 'The Worldwide Trend to High Participation Higher Education: Dynamics of Social Stratification in Inclusive Systems'. *Higher Education* 72(4): 413–34.

Marginson, Simon. (2018). 'Public/private in Higher Education: A Synthesis of Economic and Political Approaches'. *Studies in Higher Education* 43(2): 322–37.

Martin, James and James E. Samuels. (2010). 'All in the Family: Proud Legacies of America's Family-owned and Operated Career Universities'. *University Business* 1 November. Online: https://www.universitybusiness.com/article/all-family (accessed 29 August 2017).

Maruyama, Fumihiro. (2002). *Shiritsu daigaku no keiei to kyōiku* [Management and education in private universities]. Tokyo: Toshindo.

Maruyama, Fumihiro. (2010). 'Public Expenditure on Higher Education in Japan'. *Higher Education Forum* 7: 53–68.

McLean, Martin. (1995). *Educational Traditions Compared: Content, Teaching and Learning in Industrialized Countries.* London: David Fulton Press.

McVeigh, Brian J. (1997). *Life in a Japanese Women's College: Learning to Be Ladylike.* London: Routledge.

McVeigh, Brian J. (2002). *Japanese Higher Education as Myth.* Armonk, NY: M.E. Sharpe.

McVeigh, Brian J. (2006). *The State Bearing Gifts: Deception and Disaffection in Japanese Higher Education.* Lanham, MD: Lexington Books.

Mehrotra, Vikas, Randall Morck, Jungwook Shim, and Yupana Wiwattanakantang. (2013). 'Adoptive Expectations: Rising Sons in Japanese Family Firms'. *Journal of Financial Economics* 108(3): 840–54.

Melin, Leif, Mattias Nordqvist, and Sharma Pramodita (eds.). (2014). *The Sage Handbook of Family Business.* London: Sage.

Menju, Toshihiro. (2017). *Genkai kokka: jinkō genshō de nihon ga semarareru saishū sentaku* [Nation on the brink: the final options for Japan in population decline]. Tokyo: Asahi Shimbun Publications.

MEXT—Ministry of Education, Culture, Sports, Science and Technology. (n.d.a). *Shiritsu gakkō kankei zeisei* [The tax system for private schools]. Online: http://www.mext.go.jp/a_menu/koutou/shinkou/07021403/003.htm (accessed 1 December 2018).

MEXT—Ministry of Education, Culture, Sports, Science and Technology. (n.d.b). *Kōdai setsuzoku kaikaku* [High school-university articulation reforms]. Online: http://www.mext.go.jp/a_menu/koutou/koudai/detail/1397731.htm (accessed 16 November 2017).

MEXT—Ministry of Education, Culture, Sports, Science and Technology. (n.d.c). *Nihon no daigaku dewa, kyōiku naiyō/hōhōtō no kaizen ga dorekurai susunde iru no deshō ka* [How advanced are improvements to educational content and methods in Japanese universities?]. Online: http://www.mext.go.jp/a_menu/koutou/daigaku/04052801/005.htm (accessed 16 November 2018).

MEXT—Ministry of Education, Culture, Sports, Science and Technology. (2004). *Shiritsu gakkōhō no ichibu o kaisei suru hōritsutō no sekō ni tsuite* [Enactment of the law amending provisions of the Private Schools Act]. Online: http://www.mext.go.jp/a_menu/koutou/shinkou/07021403/004/003.htm (accessed 1 October 2018).

MEXT—Ministry of Education, Culture, Sports, Science and Technology. (2007). *Heisei 19nendo daigakutō setchi ni kakawaru kifukōi (henkō) ninkago no zaisei jōkyō oyobi shisetsutō seibi jōkyō chōsa ryūi jikō* [Points of concern arising from survey of finances and facilities following approval of acts of endowment relating to university establishment, 2007]. Online: http://www.mext.go.jp/a_menu/koutou/shinkou/07021403/006/008/001.htm (accessed 3 May 2017).

MEXT—Ministry of Education, Culture, Sports, Science and Technology. (2012). *Horikoshi gakuen (gunmaken) no zaigakusei to hogosha no minasama e* [To all current students of Horikoshi Gakuen (Gunma prefecture) and their parents and guardians]. Online: http://www.mext.go.jp/a_menu/koutou/shinkou/07021403/1327280.htm (accessed 6 October 2017).

MEXT—Ministry of Education, Culture, Sports, Science and Technology. (2013). *Daigaku nyūgakusha senbatsu, daigaku kyōiku no genjō* [Current state of student admissions and education in universities]. Online: http://www.kantei.go.jp/jp/singi/kyouikusaisei/dai11/sankou2.pdf (accessed 1 October 2018).

MEXT—Ministry of Education, Culture, Sports, Science and Technology. (2014). *Wakamono no kaigai ryūgaku o torimaku genjō ni tsuite* [Conditions surrounding study abroad by young people]. Online: https://www.cas.go.jp/jp/seisaku/ryuugaku/dai2/sankou2.pdf (accessed 19 October 2017).

MEXT—Ministry of Education, Culture, Sports, Science and Technology. (2015). *Shiritsu daigaku no keiei jōkyō ni tsuite* [Operating conditions in private universities]. Online: http://www.mext.go.jp/component/a_menu/education/detail/__icsFiles/afieldfile/2017/02/15/1381780_8.pdf (accessed 16 September 2018).

MEXT—Ministry of Education, Culture, Sports, Science and Technology. (2016). *Monbu kagaku daijin no shokatsu ni zokusuru gakkō hōjin no okonau koto no dekiru shūeki jigyō no shurui o sadameru ken* [Stipulation of types of profit-making activities allowed for private school corporations under the jurisdiction of the Minister of Education, Culture, Sports, Science and Technology]. Online: http://www.mext.go.jp/b_menu/hakusho/nc/1374659.htm (accessed 8 April 2018).

MEXT—Ministry of Education, Culture, Sports, Science and Technology. (2017a). *Monbu kagaku tōkei yōran* [Statistical overview of education, culture, sports, science and technology]. Online: http://www.mext.go.jp/b_menu/toukei/002/002b/1383990.htm (accessed 19 March 2018).

MEXT—Ministry of Education, Culture, Sports, Science and Technology. (2017b). *Shigaku josei ni kansuru sankō shiryō* [Reference materials on private school subsidies]. Online: http://www.mext.go.jp/b_menu/shingi/chousa/koutou/073/gijiroku/__icsFiles/afieldfile/2017/02/14/1381731_2.pdf (accessed 19 March 2018).

MEXT—Ministry of Education, Culture, Sports, Science and Technology. (2017c). *Heisei 29nendo kokkōshiritsu daigaku/tanki daigaku nyūgakusha senbatsu jisshi jōkyō no gaiyō* [Overview of student admissions in national, public and private universities and junior colleges, 2017 academic year]. Online: http://www.mext.go.jp/b_menu/houdou/29/12/1398976.htm (accessed 4 August 2018).

MEXT—Ministry of Education, Culture, Sports, Science and Technology. (2017d). *Heisei 29nendo kagaku kenkyūhi josei jigyō no haibun ni tsuite* [Allocations of Grants-in-Aid for Scientific Research, 2017 fiscal year]. Online: http://www.mext.go.jp/a_menu/shinkou/hojyo/__icsFiles/afieldfile/2017/10/10/1396984_01_1.pdf (accessed 7 September 2018).

MEXT—Ministry of Education, Culture, Sports, Science and Technology. (2017e). *Kokkō shiritsu daigaku no jugyōryōtō no suii* [Change over time in national, local public and private university fees]. Online: http://www.mext.go.jp/a_menu/koutou/shinkou/07021403/__icsFiles/afieldfile/2017/12/26/1399613_03.pdf (accessed 2 March 2018).

MEXT—Ministry of Education, Culture, Sports, Science and Technology. (2017f). *Kōtō kyōiku no shōrai kōsō ni kansuru kiso dēta, 2017* [Basic data on the future of higher education 2017]. Online: http://www.mext.go.jp/b_menu/shingi/chukyo/chukyo4/gijiroku/__icsFiles/afieldfile/2017/04/13/1384455_02_1.pdf (accessed 11 August 2018).

MEXT—Ministry of Education, Culture, Sports, Science and Technology. (2018a). *Gakkō kihon chōsa kekka no gaiyō* [Basic schools survey: outline of results]. Online: http://www.mext.go.jp/b_menu/toukei/chousa01/kihon/kekka/1268046.htm (accessed 11 April 2019).

MEXT—Ministry of Education, Culture, Sports, Science and Technology. (2018b). *Shiritsu gakkō no keiei jōkyō ni tsuite* [Operating conditions in private universities]. Online: http://www.mext.go.jp/component/a_menu/education/detail/__icsFiles/afieldfile/2018/02/16/1401001_7_1.pdf (accessed 6 December 2018).

MEXT—Ministry of Education, Culture, Sports, Science and Technology. (2018c). *Shiritsu daigaku tō no heisei 29nendo nyūgakusha ni kakawaru gakusei nōfukintō chōsa kekka ni tsuite* [Results of survey of student fees for 2017 academic year enrollees in private universities]. Online: http://www.mext.go.jp/a_menu/koutou/shinkou/07021403/1412031.htm (accessed 26 March 2018).

MEXT—Ministry of Education, Culture, Sports, Science and Technology. (2018d). *Kōritsu daigaku ni tsuite* [Local public universities]. Online: http://www.mext.go.jp/a_menu/koutou/kouritsu/index.htm (accessed 4 December 2018).

MEXT—Ministry of Education, Culture, Sports, Science and Technology. (2018e). *Heisei 28nendo daigakutō ni okeru sangaku renkeitō jisshi jōkyō ni tsuite* [Status of university-industry partnerships, 2016 fiscal year]. Online: http://www.mext.go.jp/component/a_menu/science/detail/__icsFiles/afieldfile/2018/02/16/1397873_02.pdf (accessed 7 September 2018).

MEXT—Ministry of Education, Culture, Sports, Science and Technology. (2018f). *Heisei 28nendo gakkō kyōin tōkei chōsa (kakuteichi) no gaiyō* [Outline of finalized data from the 2016 statistical survey of academic staff]. Online: http://www.mext.go.jp/b_menu/toukei/chousa01/kyouin/kekka/k_detail/1395309.htm (accessed 11 April 2019).

MEXT—Ministry of Education, Culture, Sports, Science and Technology. (2018g). *Tōkyō 23ku no daigaku no teiin yokusei ni kakawaru zanteitekina taiō* [Provisional measures to restrict enrolment capacity of universities in the 23 wards of Tokyo]. Online: http://www.mext.go.jp/b_menu/shingi/chukyo/chukyo4/042/siryo/__icsFiles/afieldfile/2018/01/26/1400706_03.pdf (accessed 5 February 2019).

MEXT—Ministry of Education, Culture, Sports, Science and Technology. (2018h). *2040nen o misueta kōtō kyōiku no kadai to hōkōsei ni tsuite* [Issues and directions for higher education looking ahead to 2040]. Online: http://www.soumu.go.jp/main_content/000573858.pdf (accessed 14 April 2018).

MEXT—Ministry of Education, Culture, Sports, Science and Technology. (2018i). *Shiritsu daigakutō keiei kyōka shūchū shien jigyō* [Intensive support project for strengthening private university management]. Online: http://www.mext.go.jp/a_menu/koutou/shinkou/07021403/002/002/1367019.htm (accessed 6 December 2018).

MEXT—Ministry of Education, Culture, Sports, Science and Technology. (2018j). *Kōtō kyōiku mushōka no seido no gutaika ni muketa hōshin no gaiyō* [Outline of policies toward implementation of a system for making higher education free]. Online: http://www.mext.go.jp/a_menu/koutou/hutankeigen/detail/__icsFiles/afieldfile/2018/12/28/1412286_001(accessed 5 February 2019).pdf.

MEXT—Ministry of Education, Culture, Sports, Science and Technology. (2018k). *Daigaku eno shingakushasū no shōrai suikei ni tsuite* [Future projection of university entrant numbers]. Online: http://www.mext.go.jp/b_menu/shingi/chukyo/chukyo4/042/siryo/__icsFiles/afieldfile/2018/03/08/1401754_03 (accessed 5 February 2019).pdf

Miller, Roy Andrew. (1982). *Japan's Modern Myth: The Language and Beyond*. New York and London: Weatherhill.

Mito, Hideonori. (2014). *Ima, naze "daigaku kaikaku" ka? Shiritsu daigaku no senryakuteki keiei no hitsuyōsei* [Why "university reform" now? The need for strategic management of private universities]. Tokyo: Maruzen Planet.

Miyajima, Koji. (2016). 'Shiritsu daigaku ni okeru governance no yūkōsei ni kansuru jisshō kenkyū' [Empirical study on the effectiveness of governance in private universities]. *Doshisha University Policy and Management* 17(2): 83–97.

Miyazawa, Setsuo (with Otsuka Hiroshi). (2000). 'Legal Education and the Reproduction of the Elite in Japan'. *Asian-Pacific Law and Policy Journal* 2(1): 1–32.

Moffatt, Michael. (1989). *Coming of Age in New Jersey: College and American culture*. New Brunswick, NJ: Rutgers University Press.

Morgan, Keith J. (1999). *Universities and the Community: Use of Time in Universities in Japan*. Hiroshima: Hiroshima University Research Institute of Higher Education, RIHE.

Morikawa, Izumi. (2007). 'Senzen no daigaku setchi (shōkaku) ninka gyōsei ni okeru shiritsu daigaku zaisei mondai' [The financial difficulties of private universities and the administration of the national sanction regarding the inauguration of universities in pre-WW 2 Japan]. *Hiroshima Shūdai Ronshū* 48(1): 1–31.

Morikawa, Masayuki. (2017). 'Occupational Licenses and Labor Market Outcomes'. RIETI Discussion Paper Series 17-E-078. Online: https://www.rieti.go.jp/jp/publications/dp/17e078.pdf (accessed 15 June 2018).

Morozumi, Akiko. (2010). *Shiritsu daigaku no keiei to kakudai/saihen* [Private university management and expansion/restructuring]. Tokyo: Toshindo.

Morozumi, Akiko. (2016). 'Shiritsu daigaku no tōgō/renkei' [Mergers and partnerships among private universities]. *Kōtō Kyōiku Kenkyū Sōsho* [Reviews in Higher Education] 133: 71–86.

Morozumi, Akiko, Tateo Kobayashi, Kuninaru Shiota, and Fumitake Fukui. (2018). 'Daigaku jōkyū kanrishoku muke kenshū/kyōiku programme no genjō to kadai' [Conditions and challenges in education/training programs for upper-level university management]. *Daigaku Keiei Seisaku Kenkyū* 8: 95–111.

Motoyama, Yukihiko and I. J. McMullen. (1997). 'The Spirit of Political Opposition in The Meiji Period: The Academic Style of the Tokyo Senmon Gakkō', in *Proliferating Talent: Essays on Politics, Thought and Education in the Meiji Era*, eds. Yukihiko Motoyama, J. S. A. Elisonas, and Richard Rubinger, pp. 317–53. Honolulu: University of Hawaii Press.

Mouer, Ross and Yoshio Sugimoto. (1986). *Images of Japanese Society: A Study in the Structure of Social Reality*. London, New York, Sydney and Henley: KPI.

Murakami Masahiro. (2003). *Hōka daigakuin: bengoshi ga fueru, shakai ga kawaru* [Professional Law School: Increasing Lawyers and Changing Society]. Tokyo: Chūō Kōron.

Murakami, Yasusuke. (1984). 'Ie Society as a Pattern of Civilization'. *Journal of Japanese Studies* 10(2): 279–363.

Nagai, Michio. (1971). *Higher Education in Japan: Its Take-off and Crash*. Trans. J. Dusenbury. Tokyo: University of Tokyo Press.

Nakai, Kōichi. (2002). *Kachi-gumi daigaku ranking* [A ranking of universities in the 'winners' circle']. Tokyo: Chuo Koron Shinsha.

Nakamura, Chūichi. (1997). 'Fuyu no jidai' no daigaku keiei [University management in the 'winter era']. Tokyo: Toyo Keizai Shimposha.

Nakamura, Chūichi. (2001). *Kokuritsu daigaku min'eika de 300 no shidai ga tsubureru* [National university privatization will cause 300 private universities to close]. Tokyo: Yell Books.

Nakamura, Chūichi. (2002). *Daigaku tōsan* [University bankruptcy]. Tokyo: Tōyō Keizai Shimpōsha.

Nakamura, Kiyoshi. (2001). *Daigaku henkaku tetsugaku to jissen: ritsumeikan no dynamism* [Philosophy and practice of university reform: the dynamism of Ritsumeikan]. Tokyo: Nikkei Jigyō Shuppansha.

Nakamuro, Makiko and Tomohiko Inui. (2013). 'The Returns to College Quality in Japan: Does Your College Choice Affect Your Earnings?' ESRI Discussion Paper Series No.306. Online: www.esri.go.jp/jp/archive/e_dis/e_dis306/e_dis306.pdf (accessed 15 June 2018).

Nakazawa, Wataru. (2014). *Naze nihon no kōkyōikuhi wa sukunai no ka: Kyōiku no kōteki yakuwari o toinaosu* [Why are public education costs so low in Japan? Reassessing the public role of education]. Tokyo: Keisō Shobō.

Narita, Katsuya and Masao Terasaki. (1979). *Daigaku no rekishi (gakkō no rekishi dai4kan)* [A history of universities (a history of educational institutions, vol. 4)]. Tokyo: Dai-ichi Hoki Publishing.

Nathan, Rebekah. (2005). *My Freshman Year: What a Professor Learned by Becoming a Student*. Ithaca: Cornell University Press.

National University Corporation Evaluation Committee. (2015). *Kokuritsu daigaku to shiritsu daigaku no jugyōryō no suii* [Change over time in national and private university tuition fees]. Online: http://www.mext.go.jp/b_menu/shingi/kokuritu/005/gijiroku/attach/1386502.htm (accessed 18 July 2017).

Newby, Howard, Thomas Weko, David Brenemann, Thomas Johanneson, and Peter Maassen. (2009). *OECD Reviews of Tertiary Education: Japan*. Paris: OECD.

NFUCA—National Federation of University Co-operative Associations. (2017). *CAMPUS LIFE DATA 2017*. Tokyo: Author.

NHK. (2019). 'Ryūgakusei ga "manabenai" 30mannin keikaku no kage de' [International students who 'can't study': in the shadows of the 300,000 international students plan], *Close-Up Gendai Plus*, 27 June 2019. Online: https://www.nhk.or.jp/gendai/articles/4300/index.html (accessed 21 January 2020).

Nihon Keizai Shimbunsha. (2005). 'Honsha shidai no chōsa kara: keiei no genjō hansū ga "fuman"' [From our survey of private universities: half are 'dissatisfied with current management]. *Nihon Keizai Shimbun*, 31 October 2005.

Nishida, Kozo. (2000). *Daigaku o reshuffle suru: kasseika eno soshiki kōdō kaikaku* [University reshuffle: reforming organizational behaviour for revitalization]. Nagoya: Kinmirai-sha.

Nishimura, Hidetoshi. (1987). 'Universities—Under Pressure to Change'. *Japan Quarterly* 34(2): 179–84.

Nottage, Luke. (2007). 'Build Postgraduate Law Schools in Kyoto, and Will They Come: Sooner and Later?' *Australian Journal of Asian Law* 7(3): 241–63.

Oba, Jun. (2009). 'Managing Academic and Professional Careers in Japan', in *Academic and Professional Identities in Higher Education: The Challenges of a Diversifying Workforce*, eds. Celia Whitchurch and George Gordon, pp. 99–111. New York: Routledge.

Obara, Kazuhito. (2005). *University leadership at private universities in Japan*. Doctoral thesis, Graduate School of Education and Information Studies Dissertation, Boston College.

Obara, Kazuhito. (2019). 'Japan: A special breed—family owned or managed universities', in *The Global Phenomenon of Family-Owned/Managed Universities*, eds. Philip G. Altbach, Edward Choi, Matthew R. Allen, and Hans de Wit, pp. 166-181. Leiden: Brill.

Obinata, Makoto. (2001). *Shiritsu daigaku no crisis management* [Crisis management for private universities]. Tokyo: Hyososha.

Obunsha Educational Information Center. (2018). '29nendo "suisen/AO" nyūgakusha, kako saikō no 44.3%' [Proportion enrolees through recommendation and AO admissions in the 2017 academic year is the highest ever: 44.3%]. Online: http://eic.obunsha.co.jp/resource/viewpoint-pdf/201801.pdf (accessed 1 March 2019).

Oe Atsuyoshi. (2003). 'Gakusei boshū to nyūgaku shiken to keiei' [Student recruitment, entrance examinations and university management]. *Kōtō Kyōiku Kenkyū* [Japanese Journal of Higher Education Research] 6: 131–48.

OECD—Organisation for Economic Cooperation and Development. (n.d.). *Education at a Glance: Centre for Educational Research and Innovation*. Online: https://www.oecd-ilibrary.org/education/education-at-a-glance_19991487 (accessed 5 August 2018).

OECD—Organisation for Economic Cooperation and Development. (1971). *Reviews of National Policies for Education: Japan*. Paris: OECD.

OECD—Organisation for Economic Cooperation and Development. (2004). *OECD Handbook for Internationally Comparative Education Statistics*. Paris: OECD Publications.

OECD—Organisation for Economic Cooperation and Development. (2017). *Education at a Glance 2017: OECD Indicators*. Paris: OECD Publishing. Online: https://doi.org/10.1787/eag-2017-55-en (accessed 21 June 2018).

OECD—Organisation for Economic Cooperation and Development. (2018a). 'Japan', in *Education at a Glance 2018: OECD Indicators*. Paris: OECD Publishing. Online: https://doi.org/10.1787/eag-2018-54-en (accessed 16 December 2018).

OECD—Organisation for Economic Cooperation and Development. (2018b). *Education at a Glance 2018: OECD Indicators*. Paris: OECD Publishing.

Ogata, Ken. (1978). *Kyōiku keizairon josetsu—shiritsu daigaku no zaisei* [Preface to educational economics—the finances of private universities]. Tokyo: Toyo Keizai Shinposha.

Ogata, Naoyuki. (2015). 'Changes to Japanese Teachers' View towards Students: Impact of Universalization', in *The Changing Academic Profession in Japan*, eds. Akira Arimoto, William K. Cummings, Futao Huang, and Jung Cheol Shin, pp. 89–102. New York, Dordrecht, London: Springer.

Ogawa, Yō. (2016). *Kieyuku 'genkai daigaku': shiritsu daigaku teiinware no kōzō* [Vanishing 'universities on the brink': the framework of insufficient enrollment at private universities]. Tokyo: Hakusuisha.

Ogawa, Yō. (2017). '2018nen no daimondai 'chūshō genkai daigaku shōmetsu' wa kaihi kanō ka' [The great problem of 2018, the 'demise of small and medium universities on the brink': is it avoidable?], *Shukan Gendai*, 30 November 2017. Online: http://gendai.ismedia.jp/articles/-/53631 (accessed 3 March 2018).

Ohno, Akira. (2008). *Genkai shūraku to chiiki saisei* [Communities on the brink and local revitalization]. Shizuoka: Shizuoka Shimbunsha.

Ohta, Souichi, Yuji Genda and Ayako Kondo. 2008. 'The Endless Ice Age: A Review of the Cohort Effect in Japan'. *Japanese Economy* 35(3): 55–86.

Okamoto Norifumi. (2016). *Shiritsu daigaku ni naniga okotte iru noka* [What is happening to private universities?]. Tokyo: Seibundo.

Okuda, Wataru. (2009). 'Shippai ga aitsugu shiritsu daigaku shisan unyō' [Successive asset management failures by private universities]. Online: https://www.murc.jp/report/rc/column/search_now/sn090202/ (accessed 17 June 2017).

Osako, Norio and Yuji Shirakawa. (2003). 'Daigaku kaikaku ga wakaru keyword 50' [50 keywords for understanding university reform]. *Aera Mook*, Special Number 93.

Ota, Hiroshi. (2014). 'Japanese Universities' Strategic Approach to Internationalization: Accomplishments and Challenges', in *Emerging International Dimensions in East Asian Higher Education*, eds. Akiyoshi Yonezawa, Yuto Kitamura, Arthur Meerman, and Kazuo Kuroda, pp. 227–52. Dordrecht: Springer.

PMAC—Promotion and Mutual Aid Corporation for Private Schools of Japan. (n.d.) *Keiei shien/jōhō teikyō* [Management support and information provision]. Online: https://www.shigaku.go.jp/s_center_menu.htm (accessed 18 June 2018).

PMAC—Promotion and Mutual Aid Corporation for Private Schools of Japan. (2007). *Shiritsu gakkō no keiei kakushin to keiei konnan eno taiō: saishū hōkoku* [Final report on management reforms and responses to financial difficulties in private schools]. Online: https://www.shigaku.go.jp/s_center_saisei.pdf (accessed 4 May 2018).

PMAC—Promotion and Mutual Aid Corporation for Private Schools of Japan. (2015). *Gakkō hōjin no keiei kaizen hōsaku ni kansuru ankēto hōkoku: daigaku/tanki daigaku hōjinhen* [Report of questionnaire survey of measures for improving management of educational corporations: corporations operating universities/junior colleges]. *Shigaku Keiei Jōhō* 30. Tokyo: Author.

PMAC—Promotion and Mutual Aid Corporation for Private Schools of Japan. (2018a). *Shiritsu daigaku/tanki daigakutō nyūgaku shigan dōkō* [Trends in applications for admission to private universities/junior colleges]. Online: https://www.shigaku.go.jp/s_center_d_shigandoukou.htm (accessed 18 December 2018).

PMAC—Promotion and Mutual Aid Corporation for Private Schools of Japan. (2018b). *Shiritsu daigakutō keijōhi hojokin* [Private university operating expense subsidies]. Online: https://www.shigaku.go.jp/s_hojo_h28.htm (accessed 18 December 2018).

PMAC—Promotion and Mutual Aid Corporation for Private Schools of Japan. (2018c). *Heisei 30nendohen konnichi no shigaku zaisei* [Private university finances today, 2018 edition]. Tokyo: Author.

PMAC—Promotion and Mutual Aid Corporation for Private Schools of Japan. (2019a). *Shiritsu daigakutō keijōhi hojokin* [Private university operating expense subsidies]. Online: https://www.shigaku.go.jp/s_kouhujoukyou.htm (accessed 15 May 2019).

PMAC—Promotion and Mutual Aid Corporation for Private Schools of Japan. (2019b). *Gakkō hōjin no keiei kaizen hōsaku ni kansuru ankēto hōkoku: daigaku/tanki daigaku hōjinhen* [Report of questionnaire survey of measures for improving management of educational corporations: corporations operating universities/junior colleges]. *Shigaku Keiei Jōhō* 33. Online: https://www.shigaku.go.jp/files/keieikaizenanke-to_h30.pdf (accessed 15 May 2019).

PMAC—Promotion and Mutual Aid Corporation for Private Schools of Japan. (2019c). *Daigaku portrait: nihon keizai daigaku* [University portrait: Japan University of Economics]. Online: https://up-j.shigaku.go.jp/school/category06/00000000673601000.html (accessed 2 January 2019).

Poole Gakuin. (2008). *Ninshō hyōka* [Accreditation]. Online: http://www.poole.ac.jp/jihee/jihee.html (accessed 19 July 2018).

Poole, Gregory S. (2010). *The Japanese Professor: An Ethnography of a University Faculty.* Rotterdam: Sense Publishers.

Poole, Gregory S. (2016). 'Administrative Practices as Institutional Identity: Bureaucratic Impediments to HE "Internationalisation" Policy in Japan'. *Comparative Education* 52 (1): 62–77.

Pounder, Paul. (2015). 'Family business insights: an overview of the literature'. *Journal of Family Business Management* 5(1): 116–27.

Powell, Margaret and Masahira Anesaki. (1990). *Health Care in Japan.* New York and London: Routledge.

Ramseyer, Mark J. (1999). 'Review of Ivan Hall's Cartels of the Mind: Japan's intellectual closed shop'. *Journal of Japanese Studies* 25(2): 365–8.

Ramseyer, J. Mark and Eric B. Rasmusen. (2015). 'Lowering the Bar to Raise the Bar: Licensing Difficulty and Attorney Quality in Japan'. *Journal of Japanese Studies* 41(1): 113–42.

Refsing, Kirsten. (1992). 'Japanese educational expansion: Quality or equality', in *Ideology and Practice in Modern Japan*, eds. Roger Goodman and Kirsten Refsing, pp. 116–29. London: Routledge.

Reis, Fabio and Rodrigo Capelato. (2019). 'Brazil: Family-founded higher education institutions', in *The Global Phenomenon of Family-Owned/Managed Universities*, eds. Philip G. Altbach, Edward Choi, Matthew R. Allen, and Hans de Wit, pp. 79–97. Leiden: Brill.

RIIHE—Research Institute for Independent Higher Education. (2012). *Shiritsu daigaku no chūchōki keiei system ni kansuru jittai chōsa* [Survey on medium- and long-term management systems in private universities]. Tokyo: Association of Private Universities of Japan.

Roberts, John G. (1973). *Mitsui: Three Generations of Japanese Business*. New York and London: Weatherhill.

Rodwin, Marc A. (2011). *Conflicts of Interest and the Future of Medicine: The United States, France and Japan*. Oxford: Oxford University Press.

Rubinger, Richard. (1982). *Private Academies in the Tokugawa Period*. Princeton: Princeton University Press.

Sacks, Peter. (1996). *Generation X Goes to College: An Eye-Opening Account of Teaching in Postmodern America*. Chicago: Open Court Publishing.

Saegusa, Mayumi. (2006). *The genesis of institutional reform: the development of the Japanese law school system*. PhD thesis, University of Illinois, Chicago.

Saegusa, Mayumi. (2009). 'Why the Japanese Law School System was Established: Co-Optation as a Defensive Tactic in the Face of Global Pressures'. *Law and Social Inquiry* 34(2): 365–98.

Saito, Takahiro. (2006). 'The Tragedy of Japanese Legal Education: Japanese "American" Law Schools'. *Wisconsin International Law Journal* 24(1): 197–208.

Saito, Rikio and Jiro Aoki, eds. (2009). *Shigaku un'ei jitsumu no subete: gakkō hōjin no governance/kihonkiteishū/zeimu* [Complete guide to private school administrative operations: governance/basic regulations/tax affairs in private school corporations]. Tokyo: Gakkō Keiri Kenkyūkai.

Saneto, Hideshi. (2015). *Gakkō hōjin handbook* [Private school corporation handbook] (7th ed.). Tokyo: Zeikei Group.

Sankei Biz. (2017). *Zenkoku 765 daigaku o 1,160 no campus goto ni chōsa* [Survey of 1,160 campuses in 765 universities nationwide]. Online: https://www.sankeibiz.jp/business/news/170926/prl1709261042041-n1.htm (accessed 26 September 2017).

Sankei Digital. (2018). 'Bestseller sakka ni kiku "2018 mondai", genjitsu to naru "daigaku tōsan no jidai"' [Best-selling author discusses the '2018 problem': the era of university bankruptcy will become a reality], *Sankei Biz*, 17 January 2018. Online: https://www.sankeibiz.jp/macro/news/180117/mca1801170700001-n1.htm (accessed 28 January 2018).

Sankei Shimbun Shakaibu, ed. (1992). *Daigaku o tou: kōhai suru genba karano hōkoku* [Universities in question: reports from the ruins]. Tokyo: Shinchosha.

Sapientia Alumni Association (2018). 'Moto eichi daigaku campus atochi no genzai to kongo no yotei' [Current status and future plans for former Eichi University campus]. *Sapientia* 29: 2. Online: https://ee65c38a-1355-4da7-9cb9-e63e58998935.filesusr.com/ugd/37067f_6d615c1173e640e487c52ce373795a95.pdf (accessed 10 August 2019).

Sato, Nobuyuki. (2016). 'The State of Legal Education in Japan: Problems and "Re-Renovations" in JD Law Schools'. *Asian Journal of Law and Society* 3: 213–25.

Sato, Susumu. (2001). *Daigaku no ikinokori senryaku: shōshika shakai to daigaku kaikaku* [University survival strategies: low-birthrate society and university reform]. Tokyo: Shakai Hyoronsha.

Sato, Yuriko. (2018). 'Kankoku to nihon no chihō shiritsu daigaku ni okeru ryūgakusei no yūchi, shien no jōkyō to cost no buntan' [Conditions and cost apportionment for international student recruitment and support in regional private universities in South Korea and Japan]. *Daigaku Ronshū* 50: 177–82.

Sawada, Akihiro. (2019). 'Tōkyō fukushi daigaku "dokusaisha tataeru kōka", moto rijichō shusshogo, odoroki no taigū to wa?' [Tokyo University of Social Welfare's "anthem in praise of the dictator": The astonishing treatment of former head after release from prison]. *AERA dot* (26 March 2019). Online: https://dot.asahi.com/aera/2019032500065. html (accessed 21 January 2020).

Schoppa, Leonard. (1991). *Education reform in Japan: A case of immobilist politics*. London: Routledge.

Sekita, Shinya. (2017). 'Dokuji shūkei! Zendaigaku shōgakukin entairitsu ranking' [Ranking of all universities based on JASSO loan default rate], *Toyo Keizai Online*, 20 April 2017. Online: https://toyokeizai.net/articles/-/168512 (accessed 30 April 2017).

Shafieyoon, Rasoul and Marjan Mansouri. (2014). 'Factors dominating the continuity and decline of family businesses'. *International Journal of Academic Research in Business and Social Sciences* 4(1): 327–43.

Shanker, M. C. and J. H. Astrachan. (1996). 'Myths and realities: Family businesses' contribution to the US economy: A framework for assessing family business statistics'. *Family Business Review* 9(2): 107–23.

Sharma, Pramodita. (2004). 'An Overview of the Field of Family Business Studies: Current Status and Directions for the Future'. *Family Business Review* 17(1): 1–36.

Sharma, Pramodita, Leir Melin, and Mattias Nordqvist. (2014). 'Introduction: Scope, evolution, and future of family business studies', in *The Sage Handbook of Family Business*, eds. Leif Melin, Mattias Nordqvist, and Sharma Pramodita, pp. 1–22. London: Sage.

Shepherd, Jessica. (2008). 'Desperately seeking students', *The Guardian*, 16 January 2008. Online: https://www.theguardian.com/education/2008/jan/15/internationaleducationnews. highereducation (accessed 22 July 2017).

Shimada, Hiroshi. (2002). *Shigo eno kyōiku shidō* [Educational responses to students talking during class]. Machida: Tamagawa University Press.

Shimano, Kiyoshi. (1999). *Abunai daigaku, kieru daigaku* 2000 [Universities that are in trouble, universities that will disappear—2000 edition]. Tokyo: Yell Books.

Shinken Ad. (2018). 'Jinendo kara no shigaku josei: teiinware no genkakuritsu o age, kyōiku no shitsu de zōgaku mo' [Private school subsidies from next year: rise in reduction rate for under-enrolled institutions, increased subsidies for educational quality]. *Between*, 29 January 2018. Online: http://between.shinken-ad.co.jp/univ/2018/01/shigakujosei.html (accessed 31 January 2018).

Shomura, Atsuko. (2017). *Igakubu no gakuhi yasui hodo hensachi takai 'hanhirei' no hōsoku ranking de kenshō* [The lower the fees the higher the *hensachi* in medical colleges: testing the law of inverse proportion through rankings]. *Aera.dot* (10 October 2017). Online: https://dot.asahi.com/dot/2017100600072.html (accessed 10 October 2017).

Snoddy, Gregory Allan. (1996). *A comparative study of the strategies to maintain enrolments at Japanese and American private institutions of higher education as a response to decline in the population of traditional age students*. Doctor of Education thesis, West Virginia University, Morgantown.

Special Advisory Council on Education. (1987). *Kyōiku kaikaku ni kansuru daisanji tōshin* [Third report on education reform]. Tokyo: National Printing Bureau.

Statistics Bureau, Ministry of Internal Affairs and Communications. (2014). *Saikin no seiki/ hiseiki koyō no tokuchō* [Recent characteristics of regular/non-regular employment]. Online: https://www.stat.go.jp/info/today/097.html#k1 (accessed 19 March 2017).

Steele, Stacey and Anesti Petridis. (2014). 'Japanese Legal Education Reform: A Lost Opportunity to End the Cult(ure) of the National Bar Examination and Internationalise Curricula?', in *The Internationalisation of Legal Education: The Future of Practice of Law*, eds. William van Caenegem and Mary Hiscock, pp. 92–121. Cheltenham, UK: Edward Elgar.

Stewart, Alex. (2003). 'Help one another, use one another: Toward an anthropology of family business'. *Entrepreneurship, Theory and Practice*, 27(4): 383–96.

Stewart, Alex. (2014). 'The anthropology of family business', in *The Sage Handbook of Family Business*, eds. Leif Melin, Mattias Nordqvist, and Sharma Pramodita, pp. 66–82. London: Sage.

Sugiyama, Yukimaru. (2004). *Gakeppuchi jakushō daigaku monogatari* [The tale of a puny university on the cliff-edge]. Tokyo: Chūō Kōron Shinsha.

Suzuki Yūga. (2001). *Daigakusei no jōshiki* [What every university student knows]. Tokyo: Shinchōsha.

Tachi, Akira. (1997). *Daigaku kaikaku: nihon to america* [University reform: Japan and the United States]. Tokyo: Tamagawa University Press.

Tada, Tomio. (2001). *Daigaku kakumei* [University revolution]. Tokyo: Fujiwara Shoten.

Taguri, Renato and John Davis. (1996). 'Bivalent attributes of the family firm'. *Family Business Review* 9(2): 199–208.

Takahashi, Satoshi. (2017). 'Neo-liberal education reform 1980s to 2000s', in *The History of Japanese Education (1600–2000)*, eds. Masashi Tsujimoto and Yoko Yamasaki. London and New York: Routledge.

Takeda, Yasumasa. (2001). *Uchinaru daigaku kaikaku: rikei daigakujin no hatsugen* [University reform from within: accounts from science and engineering professors]. Tokyo: Gakkai Shuppan Center.

Takei, Kazuyoshi. (2016). 'The Evolution of Japanese Family Business Governing Principles', *FFI Practitioner*, 17 August 2016.

Tamrat, Wondwosen. (2018). 'Family-owned private universities in Africa'. *International Higher Education* 95: 23–4.

Tanaka, Masahiro. (2007). 'Ideals and Realities in Japanese Law Schools: Artificial Obstacles in the Development of Legal Education'. *Higher Education Policy* 20(2): 195–206.

Tanaka, Masahiro. (2016). 'Japanese Law Schools in Crisis: A Study on the Employability of Law School Graduates'. *Asian Journal of Legal Education* 3(1): 38–54.

Tanaka, Ryūichi. (2019). 'Recent Debates on Public-Private Cost Sharing for Higher Education in Japan'. *Social Science Japan Journal* 22(2): 271–6.

Taylor, Laurie. (2000). 'Relatively Successful', *The Guardian*, 19 July 2000.

TBS Radio. (2017). 'Sudeni 4wari ijō ga teiinware!? Shiritsu daigaku no kongo o kangaeru' [Already 40% are under-enrolled!? Considering the future of private universities], 8 March 2017. Online: https://www.tbsradio.jp/126181 (accessed 23 December 2018).

Teichler, Ulrich. (1997). 'Higher Education in Japan: A View from Outside'. *Higher Education* 27: 275–98.

Teichler, Ulrich. (2019). 'The Academic and Their Institutional Environment in Japan: A View from Outside', *Contemporary Japan* 31(2): 234–263.

Toivonen, Tuukka and Yuki Imoto. (2012). 'Making sense of youth problems', in *A Sociology of Japanese Youth: From Returnees to NEETS*, eds. Roger Goodman, Yuki Imoto, Tuukka Toivonen, pp. 1–29. London: Routledge.

Tokai Higher Education Research Institute. (2001). 'Tokushū: daigaku zennyū jidai no kyōiku jissen o tou' [Special feature: exploring educational practice in the era of open admission to university]. *University and Education* 29: 4–48.

Tose, Nobuyuki and Kazuo Nishimura. (2001). *Daigakusei no gakuryoku o shindan suru* [Diagnosing university students' academic abilities]. Tokyo: Iwanami Shoten.

Toyo Keizai. (2018). 'Tokushū: daigaku ga kowareru' [Special feature: universities in breakdown], *Shūkan Tōyō Keizai*, 10 February 2018.

Trow, Martin. (1973). *Problems in the Transition from Elite to Mass Higher Education*. Berkeley, California: Carnegie Commission on Higher Education.

Tsuda, Takeyuki. (1993). 'The Psychological Functions of Liminality: The Japanese University Experience'. *The Journal of Psychohistory* 20(3): 305–30.

Umakoshi, Toru. (2004). 'Private higher education in Asia: Transitions and development', in *Asian Universities: Historical Perspectives and Contemporary Challenges*, eds. Philip Altbach and Toru Umakoshi, pp. 33–49. Baltimore: Johns Hopkins University Press.

Umezu, Kazuro. (2001). *Tsubureru daigaku nobiru daigaku: karakuchi saiten* [Universities that will go bust and those that will grow: a candid analysis]. Tokyo: Yell Books.

University Council. (1991). *Heisei 5nendo ikō no kōtō kyōiku no keikakuteki seibi ni tsuite* [Planned development of higher education from 1993 onward]. Report 17 May 1991. Online: http://www.mext.go.jp/b_menu/shingi/chukyo/chukyo4/gijiroku/030201fe.htm (accessed 10 June 2017).

University Council. (1998). *21seiki no daigakuzō to kongo no kaikaku hōsaku ni tsuite— kyōsōteki kankyō no naka de kosei ga kagayaku daigaku* [A vision of universities in the 21st century and approaches to reform: Distinctive universities in a competitive environment]. Online: http://www.mext.go.jp/b_menu/shingi/old_chukyo/old_daigaku_index/toushin/1315917.htm (accessed 10 June 2017).

University Council. (2000). *Daigaku nyūshi no kaizen ni tsuite* [Improving university admissions]. Online: www.mext.go.jp/b_menu/shingi/old_chukyo/old_daigaku_index/toushin/1315961.htm (accessed 17 June 2017).

University Journal Editorial Committee. (2017). 'Abe seiken no daigaku kyōiku zenmen mushōka, zaimushō ga hantai o hyōmei' [Ministry of Finance expresses opposition to Abe government's full-scale subsidization of university fees], *University Journal Online*, 6 November 2017. Online: https://univ-journal.jp/16667/ (accessed 18 November 2017).

Usami, Hiroshi. (2000). *Daigaku no jugyō* [Teaching in universities]. Tokyo: Toshindo.

Ushiogi, Morikazu. (2002). 'Shijō kyōsōka no daigaku keiei' [University management under market competition]. *Kōtō Kyōiku Kenkyū* [Japanese Journal of Higher Education Research] 5: 7–26.

Van den Berghe, Pierre. L. (1973). *Power and Privilege at An African University*. London: Routledge and Kegan Paul.

Vincent-Lancrin, Stéphan. (2008). 'What is the impact of demography on higher education?', in *Higher Education to 2030: Volume 1, Demography*, ed. Centre for Educational Research and Innovation. Paris: OECD.

Wagatsuma, Hiroshi and Arthur Rosset. (1986). 'The Implications of Apology: Law and Culture in Japan and the US'. *Law Society Review* 20(4): 461–97.

Walker, Patricia. (2007). 'System transition in Japanese short-term higher education: What future for the Japanese junior college in crisis?', *Compare*, 37(2): 239–55.

Walsh, Bryan. (2005). 'As Japan's Population Ages, Its Universities Face Bankruptcy As Enrollment Plunges', *Time Asia*, 4 July 2005.

Watanabe, Takashi. (2017). *Shiritsu daigaku wa naze ayaui noka* [Why private universities are at risk]. Tokyo: Seidosha.

Watson, Andrew R. J. (2016). 'Changes in Japanese Legal Education'. *Journal of Japanese Law* 21(41): 1–54.

Wheeler, Greg. (2012). 'The *Akahon* Publications: Their Appeal and Copyright Concerns'. *Shiken Research Bulletin* 16(1): 23–6.

Whitley, Richard. (2019). 'Changing the nature and role of universities: The effects of funding and governance reforms on universities as accountable organizational actors', in *The Oxford Handbook of Higher Education Systems and University Management*, eds. Gordon Redding, Anthony Drew, and Stephen Crump, pp. 63–87. Oxford: Oxford University Press.

Wilson, Matthew, J. (2014). 'Seeking to Change Japanese Society through Legal Reform', in *Critical Issues in Contemporary Japan*, ed. Jeff Kingston, pp. 265–75. London and New York: Routledge.

Wisniewski, Richard. (2008). 'The Averted Gaze'. *Anthropology and Education Quarterly* 31(1): 5–23.

Working Group on the Advancement of Private Universities, MEXT. (2017). *Shiritsu daigakutō no shinkō ni kansuru kentō kaigi giron no matome* [Summary of discussions in the Working Group on the Advancement of Private Universities]. Online: http://www.mext.go.jp/b_menu/shingi/chousa/koutou/073/gaiyou/1386778.htm (Accessed 5 May 2018).

Wright, Ewan and Hugo Horta. (2018). 'Higher Education Participation in "High-Income" Universal Higher Education Systems: "Survivalism" in the Risk Society'. *Asian Education and Development Studies* 7(2): 184–204.

Yamada, Reiko. (2001). 'University policy in the post-massification era in Japan: Analysis of government educational policy for the 21st century'. *Higher Education Policy* 14: 277–91.

Yamada, Reiko. (2018). 'Impact of Higher Education Policy on Private Universities in Japan: Analysis of Governance and Educational Reform through Survey Responses'. *Higher Education Forum* 15: 19–37.

Yamagishi, Shunsuke. (2001). *Daigaku kaikaku no genba e* [To the front lines of university reform]. Machida: Tamagawa University Press.

Yamamoto, Kiyoshi. (1999). 'Japan: collegiality in a paternalist system', in *Managing Academic Staff in Changing University Systems: International Trends and Comparisons*, ed. David Farnham, pp. 311–23. Buckingham, UK: Open University Press.

Yamamoto, Kiyoshi. (2004). 'Corporatization of National Universities in Japan: Revolution for Governance or Rhetoric for Downsizing?' *Financial Accountability and Management* 20(2): 153–81.

Yamamoto, Shinichi. (2002). 'Daigaku no soshiki keiei to sore wo sasaeru jinzai' [Staffing issues under the new management of universities]. *Kōtō Kyōiku Kenkyū* [Japanese Journal of Higher Education Research] 5: 87–108.

Yamamoto, Shinichi. (2005). 'Government and the National Universities: Ministerial Bureaucrats and Dependent Universities', in *The 'Big Bang' in Japanese Higher Education: The 2004 Reforms and the Dynamics of Change*, eds. Jerry S. Eades, Roger Goodman, and Yumiko Hada, pp. 94–105. Melbourne: Trans Pacific Press.

Yamamoto, Shinichi. (2012). 'Japan: Lifelong Learning and Higher Education in Japan', in *Global Perspectives on Higher Education and Lifelong Learners*, eds. Maria Slowey and Hans Schuetze, pp. 217–29. New York and London: Routledge.

Yamamoto, Shinichi. (2019). 'The Value of Degrees and Diplomas in Japan', in *Preparing Students for Life and Work: Policies and Reforms Affecting Higher Education's Principal Mission*, eds. Walter Archer and Hans G. Schuetze, pp. 141–56. Leiden; Boston: Brill.

Yamanoi, Atsunori. (2007). *Nippon no Daigaku Kyōju Shijō* [The academic marketplace in Japan]. Tokyo: Tamagawa University Press.

Yamasaki, Hirotoshi. (2015). 'Higher Education and Society', in *The Changing Academic Profession in Japan* (The Changing Academy Vol. 11), eds. Akira Arimoto, William K. Cummings, Futao Huang, and Jung Cheol Shin, pp. 213–20. Dortrecht: Springer.

Yamazaki, Sono, Koji Miyajima, and Yoshio Itaba. (2018). *Kore kara no daigaku keiei— governance, management, leadership* [University administration into the future— governance, management, leadership]. Kyoto: Kōyō Shobō.

Yomiuri Shimbun Educational Network. (2017). *Daigaku no jitsuryoku 2017* [The power of universities 2017]. Tokyo: Chūōkoron-Shinsha.

Yomiuri Shimbun Ōsaka Honsha. ed. (2002). *Tsubureru daigaku, tsuburenai daigaku* [Universities that will go bust and those that won't]. Tokyo: Chūō Kōron Shinsha.

Yonezawa, Akiyoshi. (2010). *Kōtō kyōiku no taishūka to shiritsu daigaku keiei: 'josei to kisei' wa nani o motarashita noka* [Massification of higher education and private university management: the effects of 'subsidisation and control']. Sendai: Tohoku University Press.

Yonezawa, Akiyoshi (ed.). (2011). *Daigaku no management: shijō to soshiki* [University management: market and organization]. Tokyo: Tamagawa University Press.

Yonezawa, Akiyoshi. (2015). 'Inbreeding in Japanese Higher Education: Inching Toward Openness in a Globalized Context', in *Academic Inbreeding and Mobility in Higher Education Global Perspectives*, eds. Maria Yudkevich, Philip Altbach, and Laura E. Rumbley, pp. 99–219. London: Palgrave Macmillan.

Yonezawa, Akiyoshi and Masateru Baba. (1998). 'The market structure for private universities in Japan', *Tertiary Education and Management* 4(2): 145–52.

Yonezawa, Akiyoshi and Futao Huang. (2018). 'Toward Universal Access Amid Demographic Decline: High Participation Higher Education in Japan', in *High Participation Systems of Higher Education*, eds. Brendan Cantwell, Simon Marginson, and Anna Smolentsveva, pp. 418–38. Oxford: Oxford University Press.

Yoshimoto, Keiichi. (2003). 'Senmongakkōno hatten to kōtōgakkōno tayōka' [Diversification in Japan's higher education system: The development of special training colleges]. *Kōtō Kyōiku Kenkyū* [Japanese Journal of Higher Education Research] 6: 57–82.

Yoshimoto, Yasunaga. (2003). *Daigaku ni wa haitta keredo* [You have got into to university, but...?]. Tokyo: Sangokan.

Yoyogi Seminar. (2018). *Nyūshi jōhō: waseda daigaku* [Admissions information: Waseda University]. Online: https://www.yozemi.ac.jp/nyushi/data/waseda/ (accessed 10 December 2018).

Yu, Kai. (2019). 'China: A publicly listed private higher education initiative', in *The Global Phenomenon of Family-Owned/Managed Universities*, eds. Philip G. Altbach, Edward Choi, Matthew R. Allen, and Hans de Wit, pp. 98-115. Leiden: Brill.

Zeugner, John F. (1984). 'The Puzzle of Higher Education in Japan: What Can We Learn From the Japanese?' *Change* 16(1): 24–31.

Index

Printed and bound by CPI Group (UK) Ltd, Croydon, CR0 4YY